Decolonization in St. Lucia

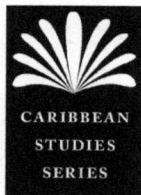

CARIBBEAN
STUDIES
SERIES

ANTON L. ALLAHAR AND SHONA N. JACKSON

SERIES EDITORS

Decolonization in St. Lucia

POLITICS AND GLOBAL NEOLIBERALISM

1945–2010

Tennyson S. D. Joseph

UNIVERSITY PRESS OF MISSISSIPPI · JACKSON

www.upress.state.ms.us

The University Press of Mississippi is a member of the Association of
American University Presses.

First printing 2011

∞

Library of Congress Cataloging-in-Publication Data

Joseph, Tennyson S. D.
Decolonization in St. Lucia : politics and global neoliberalism, 1945–2010
/ Tennyson S. D. Joseph.
p. cm. — (Caribbean studies series)
Includes bibliographical references and index.
ISBN 978-1-61703-117-5 (cloth : alk. paper) —
ISBN 978-1-61703-118-2 (ebook)
1. Saint Lucia—History—Autonomy and independence movements.
2. Decolonization—Saint Lucia—History. 3. Saint Lucia—Politics and
government—20th century. 4. Saint Lucia—Politics and government—
21st century. 5. Neoliberalism—Saint Lucia—History. 6. Globalization—
Political aspects—Saint Lucia—History. 7. Saint Lucia—Economic
conditions. I. Title.
F2100.J67 2011
972.9843—dc22   2011004068

British Library Cataloging-in-Publication Data available

This book is for my daughters, Nzingha and Choiselle

For the better understanding of the Caribbean, which we should, across generations, seek to create in fulfillment of the dreams of our freedom-fighting forebears, from Jean Jacques Dessalines to Walter Rodney

May their spirit of resistance and honesty of purpose continue with your generation.

Contents

Contents

Tables

Acknowledgments

It is always misleading to trace the origins of a book strictly from the point at which the formal writing process actually begins, for long before the writing commences there are ideas, experiences, questions, and influences that provide the primeval matter that shapes the content of the final product. This holds particularly strongly in the case of this book, given its genesis in questions that held my interest as a research student in the Caribbean and the United Kingdom long before the possibility of its publication had ever been contemplated.

In acknowledging the many people who have contributed to the appearance of this book, I must begin with the persons who nurtured the tender saplings of my earliest ideas during my days of postgraduate study. In this regard, special mention must be made of George Belle, dean of the Faculty of the Social Sciences at the University of the West Indies (UWI) in Barbados, who first exposed me to the implications of globalization for the sustainability of the antisystemic responses that had shaped the nationalist stances of Caribbean states since the decade of the 1970s. Indeed, too, it was George Belle who had first introduced to me the notion of "recolonization" as an analytical category for capturing what was novel in globalization, beyond the previous concerns of "neocolonialism." In a direct sense it is the spirit of that early instruction that has shaped the ideas and concerns of this book.

While Barbados and Cave Hill Campus provided understanding of the theoretical questions central to this book, it was under the guidance of Geoffrey Hawthorne of the University of Cambridge that specific focus was placed on linking theory to the empirical realities of St. Lucia. Geoff's interventions were critical, and his insights were invaluable in allowing me to refine my own theoretical understanding of the impact of globalization on the political economy of newly decolonized states like St. Lucia.

My researches in the United Kingdom, however, were not confined to the halls of Cambridge University. Indeed, a postgraduate fellowship at the Institute of Commonwealth Studies (ICS), University of London, from 1999 to 2000 provided me with real succor at the most challenging time of my studies and facilitated the successful completion of the research project. Not only did the

ICS postgraduate fellowship provide me with an office and a Caribbean library two floors below, but, more specially, it placed within my reach a number of academic and spiritual guides who assisted my research along the way, namely Pat Caplan, Peter Lyon, and Richard Bourne. Most special of all was Mary Turner, who provided the concrete guidance that saw the project through to completion.

The influences behind the book were, however, not only academic. Indeed, my immediate postdoctoral years were spent actively involved in the political life of St. Lucia, when I served first as the political attaché to the prime minister of St. Lucia as well as a candidate in the 2006 general election, and later, for a brief period, as a senator in the parliament of St. Lucia. Indeed, many of the amendments to the original project have been informed and refined by actual concrete political experiences. In this regard, the book would not have been possible without the insights shared by many colleagues actively involved in political struggle in St. Lucia between 2001 and 2006. I thank them all, and above all, I thank the people who struggled with me and deepened my understanding of St. Lucia.

The book would simply not have been possible had the University Press of Mississippi not deemed it worthy of publication. It is to Anton Allahar of the University of Western Ontario that I owe the biggest debt of gratitude, for it was at his gentle prompting, while at a conference in Jamaica, that I was moved to submit the manuscript for consideration. I am also eternally grateful to the Editorial Board at the University Press of Mississippi, and in particular Craig Gill, for sincerely believing that the work was important enough to be made available in book format for a wider audience, and for their quiet guidance throughout the process. A special thanks to Robert Burchfield for his insightful editorial suggestions.

Finally, I must thank my research assistant, Chatoyer Bobb, who accompanied me to St. Lucia in February 2009 to undertake the fieldwork and interviews that facilitated the writing of the closing chapters.

Despite the many minds that shaped it, any shortcomings, weaknesses in interpretation, and historical and factual inaccuracies remain entirely my responsibility.

Decolonization in St. Lucia

Introduction

This work explores the impact of global transformation upon the independence experience of St. Lucia, which attained its independence in the immediate post–Bretton Woods order in which a global framework had emerged that afforded little space for a radical shift in the internal role of the state in the postindependence period. Consequently, the concept of "limited sovereignty" became the defining feature of St. Lucia's understanding of the possibilities of independence (Thorndike 1979a, 603; Lewis 1953, 118–119).

In this work, the concept of neoliberal globalization is associated, in line with the perspectives of David Harvey (2005) and William Robinson (2008), with the economic and political transformations resulting from the erosion of key features of the postwar Bretton Woods "embedded neoliberal" order in the early to mid-1970s. While I am not suggesting that the Bretton Woods order was established with the advancement of postcolonial sovereignty as its main aim, I do argue that these global transformations have rendered unworkable many of the assumptions and strategies upon which the national self-determination project had been pursued in the Caribbean in the post-1945 period. I propose that globalization holds far wider implications for the internal sovereignty of the weak, postcolonial Caribbean states than it does for the longer established, more powerful states in the world system. For the powerful states, "the real issue is not sovereignty, but the relative autonomy of the state and the limit to its actions" (Bogues 1994, 8). For the newly decolonized states of the Caribbean, however, these global transformations hold implications for the assumptions of independence itself, because they have eroded the conditions that shaped the strategies through which independence was pursued. Further, the historical openness of Caribbean societies and their dependence upon the global economic system (Clapham 1996, 245) exacerbate their vulnerabilities. While the notion of "limited sovereignty" had been pervasive in several Caribbean states before and after the collapse of the West Indies Federation in 1962 (Thorndike 1979a), the process of globalization calls for a reexamination of the assumptions of sovereign statehood in light of its impact on the pursuit of sovereignty and national self-determination.

Specifically, it is important to isolate the impact of the shift—from the embedded neoliberalism of the postwar Keynesian order to the period of hegemonic neoliberalism from the 1980s and beyond—on the postcolonial state and its decolonization. This shift has seen a wholesale redefinition of the role of the state from a guarantor and protector of national economic and political interests, to a facilitator of transnational capital. Robinson (2008) identifies this post-1980s period of global neoliberalism as being marked by four key developments, all of which have impacted upon the shift in the role of the independent state from its anticolonial genesis. These include:

1. A new capital labor relation based on deregulation and "flexibization" of labor.
2. A new round of extensive and intensive expansion . . . through the reincorporation of major areas of the former Third and Second worlds into the world capitalist economy. . . .
3. The creation of a global legal and regulatory structure to facilitate what were emerging globalized circuits of accumulation, including the creation of the World Trade Organization.
4. The imposition of the neoliberal model on countries throughout the Third world, and also the First and former Second worlds, involving structural adjustment programs that created the conditions for the free operation of capital within and across borders and the harmonization of accumulation conditions worldwide (ibid., 16).

This work pursues the analysis of this new neoliberal global order with the specific focus on its impact on the historical experience of decolonization and independence in St. Lucia. I identify key episodes in the historical and contemporary experience of St. Lucia in which globalization can be seen to have affected the theoretical assumptions and practical expressions of national sovereignty. In these periods, conflicts over the meanings and expectations of independence, the character of the St. Lucian state in its role as domestic and international actor, and the degree of internal economic and political reform undertaken are particularly acute. These conflicts provide the basis for the analytical interpretations of the impact of globalization on the independence experience. Central to this analysis is the tension in the role of the state as a facilitator of domestic aspirations, on the one hand, and as a conduit for global economic adjustment, on the other. As a result, the national development project in St. Lucia vacillates between conformist and antisystemic notions, and between economic considerations of development and political concerns of anticolonial reform. In each phase, I identify the impact of global realities in shaping the processes inherent in the fluctuation between these tendencies.

By focusing on the specificity of the St. Lucian experience, this book advances discussion of Caribbean nationalism and decolonization. There currently exist studies on the politics of decolonization in Jamaica (Munroe 1972; Hart 1989, 1999; Post 1969, 1978; 1981), Trinidad and Tobago (Ryan 1972; Oxaal 1968), Guyana (Jagan 1954), and Barbados (Belle 1977, 1988), but none on St. Lucia. In addition, many of the existing writings on St. Lucian politics have been undertaken in response to political crises and have been written with a heavy dose of journalistic flair (Wayne 1977, 1986, 2010; Francois 1977; Odlum n.d.a, n.d.b.; Dabreo 1981, 1982; James n.d.; Francois 1994, 1996). I rely on such works mainly as primary material and view them as indications of political tendencies or "public responses," rather than as analytical contributions to understanding the political economy of St. Lucia. As a result of its specific focus on the independence experience of St. Lucia under globalization, this book presents new empirical data relevant to the study of Caribbean decolonization, markedly different from the concerns pursued in earlier studies on the politics of decolonization elsewhere in the Caribbean. The book therefore raises new insights into the politics of nationalism and decolonization in the Caribbean by focusing on the question through the prism of the impact of globalization on the independence experience. It focuses on the assumptions and strategies of the early nationalist experience, and demonstrates the impact of globalization on practical and philosophical expressions of independent statehood up to the first decade of the twenty-first century. Its principal aim is to provide an understanding of the impact of the global political economy on the internal politics of small, peripheral, postcolonial states.

Why St. Lucia?

There are a number of specific features of the St. Lucian historical experience that make it relevant to the study of the impact of global neoliberalism on the assumptions of independent statehood in the Caribbean. Most important is the fact that St. Lucia's incorporation into the world economic system resulted in a situation in which notions of economic backwardness and political unviability featured very prominently in shaping the pace and character of its decolonization. The pervasive view of St. Lucia's "backwardness" as an argument against formal sovereignty has been described as tentative anticolonialism, and will be explored more fully in Chapter 2. These notions of backwardness pertained both to the character of the internal economy of St. Lucia and to the constitutional development and political democratization of the territory. These factors delayed the progress of St. Lucia toward independence well into the era of global neoliberalism, thus fundamentally affecting its postcolonial experience.

St. Lucia's incorporation into the European economic system was slow, gradual, and uneven (Louis 1981, 11–15). This resulted in the underdevelopment of the plantation system (Beckles 1990, 6). Valued primarily as a military outpost (see Breen 1844, 67–68), the perpetual insecurity engendered by war and constantly revolving metropolitan overlordship militated heavily against the development of St. Lucia as an agricultural colony (Jesse 1964, 22; Easter 1965, 2). It was not until the period following the 1763 Treaty of Paris and "a full century behind other Caribbean territories in terms of colonial exploitation" (Barrow 1992, 14) that St. Lucia commenced the development of the slave plantation economy. Further economic disruption occurred during the French Revolution (Easter 1965; Breen 1844, 78) and in the later period of the "Brigand wars" when blacks, emancipated by the French National Assembly, resisted British attempts to restore slavery (Gaspar 1997; Devaux 1997).

Unchallenged British control of the territory was achieved as late as 1814 when the slave mode of production was well into its decline. As a consequence, the dominant economic pattern in St. Lucia was the growth of an independent peasantry (Romalis 1968, 35; Acosta and Casimir 1985; Louis 1981; Adrien 1996). This experience has led to the suggestion that the "fabric of St. Lucian society has not been patterned by a close relationship with the outer world" and that "political interferences of colonial powers had a scant impact on the content of locally created economic and social organizations" (Acosta and Casimir 1985, 4). This contention, however, ignores the extent to which this historical experience affected the character of the future excision from colonial control. Indeed, it is this experience that shaped future concerns about the territory's "unreadiness" for self-government.

One of the clearest consequences of the relatively weaker expression of the plantation economy was that it militated against St. Lucia's political and constitutional development. While the older British colonies, such as Barbados, had a long experience of white-dominated local parliaments, St. Lucia "until 1925 never had an elected legislature" (Alleyne n.d., 19). Although other Caribbean territories such as Guyana also experienced similar colonial histories, these societies were always viewed as having significant potential for economic exploitation. Further, the largely peasant-based existence of the St. Lucian underclass served to reduce its level of anger against the colonial order. This was seen particularly during the period of anticolonial revolt in the 1930s when the St. Lucian political scene remained relatively calm (Bolland 1995, 79; Lewis 1977, 21; SL Leg. Coun., 14 June 1938). These economic and political realities influenced the political economy of St. Lucia well into the decolonization period (Harris 1960, 65). Salz (1961, 4) described the politics of St. Lucia during this period as "on the whole less agitated or at any rate, less spectacular than has been and is the case in many of the other West Indian islands." Arguing that it would be difficult "to point to any one single event as [a] decisive turning point" or "as productive of an abrupt and definite break of a given social order," he saw little "inner logic" or "inner dynamics" at work in the early nationalist period. He saw instead the influence of "external circumstances and stimuli; events not under the control of St. Lucia, and a factor of 'timing' at work" (ibid.). Thus the political economy of St. Lucian decolonization involved a process in which social and political change was dependent upon changes in the larger and more "economically advanced" Anglophone Caribbean territories, further reinforcing notions of tentative anticolonialism. These factors delayed constitutional decolonization (see Lewis 1968, 145) and allowed global structural realities to intervene more directly in shaping the pattern of postcolonial development in St. Lucia.

These realities shaped the movement into political independence in St. Lucia under John Compton's United Workers' Party (UWP) in the late 1970s. In stark contrast to the experience of the Caribbean states that decolonized in the early to mid-1960s, the interventionist state involved in social and economic engineering on behalf of a previously marginalized population remained alien to the St. Lucian experience. In financial, technological, and ideological terms, the outlines of neoliberal globalization were beginning to take shape and were questioning the definition of the state as a mechanism that could limit the impact of global capital within the domestic sphere. Motivated both by the need to defeat the socialist alternative and by his own reading of the international environment, Compton's economic agenda stressed the role of the sovereign state as a facilitator of global capital (see *The Voice* [Independence Supplement], 19 February 1979). The defeat of Compton's government three months after formal independence by a socialist-inspired St. Lucia Labour Party (SLP) revealed even more clearly the limits of the newly won independence. Not only did the SLP administration collapse within two and a half years due to a combination of internal ideological splits, the hostility of domestic capital, and an unfavorable international environment, but the regime was unable to pursue its project of antisystemic economic nationalism (Duncan 1980, 12–14). In the unfolding global political-economic environment of the 1980s and the 1990s, the constraints on the independent state were to increase with the adjustments in the global banana market and the later global economic crisis in the new millennium. The St. Lucian experience therefore serves as a useful case study of a small state whose historical and contemporary evolution meant that its independence has been largely circumscribed by global neoliberalism.

CHAPTER I

Conceptual Issues

Sovereignty, Nationalism, and Independence in the
Era of Global Neoliberalism

The impact of global neoliberalism on the practice of sovereignty of the independent nation-state has given rise to a wide body of reflection (see, for example, Agnew 2009; Sassen 1996, 1998; Harvey 2005; and Robinson 2004, 2008). The work of Robinson in particular is key to understanding the impact of global neoliberalism for the independence experience of St. Lucia. In contrast to the widely held viewpoint that globalization has brought about the end of the nation-state or the death of sovereignty, Robinson (2008), in contrast, sees the state as being transformed to serve the needs of a transnational capitalist class as distinct from a traditionally understood "national interest." Thus the state has been transformed into a "neoliberal state" whose role is to "serve global (over local) capital accumulation, including a shift in the subsidies that states provide, away from social reproduction and from internal economic agents and toward transnational capital" (ibid., 33). In a context where St. Lucia gained its independence in 1979, the very moment leading to the rise of global neoliberalism—the decade of the 1980s—Robinson's formulation provides a useful framework for understanding the independence experience of St. Lucia in the era of global neoliberalism.

The central theoretical assumption of this work is that a process of globalization has shaped the experience of decolonization and independence and has shaped the meaning and practice of the notion of sovereignty in St. Lucia. This shift in the understanding of sovereignty has meant specifically that at the very point of its birth as an independent nation-state, the instrumentality of sovereign statehood was consciously tailored to facilitate St. Lucia's incorporation into the emerging global neoliberal order as its principal purpose. This stands in stark contrast to the experiences of Caribbean states such as Jamaica, Trinidad and Tobago, and Barbados, which embarked on formal decolonization under global conditions that were shaped by Keynesianism as distinct from neoliberalism.

Exploring Global Neoliberalism

While the buzzword of "globalization" enjoys popular usage (Scholte 1996), the extent and reality of globalization remain a contentious issue. Klak (1998c, 4) has classified the debate on globalization "in terms of whether globalization trends are interpreted as positive or negative with respect to global and national distributions of power, wealth, and development, and political and economic struggles over resources." Similarly, Tabb (1997b, 21) sees the conflict as lying between the view of the international economy as one that "subsumes and subordinates national level processes" and a more "nuanced" view that gives a major role to national-level policies and actors, and the central position not to inexorable economic forces but to politics.

However, the situation is complicated by the presence of varying degrees of skepticism over the existence of globalization. On the one hand, there is a tendency to reject wholesale the idea of globalization, while, on the other, there exist varying degrees of circumspection in the application of the concept. Thus Held (1998) distinguishes between "hyper," "strong," or "extreme" globalizers and "weak," "nuanced," or "soft" globalizers. As a result, many researchers avoid using the term "globalization," fearing that it obfuscates more than illuminates (Amoore et al. 1997).

A major argument of the skeptics is that the "level of integration, interdependence, openness . . . of national economies in the present is not unprecedented" (Hirst and Thompson 1996, 49). These writers suggest, for example, that the "level of autonomy under the Gold Standard up to the First World War was much less for advanced economies than it is today." While acknowledging a degree of change, they seek to "register a certain scepticism over whether we have entered a radically new phase in the internationalization of economic activity" (ibid.). Similarly, D. M. Gordon (1988, 54) contends that "we have been witnessing the decay of the postwar global economy rather than the construction of a fundamentally new and enduring system of production and exchange." In a related argument, Hirst and Thompson (1996, 49–50) suggest that the tendency to oscillate between autonomy and interdependence is a normal feature of states within the international system.

Others reject globalization on the basis that the developments associated with the concept are confined to a very small sector of world economic activity. Thus Ruigrok and Van Tuldor (1995, 151) argue that "what is often referred to as 'globalization' is perhaps better described as triadization." They maintain that in "the 1980s internationalization of trade and investments was largely limited to the United States, the European Community and Japan as well as East and South East Asia." Further, these writers challenge the idea that the activities of the major multinational firms indicate a process of globalization since key functions like management decisions remain "firmly under domestic control" (ibid., 159).

The concept of globalization is also questioned within the neo-Marxist perspective, which sees the notion as an "ideological construct" that denies the capacity for resistance to the dictates of capitalism. Wood (1997b, 23), for example, describes "the conventional wisdom about globalization" as "an excuse for the most complete defeatism and for the abandonment of any kind of anti-capitalist project."

Another argument raised against globalization is the centrality of the nation-state in facilitating the process of global integration. Thus Amoore et al. (1997, 186) suggest that while "the nature of intervention may have changed ... the state has not necessarily diminished in its significance to contemporary capitalism." Consistent with this argument is the emphasis placed by writers on the legitimation function of the state given the absence of competing centers of legitimacy at the global level (Hirst and Thompson 1995, 431). Given the continued relevance of the state, such writers conclude that "we should ditch the over-fashionable concept of 'globalization' and look for less politically debilitating models" (Hirst and Thompson 1996, 185–186).

A close examination of the ideas of the skeptics reveals that their objections are largely a response to the inflated claims of the "hyperglobalizers," and to the "politically debilitating" consequences of the concept. Ohmae (1990, 1993) is typical of such "hyperglobalizers." He speaks of a "borderless world" in which the nation-state has become "unnatural" and "dysfunctional." Despite their hostility to the claims of the "hyperglobalizers," however, the skeptics generally recognize that significant changes have taken place in the global political economy since the mid-1970s. For example, D. M. Gordon (1988, 25) identifies an "erosion of the social structure of accumulation which conditioned international capitalist prosperity during the 1950s and 1960s." Similarly, Hirst and Thompson (1995, 409) concede that the "nation-state's capacity for governance [has] changed and in many respects (especially as national macro-economic managers) [has] weakened considerably in recent years."

Despite their differences, it is clear that most of these commentators recognize and accept that the global environment since the mid-1970s has fundamentally transformed the role of the state in particular as it relates to its domestic political role as facilitator of a distinct "national interest." Instead, under neoliberal globalization the state has been reconfigured through ideological, economic, and political (including military) means to serve as a facilitator of the interests of what Robinson (2004) calls a transnational capitalist class, overturning the previous Keynesianism that had facilitated a more equitable distributive and social function for the state. It is through the prism of the impact of global neoliberalism in shifting the role of the independent state to that of facilitator of global capital that this work utilizes the concept of globalization in understanding the independence experience of St. Lucia.

This work identifies a transition from a post-1945 world order to a post-1970 global order that raised challenges to the strategies that had defined the independence project. The concept of globalization adopted identifies with the perspective of Stephen Gill (1993a, 9), who describes a process of transformation at three interrelated levels:

> (i) "economic," including the restructuring of global production, finance and exchange which challenges previous sets of arrangements and forms of economic organization; (ii) "political," that is in terms of institutional changes including forms of state, the internationalization, transnationalization and indeed globalization of the state . . . ; and (iii) "socio-cultural," that is (in part) the way global restructuring at the political and economic levels also entails challenges to embedded sets of social structures, ideas and practices, thus promoting, as well as constraining the possibilities of change.

When to this is added the greater mobility of finance capital facilitated by new communications technologies, the specific sense of globalization as a set of processes limiting the state as defender and promoter of national interests and in particular as engaged in postcolonial social interventions to reverse colonially induced weaknesses can be readily understood.

The concept of globalization relevant to the St. Lucian experience and used in this work is concerned with the processes that have challenged the assumptions, strategies, and structures through which the decolonization project in the Anglophone Caribbean had been pursued. The concept of globalization adopted here therefore recognizes the presence of objective material conditions that have rendered previous postcolonial strategies and approaches unworkable. At the same time, it rejects the view that the state has become a meaningless actor in the social, political, and economic realm. Such a view addresses the concerns of the skeptics by avoiding the inflated claims of the hyperglobalizers, and is consistent with the view expressed by Saskia Sassen (1998, 199) that

> even though transnationalization and deregulation have reduced the role of the state in the governance of economic processes, the state remains as the ultimate guarantor of the rights of capital whether national or foreign. Firms operating transnationally want to ensure the functions traditionally exercised by the state in the national realm of the economy, notably guaranteeing property rights and contracts. The state here can be conceived as representing a

technical administrative capacity which cannot be replicated at this time by any other institutional arrangement; further, this is a capacity backed by military power.

Exploring Sovereignty in the Era of Global Neoliberalism

Given the impact of global neoliberalism on the functions of the role of the state, a wide body of literature has been churned out involved with the issue of rethinking the concept of sovereignty within the social sciences. Sassen (1996, 1998), Agnew (2009), Jackson and James (1993), Jackson (1990, 1992, 1998), Williams (1996), Camilleri and Falk (1992), and Morris (1998) have all examined the implications of globalization for the sovereignty principle. These works reveal two opposing tendencies. One tendency stresses the continuing juridical significance of the sovereignty principle as an indication of its relevance in the existing global context. A second tendency views the new global situation as dissolving the "internal/external distinction crucial to the orthodox definition of sovereignty" (Williams 1996, 118). To such writers:

> if the line between internal supremacy and external equality can no longer be maintained, sovereignty must be reformulated. If globalization has blurred the distinction between national and international, transformed the conditions of national decision-making, altered the legal framework and administrative practices of states, obscured lines of responsibility and changed the institutional and organizational content of national politics, then sovereignty as a doctrine is of limited relevance. In this sense, globalization refers to more than the erosion of autonomy. It highlights a change in the political landscape and requires an adaptation of political practice. (ibid.)

The writers who see few implications for national sovereignty in the process of globalization argue that the state remains a central institution of political power both in its domestic and international functions. For example, Jackson and James (1993, v–vi) hold that "whether new nations are being formed out of the ruins of multi-ethnic states or whether novel international communities are coming into existence by the co-operative actions of independent governments, the state remains the focus." Such writers argue that despite the expansion of the "orbit of international law . . . far from withering away in the twentieth century, the independent state has everywhere become the standard form of territorial political organization" (ibid., 4). Far from recognizing a diminution in the significance of sovereignty, these writers maintain that "in many respects a major effect has been to enhance that significance" (ibid., 6). These works place strong emphasis on juridical sovereignty as the "ground rule" that "identifies who among territorial bodies, is eligible to pass through the gate which stands at the entrance to international society" (A. James 1984, 2). Relatedly, these works point to the absence of alternative global and domestic sources of authority adequately performing the functions of the sovereign state.

Those writers who defend the relevance of sovereignty commonly argue that "at no time in history were states able to exercise all the rights they claimed." "Absolute power," such writers argue, "is a myth" (Williams 1996, 114). To such writers, the theoretical conceptualization of sovereignty has failed to reflect the practical workings of the concept. They argue that while the theoretical notions of sovereignty generally overstate the absence of limits to the internal power of states, in practice such limitations are commonplace. While such writers recognize the impact of globalization in eroding the power of states, they place greater emphasis on the need to bring the theoretical notions of sovereignty closer to its practical workings (see Morris 1998).

Agnew (2009, 2), for instance, argues that "states have never exercised either total political or economic-regulatory monopolies over their territories. Indeed, some states, perhaps a majority, may have aspired to exert sovereignty in some respect or other but have never entirely succeeded in doing so." As a result, he rejects the "linear story about recent globalization undermining a long-established state territorial sovereignty" and instead seeks to emphasize how "globalization has merely further complicated an already complex relationship between sovereignty and territory" (ibid.).

While the practice of sovereignty has entailed far greater limits to state power than classical notions of sovereignty have allowed, writers working within a framework of anticolonialism and radical decolonization criticize notions such as those expressed by Morris and Agnew as tending to ignore the role of sovereignty as a tool for anticolonial resistance. They see such works as failing to address the impact of neoliberal globalization on the national self-determination project of postcolonial states. Particularly troubling from the anticolonial perspective is the emasculation of the state as a guarantor of internal democracy under neoliberal globalization. This emasculation is reflected, in intellectual terms, in arguments that suggest that sovereign statehood may not necessarily be the most effective guarantor of the rights of citizens (Hintjens 1995). Such arguments call for the identification of new modes of social organization and new institutional frameworks through which citizen participation and policy legitimacy can be established, and for the very redefinition of the idea of citizenship itself (see, for example, Premdas 2002). Related to this is the argument that globalization does not necessarily mean a negation of a sovereign people, since such sovereignty can be better expressed at other levels, as in supranational forms of power, for example.

However, while it is true that the radical thinkers who seek to defend the earlier anticolonial agenda of the state have remained largely impervious to the adjusted notions of citizenship, sovereign expression, and the idea of transnational politics, their concerns remain relevant when the extent to which the modern state has been redefined to function as a promoter of the interests of transnational capital is taken into consideration. Hoogvelt (1997, 131), for example, observes that while some writers "make rather much of the continuing, indeed in some cases apparently enhanced exercise of sovereignty and regulation by national governments . . . , much of this regulation amounts in effect to no more than a regulation *for* globalization." She argues that "it is this confusion over regulation and deregulation that explains why there is so much controversy . . . between those who hold so called 'declinist' views of the nation-state, and those who claim to observe a strengthening of national authority" (ibid., 139).

A similar point about the role of the state in regulating for globalization has been made by Saskia Sassen. She argues that the state has been centrally involved in the "emerging transnational governance system," but it is a state "that has itself undergone transformation and participated in legitimating a new doctrine about its role in the economy. Central to this new doctrine is a growing consensus among states to further the growth and strength of the global economy" (Sassen 1996, 23).

In short, under global neoliberalism, while sovereignty might have been redefined to reflect the role of the state as a promoter of the interests of a transnational capitalist class, it is clear that the sovereign state remains central to the task of defending such interests.

This emergence of a global hegemonic bloc promoting the interests of transnational capital at the expense of other social objectives reinforces the critical perspective of the anticolonial theorists. Thus, while it is true that many sovereign states readily participate in the process of neoliberal adjustment to globalization, it is also true that national policy makers have implemented such policies in the face of hostile opposition from their electorates. Moreover, an important point emphasized by Hoogvelt is that this impulse for regulation emanates largely from the global economic environment rather than from the local political sphere, thus undermining the notion of the "consent of the governed." Such a scenario supports the notion of "glocalization" advanced by Peck and Tickell (1994, 324–325), in which "supra-national regulatory systems have inherited power without responsibility" while local government entities "have been conferred responsibility without power." A clear distinction is made between the authority that states continue to enjoy and the power to determine their internal economic relations. In other words, it is the democratic aspects of the national self-determination project that are most directly threatened by neoliberal globalization.

David Held (1998) has presented one of the clearest arguments that globalization has undermined national self-determination. He argues that prior to the onset of globalization, it was taken for granted that "all the key elements of self-determination . . . could be neatly meshed with the spatial reach of sites of power in a circumscribed territory" (ibid., 2). Held's main conclusion is that in the present context, such assumptions are no longer sacrosanct. While Held does not contend that "national sovereignty today . . . has been wholly subverted," he argues that the "autonomy of democratically elected governments has been, and is increasingly constrained by sources of un-elected and unrepresentative economic power" (ibid., 9, 14).

As a result of these developments, there is a growing tendency within political science toward a normative stance that views postcolonial independent statehood as largely dysfunctional. In contrast to the decade of the 1960s, when a greater moral legitimacy was attached to postcolonial independent statehood, the period of globalization has witnessed a growing tendency to underplay its significance. In the present period, values such as "interdependence" and "cooperation" are now more widely emphasized than the value of the independent state as a bulwark against external domination (Krasner 1993, 301; Rosenau 1995, 95). Adam Watson's work (1997) typifies such a tendency. In a discussion on the relations between newly decolonized states and powerful Western hegemonic states, Watson advocates a return to greater external control of postcolonial states. According to Watson (ibid., 67),

> the Western powers see themselves as having responsibilities towards the peoples of the new states, not just their governments. In discussing their responsibilities they now increasingly often . . . overstep the theoretical line that bars foreigners from interference with the domestic governance of states. . . . Overstepping that line was, in one sense, the essential feature of colonialism. The pendulum, after swinging far towards a host of new independences . . . is now swinging back towards limits and restraints on the new states.

Watson identifies benefits in this development for the formerly colonized states. He argues that "the evidence is that hegemonic pressure and where necessary intervention have done much to promote peace, prosperity and especially rights of individuals, in newly independent ex-colonies and in other ill-governed states like Haiti" (ibid., 121).

This notion of a "dysfunctional" postcolonial sovereignty is also identifiable in R. H. Jackson's (1990) concept of "quasi-states." Jackson emphasizes that the sovereignty of most postcolonial states is largely juridical in nature and exists solely on the basis of the "goodwill" of more powerful entities. He sees the sovereignty of small, weak states as largely "negative sovereignty." While "positive sovereignty" refers to the ability of states to deliver goods and services to the population and to resist the interference of other states, "negative sovereignty" emphasizes prohibitions against the internal population (ibid., 29). Thus the "juridical cart is now before the empirical horse," resulting in a "rather different sovereignty regime with an insurance policy for marginal states" (ibid., 23–24). As a result of the internal failures of many of these states, Jackson (1998), along with Peter Lyon (1993), advocates a return to a form of "trusteeship" or "guardianship" over such states. In the context of the Caribbean, Hintjens's (1995) call for "alternatives to independence" shares Jackson's assumptions about the failure of the statehood project. According to the "alternatives to independence" perspective, "if decolonization is to be equated with postcolonial liberation, it cannot be confined to national liberation; it should result in previously excluded and segregated people securing access to improved levels of economic, social and political rights" (ibid., 28).

A similar, though differently argued reflection on the need to relax the fixation with state-centric sovereignty in the Caribbean has been made by Matthew Bishop and Anthony Payne (2010) in a work that was specifically concerned with the failure of the integration movement in the Caribbean. Framing their argument in the perspective that regional elites have "doggedly attached themselves to a somewhat reductionist notion of sovereignty, characterized by a narrow, state-centric and largely 'zero-sum' understanding of the term," Bishop and Payne argue that the "conventional Caribbean understanding of sovereignty and statehood needs to be opened up, unpicked and discussed in a frank and open debate with the people of the region" (ibid., 2, 5). While they were writing strictly in an attempt to show how the traditional understanding of sovereignty has served to restrict the movement to a regional framework of governance in the Caribbean, their arguments nevertheless demonstrate the manner in which notions of poststate-centric sovereignty have been imagined away from its anticolonial moorings. In this sense, therefore, they also prescribe "alternatives" to the traditional understanding of sovereignty in the Caribbean.

While the frustration of writers like Bishop and Payne with the failure of the integration project in the Caribbean is a valid concern, their isolation of nonstate-centric readings of sovereignty do not place them in opposition to radical anticolonialists who also identify the need for a regional solution as a way out of the postcolonial democratic and development challenges confronting the

Caribbean. Thus Caribbean radicals, as a group, are not homogenously attached to traditional sovereignty for its own sake, as is implied in Bishop and Payne's analysis. What Caribbean radicals do share in common is an opposition to external forms of domination and a historical suspicion toward external sources of economic exploitation of Caribbean people and resources.

This less-than-vigilant attitude toward external sources of domination and exploitation tends to pervade the perspectives such as those presented by Hintjens (though less so in the case of Bishop and Payne), which call for alternatives to the state-centric notions of sovereignty. The weakness of such perspectives lies in the fact that they tend to ignore the history of the anticolonial independence project as a mechanism for resisting such domination and exploitation. This neglect of the history of the anticolonial struggle is evident in Jackson's (1990) claim that postcolonial sovereignty exists through the "goodwill" of more powerful states. This assertion is no doubt influenced by the perceived military limitations of postcolonial states. What these perspectives often forget is that the sovereignty of small, weak states like St. Lucia, albeit largely juridical, does not exist solely because of the ability of such states to defend themselves militarily against a more powerful state. Instead, their sovereignty exists as a consequence of the historical and factual occurrence of a global anticolonial movement between 1945 and 1980, part of which involved significant military defeats for colonialism. It was this global defeat that rendered the colonial condition untenable.

Viewed in this way, the sovereignty of weak states like St. Lucia is not as aberrant as is often suggested. Indeed, one of the central features of the nationalist experience of the Anglophone Caribbean states is the extent to which concerns about political democracy and social and economic equality motivated the thrust toward independence (Bell 1967, 1980). Similarly, the period of early postcolonial state construction has benefited a far wider cross section of the Caribbean population than is assumed by Clapham's analysis (see Domínguez 1993).

Arguments such as those presented by writers like Jackson reflect a reduced sensitivity toward global inequalities. These inequalities initially shaped the nationalist movements in the Anglophone Caribbean, and, by ignoring them, such writers understate the extent to which neoliberal globalization has frustrated the capacity of postcolonial social formations to advance the projects that had shaped the decolonization movement from its earliest genesis. Such a tendency validates Hurrell and Woods's (1995, 447) assertion that "neglected in liberal and other writings about globalization is one particularly important feature of world politics: inequality." Slater (1996, 27) has described this neglect as reflecting a "limiting, enclosed and particularly centered position that is characterized by a crucial historical and geopolitical amnesia." This tendency, he argues, is "conducive to the preservation and continued development of a distorted 'world view' since it allows for the historical erasure of imperial politics, and additionally represses the record of contemporary forms of Western power over the non-west [*sic*]."

In response to this tendency, writers adhering to an imperialism, dependency, and neo-Marxist framework have sought to identify in neoliberal globalization historical continuities of exploitation of formerly colonized states. One tendency within this perspective identifies a process of "recolonization" in the developments associated with globalization (Gruhn 1983; Raghavan 1990; Duncan 1995a; Belle 1996). While this notion tends to understate the continuing relevance of the sovereign state as a domestic anchor for global neoliberalism, its strength lies in the recognition of the increased capacity of transnational capital to influence the internal development options of independent states.

Kathy McAffee (1991, 70–72), for instance, sees the new global political-economic environment as facilitating a "new level of control" of the Caribbean territories that parallels that which existed during the colonial era. Similarly, Belle (1996, 19) has argued that "neocolonialism" no longer suffices as a basis for explaining the relation between the postcolonial world and the developed West. According to this view, the existing global political-economic environment is qualitatively different from that which existed when notions of neocolonialism were formulated by the likes of Kwame Nkrumah, Frantz Fanon, and Amilcar Cabral, in which there was a belief that the independent state was somehow operating below its transformatory potential. In contrast, Belle argues that under neoliberal globalization, the real question is not the underperformance of the state (or the comprador nature of its elites), but its incapacity to engage in anticolonial development strategies or to act in a manner contrary to the interests of transnational capital.

The Utility of Sovereignty and National Self-Determination: Exploring a Normative Stance for St. Lucia

These conflicting interpretations of the impact of globalization upon national sovereignty reflect divergent normative stances on the "desirability" of postcolonial sovereignty. Thus the extreme neoliberal perspective that identifies economic benefits in the openness of societies to global economic processes is sympathetic to any structural changes that weaken the capacity of the sovereign state to frustrate the objectives of global capital (Ohmae 1990, 1993). In this view, the independent state is seen as a barrier to economic progress. On the other hand, those writing from a third world or anticolonial perspective generally lament the redefinition of the state away from Keynesian-type social interventionist objectives. Within this perspective, global economic processes are held responsible for the economic underdevelopment of the third world. The independent postcolonial state is therefore seen as a mechanism through which external economic exploitation can be limited. Similarly, given the importance of individual liberty and "economic rationality" to mainstream liberalism, the normative stance adopted is one that embraces "interdependence" and searches for alternative institutional frameworks through which transnational modes of citizenship, participation, and democratic inclusion can emerge as the traditional understanding of state-centric sovereignty proves less workable.

These conflicting normative interpretations of the impact of neoliberal globalization on state sovereignty are also reflected in theories of nationalism. In periods where the scope and power of the international economic system are seen as an inexorable force overriding the nation-state, nationalism is viewed as "irrational" by those sympathetic to such internationalization and as "inefficacious" by those supportive of national liberation. In periods where state autonomy appears to be gaining ascendancy over internationalization, the theories largely tend to favor such nationalism. Thus, among radicals, nationalism is seen as a "logical" internal response to external repression, while among conservatives and liberals it is seen as an indication of "modernization" (Sathyamurthy 1983, 6–10).[1]

One weakness of the dominant theories of nationalism is their undervaluation of the political question of the seizure or establishment of state apparatus and their overemphasis on the ideological and cultural dimension of nationalism. Among such theories are Benedict Anderson's notion of "imagined communities" (Anderson 1983), Gellner's work (1964), and Marxist theories of nationalism such as those of Hobsbawm (1977, 1990) and Nairn (1975, 1977). To these theorists, nationalism, like religion, is an "irrational" development. Gellner (1964, 153), for example, asks: "Could one think of a sillier, more frivolous consideration than the question concerning the native vernacular of the governors?" Similarly, Nairn's view of nationalism as "janus faced" and as a "pathology" and a "neurosis" that defies theoretical clarification also reflects this tendency (Nairn 1975, 1977; see Blaut 1987, 80).

These largely "negative" readings of anticolonial nationalism stand in marked contrast to what obtained in the 1950s and 1960s (Emerson 1960), where independence was viewed as part of a process of modernization. However, Blaut (1987) argues that despite the generally more sympathetic treatment of anticolonial nationalism in the 1960s, one common weakness has been to underplay the specific intent of indigenous populations to utilize the nation-state as a tool to resist the economic and political exploitation of the West. In Blaut's view, such works deny the "conflict" element inherent in third world nationalism (ibid.). Instead of viewing colonialism as a mechanism of political domination to facilitate Western economic exploitation, it was presented as having laid the foundations for the modern nation-state in a developmentally linear and conflict-free manner (see Emerson 1960, 43–49).

Blaut's main objection to these theories is that they present "no material economic or social reason why people . . . strive to acquire an independent state for themselves, or fight against such efforts at secession, or strive to annex someone else's territory to their own state or empire" (Blaut 1986, 5). Instead, Blaut (ibid., 6–7) sees nationalism as "one kind of political struggle for state power. . . . It is a kind of political process which . . . functions as a neutral tool or implement, one that has been put to use by a variety of classes and cultures for a variety of ends: democratic, autocratic, and otherwise." This view of nationalism as a "neutral" tool is not intended to deny that one group may win political advantage over a rival group. Instead, nationalism is politically neutral in the sense that the mechanism of nationalism can be utilized by a wide variety of political groups with a wide range of political ideologies, all for their own ends.

It is upon such a basis that the impact of neoliberal globalization on St. Lucian decolonization can be properly assessed. While this work does not assume that with independence came an autonomous moment or possible moments when St. Lucia could have pursued alternatives that ran counter to global hegemonic perspectives, it analyzes the St. Lucia experience on the basis of the pervasiveness of demands for such an alternative and the varying extents to which such alternatives were favored or frustrated by the vagaries of domestic and international politics. The continuous articulation and eventual retreat of an alternative to the interests of neoliberal globalization are traced throughout the independence experience of St. Lucia. The accommodation to global capital, and the resultant domestic resistance to it and the politics emergent therefrom, forms the basis for the exploration of the independence experience of St. Lucia. Writers such as David Harvey (2005) and William Robinson (2008) have shown that under neoliberal globalization, the role of the state has shifted from representing domestic populations and economies to facilitating the mobility of capital, and this work isolates the specific consequences and implications of this shift in the case of St. Lucia.[2]

CHAPTER 2

Tentative Anticolonialism

Implications for Decolonization under Globalization, 1940–1970

The Social Structure of Colonial St. Lucia and the Challenge of Working-Class Nationalism

The period surrounding the publication of the reports of the Wood and Moyne commissions of inquiry into West Indian social and economic conditions in 1922 and 1938, respectively (see Cmnd. 1679 [1922]; Cmnd. 6607 [1945]), provides a useful context in which to examine the internal colonial relations of St. Lucia. This period coincides with a phase of economic and social upheaval that sparked the popular nationalist movements in the West Indies. It is in response to these upheavals that the Wood and Moyne commissions were activated and resultant shifts in colonial policy, culminating in eventual decolonization, can be identified.[1] The period therefore provides a useful platform from which to explore the political and economic objectives of working-class nationalism.

In this period, St. Lucia was "not only one of the poorest areas of the West Indies but was regarded as one of the slums of the Commonwealth and among the most poverty stricken areas of the new world" (O'Loughlin 1968, 46).[2] The Moyne Commission (Cmnd. 6607 [1945], 410) noted the existence of a large urban, unemployed, slum-dwelling class reliant on the coaling trade as its main source of employment, but whose plight was exacerbated by the decline of the steamship (see Annual Colonial Report [St. Lucia] 1931).[3] This urban unemployment problem was aggravated by the existence of an economy of "notorious artificiality," associated with the availability of high-paying, short-term employment opportunities (see Lewis 1968, 149–150). This was seen, for example, in the period of the construction of U.S. military bases in the south of the island during World War II and the reconstruction of the city of Castries after a disastrous fire in 1948 (ibid.). The urban unemployed were therefore largely averse to agricultural labor, which was low paying and highly seasonal in nature due to the rhythms of the dominant sugar industry.

The sugar plantation dominated the St. Lucian economy in this period, and the main challenges to the colonial order emerged there. A commission investigating the West Indian sugar economy in 1930 noted prophetically that "sugar can no longer be produced except at a loss . . . ; serious distress may result among large numbers of the population, and that Governments of certain colonies may experience great financial difficulty in maintaining essential services" (Cmnd. 3517 [1930], 3). While the report observed that the sugar industry was not as critical to St. Lucia as it was to other territories,[4] with sugar exports contributing to as much as 45 percent of the territory's export revenues, it was believed that any shortfall would lead to severe social crises. Out of a population of about 56,917, 6,900 people were estimated to be employed directly in the sugar industry (ibid., 85–86). Wages in the sugar industry were extremely low, ranging between one to two shillings per day for men, but nevertheless represented the highest-paying section of the agricultural sector.

These economic conditions were reflected in the social conditions of the majority of the population. Rural society during this "prebanana" period was described as "brutally feudal" and marked primarily "by an oppressed peasant proprietary class fighting to maintain its precarious existence within a hostile environment" (Lewis 1968, 160).[5] Housing conditions were described as being "of a primitive character" (see Annual Colonial Report 1932, 7) in which "it was typical to find the entire family living in a single room" (Lewis 1977, 16). Many plantation workers lived in these "primitive conditions" in plantation-owned barracks, and as late as the mid-1960s there was a high incidence of diseases such as bilharzia and hookworm (O'Loughlin 1963, 89) and an estimated illiteracy rate of 70 percent (Romalis 1968, 30). St. Lucia's social problems were described as being more urgent than its economic problems (O'Loughlin 1968, 43, 72). These social problems were exacerbated by a marked rural-urban socioeconomic disparity fostered by the colonial government's failure to extend its administration and social services to the rural sector (Lewis 1968, 150).

The society's internal class relations reflected its historical evolution as a slave-based plantation society. A small European element, largely French in ancestry, dominated the society economically, politically, and culturally. While this group had significant commercial interests in the Castries capital, its hegemony was most apparent in the sugar plantation sector (Jackson Commission Report 1957, 3). One of the dominant families in the plantation sector was the Devaux family. In 1952 three plantations, the Roseau, Cul-de-sac, and Dennery plantations, were engaged in the manufacture of sugar. Two of these were owned by the Devaux family and the third by Denis Barnard (ibid.).

The local and British colonial administration was most responsive to the economic interests of the planter class. One of the stated aims of the British government was to "maintain in these colonies as a condition of progress and stability a European element," an objective whose realization depended upon "the prosperity of the sugar industry" (British HC Sessional Papers, 4 July 1922, 235). While this was advocated for the entire Caribbean region in the 1920s, due to considerations of economic underdevelopment the principle continued to be applied in St. Lucia long after it had been abandoned elsewhere.[6] Planters therefore featured prominently as nominated officials in the local assembly, reflecting the centrality of their interests to the colonial order (Salz 1961, 25). Politically aligned to the propertied European element was a "brown-to-white" business and professional middle class (Midgett 1983). The position of this class reflected an ethnocentric policy of democratization designed to co-opt "those of mixed race" of "exceptional capacity and intelligence" whose "essential sanity" and "remarkable loyalty to the throne" (Cmnd. 1679 [1922], 79) would pose no challenge to British colonial objectives. Collectively, therefore, this group comprised the principal local beneficiaries of the colonial system.

The political dominance of this group was facilitated by rigid property and literacy franchise qualifications that shaped the composition of the St. Lucia Legislative Council well into the 1950s (Cmnd. 6607 [1945], 379) (see Table 2.1). Planters and propertied Euro–St. Lucians such as Harold Devaux, Andre Duboulay, Clive Beaubrun, and Grace Augustin were nominated throughout this period. Similarly, businessmen and professional middle-class persons such as L. F. McVane, Allen Lewis (an attorney and brother of future Nobel laureate W. A. Lewis), Garnet Gordon (an attorney), F. J. Carasco (a businessman), and R. G. H. Clarke (a druggist) were the main political beneficiaries of limited representative government between the 1930s and 1950s (see Midgett 1983, 125; SL Leg. Coun. 1930–1957).

The political dominance of the propertied class was a reflection of the mild nature of the 1930s labor revolts in St. Lucia (Lewis 1977, 38; Bolland 1995). Indeed, the main beneficiaries of the shift in colonial policy following the 1930s revolts were the local sympathizers with colonialism. In stark contrast to what was taking place in St. Lucia, in Jamaica in 1944, following the 1930s riots, the granting of universal adult suffrage ushered in labor radicals like Alexander Bustamante and nationalist reformers like Norman Manley. It was not until the attainment of universal adult suffrage in 1951 that wholesale political control of the local assembly by representatives of the black majority was possible in St. Lucia (Salz 1961, 136–140). Thus the propertied sections of the society exerted a tremendous influence over the process of change that had been unleashed by the popular labor upheavals of the 1930s.

Table 2.1. Number of electors in the 1930s Anglophone Caribbean		
Country	No. of Electors	% of Population
Antigua	1,048	3.06
The Bahamas	13,146	21.97
Barbados	6,359	3.30
British Guiana	9,578	2.84
British Honduras	1,156	2.00
Dominica	1,124	2.46
Grenada (1921)	--	3.25
Jamaica	61,621	5.22
Montserrat	260	1.90
St. Kitts and Nevis	1,628	2.30
St. Lucia	1,509	2.18
St. Vincent	1,598	2.78
Trinidad and Tobago	30,911	6.64
Source: Hart 1998, 109.		

It was in opposition to these social, political, and economic conditions that a characteristically working-class labor nationalism can be identified.[7] The origins of this popularly based labor nationalism can be traced to the entry, from 1945 onward, of a group of young radicals such as George Charles and Martin JnBaptiste into the St. Lucia Cooperative Workers' Union (SLCWU), an organization that had been largely dominated by middle-class elements since its formation in 1939. Working-class nationalism sought political transformation in order to improve the economic and social conditions of the laboring population. This was seen as more urgent than the question of the broader economic viability of the state. This orientation evolved out of the Crown Colony government experience, in which the state had primarily served the interests of the elite minority section of society. Working-class nationalists rejected the notion of the neutral state and widely expected constitutional democratization to reverse the existing political and economic order (Phillips n.d., 22). These aims are clearly evident in an article in the *Workers' Clarion* (14 September 1957, 1):[8]

> In the struggle by the working class for improved conditions, it is hardly expected that any government operating within the framework of a capitalist society can be neutral. Both the law and the Administration of a capitalist society are directed essentially to support employers. . . . It is therefore no cause for surprise that the Administration . . . can and usually does, under the guise of protecting the "interests of the community" consciously or unconsciously

perpetuate low living standards by the club of the policeman or the bayonet of the soldier. . . . We are not prepared to commit St. Lucia to a Federation[9] as a country which . . . is governed by a few planters and capitalists who keep the bulk of the workers in economic servitude.

The largely rural, agricultural mass base and the lower-middle-class origins of its leadership shaped the economic goals of the St. Lucia Labour Party (SLP).[10] Though falling short of advocating the welfare state due to the "limitations of finance," the SLP tended to "prefer popular extensions of the social services to the less spectacular measures of economic development" (PRO-CO 1031/2178, 4 June 1958). In its 1957 manifesto, the party advocated that lands "not specifically reserved for forestry or other purposes should be made available to peasants to be developed along approved lines" (SLP 1957, 2). The economic program of the party was redistributive rather than productive in focus:

We must realize that in many of these islands there is too great a disparity between the "haves" and the "have nots." There are yet far too many people who despite political freedom yet live in perpetual bondage of debts, poverty, ignorance, and disease. There is in a primarily agricultural community, far too large a weak peasantry, too poor to own the simple tools needed to cultivate their fields and whose chief pre-occupation is survival. (*Workers' Clarion*, 9 January 1958, 1)

The SLP proposed to "attack this problem by a pincer movement, one aim being to provide incentives for the production of greater wealth by developing through our own efforts, and where possible, by outside assistance, our natural resources. The other aim being a more equitable distribution of wealth, whether at present in existence, or subsequently reproduced" (*Workers' Clarion*, 9 January 1958, 1). The party was fully aware of ruling-class opposition to these objectives since "more even distribution of wealth threatens the destruction, indeed in some sense, is the destruction of the very pillars on which the existing society is based" (*Workers' Clarion*, 30 January 1958, 1). Working-class nationalists advocated a far more extensive role for the state than was envisaged by the beneficiaries of colonialism, who, as will be seen later, were more concerned about issues of productivity.

Working-class nationalism was robust in its pursuit of self-government, but was less sensitive to the economic foundations of a future sovereign state. Much of its approach to decolonization suggested a subordination of the broader economic development of the country to the trade union considerations of the welfare of its working-class constituents. Indeed, working-class nationalism and the demand for decolonization itself emerged as an adjunct to the industrial pursuits of labor. One of the early founders of the SLP, George Charles, saw little difficulty in declaring that the SLP, which was established in March 1949 (Kunsman 1963, 609), had evolved as the "political arm" of the SLCWU (Charles 1994, 33). Charles's explanation for the rationale for this development confirms the subordination of the political goal of self-government to the industrial concerns of the labor movement and indicates the labor movement's inherent opposition to the existing economic and political interests. According to Charles, the goal of state power was pursued because trade unions were frustrated by the existing colonial power structure:

> The trade unions were struggling for increased wages. We found that that was not enough because in many cases the persons who blocked the union in its demands were the very persons in government. So therefore, the question arose simply, well that the only thing to do, go in and get inside. And the only way to get inside was through universal adult suffrage. . . . So the struggle was universal adult suffrage and when it was accorded then you had to have the industrial arm and the political arm. The Labour Party was really the political arm, so that we did not at least try to differentiate. (Charles, interview)

The operationalization of working-class nationalism can be further analyzed by examining two major sugar strikes: the Brown strike of 1952 and a five-week strike in 1957. The Brown strike derived its name from the role played by W. G. Brown, an independent member of the St. Lucia Legislative Council, in leading a strike of sugar workers in the Roseau valley for pay increases. A number of features of the Brown strike were consistent with the politics associated with political unionism. The strike followed closely upon the attainment of universal adult suffrage in 1951 and reflected the fact that the vote was being used to elect trade unionists to the legislature. Indeed, the 1952 strike was linked to the fact that Brown had made pay increases to members of his Roseau Peasants and General Workers Union (RPGWU) a central plank of his electoral campaign. Further, the RPGWU had itself been formed to facilitate Brown's electoral ambitions. It provided exclusive representation for workers on the Roseau sugar estate, which was situated in Brown's electoral district. However, Brown's actions eroded the SLCWU's membership and placed pressure on the older SLCWU to outperform Brown in the delivery of pay increases to workers, thus heightening the link between political democratization and industrial conflict (Malone Commission Report 1952). Nationalism therefore became firmly associated with improvements in the economic position of workers and intensified agitation against the plantocracy.

One of the planters' earliest responses to the working-class trade unionist challenge was to threaten to cease sugar production since trade unionism
meant that the planters could no longer unilaterally control and determine
wage levels (Malone Commission Report 1952, 45). Following the Brown
strike, the two sugar companies owned by Harold Devaux—the Roseau and
Cul-de-sac sugar companies—went into voluntary liquidation. They were replaced by Sugar Manufacturers Ltd., a public liability company with a nomi-
nal capital of $2 million, with the government owning $250,000 in ordinary
shares.

The processes unleashed by the Brown strike found a sharper expression
in the 1957 strike. While the Brown strike had been quickly diffused,[11] the
1957 sugar strike was marked by a greater level of militancy by strikers and a
more coercive response by the colonial authorities. The strike started spontaneously on the Roseau estate on 25 March 1957, but was quickly taken over
by the SLCWU and spread to all the major estates in the country (Jackson
Commission Report 1957, 12). Under John Compton's leadership, roadblocks
were mounted and nonstrikers intimidated. The violence and economic disruption lasted for nearly six weeks. The strike was quelled by the deployment
of Grenadian and Barbadian police reinforcements and the posting of three
British warships in and around Port Castries (see Charles 1994, 48). Scores
of persons were taken to court between 3 and 26 April 1957 and charged with
offenses ranging from the use of weapons to disorderly behavior and intimidation. Many were fined between $40 and $50 and received jail sentences of
between three and six months (see PRO 1031/2809, 27 April 1957).

Following the 1957 strike, one of the critical contradictions in the islands' recently introduced constitutional status of "full ministerial system" was brought
sharply to the fore. The "full ministerial system" had seen the elevation of a
certain number of elected members to the status of "ministers" with executive
responsibility over designated portfolios (see Table 2.2). As a result of the strike,
ministers who had retained their leadership posts in the trade unions came under sharp criticism. The conflict between their roles as managers of the economy
as a whole and their roles as trade union leaders became, as will be seen later, a
central basis for opposition to the tactics of working-class nationalists.

The 1957 strike completed the destruction of the sugar plantocracy set in motion by the Brown strike. In 1961 the majority of shares of Sugar Manufactures
Ltd. were sold to Van Geest, of Geest Industries Ltd., a leading British investor
in agricultural production. This drew the St. Lucian economy more firmly into
the global economy as a banana producer. The economy therefore witnessed
a transition from local planter domination to domination by global capital,
which drew into its orbit the small landholders as banana producers.

Table 2.2. Constitutional development in St. Lucia, 1924–1967		
YEAR	**GOVERNMENTAL STRUCTURE**	**ADVANCE INITIATED**
1924	EXEC. COUNCIL: Governor and chief officials, e.g., Principal Law Officer Colonial Secretary Treasurer Nominated Officials LEGIS. COUNCIL: 6 ex-officio members 3 nominated members 3 elected members (Governor with casting vote)	Elected representatives in Legis. Council Franchise qualification: £30 annual net income Ownership of property valued at £150/ Rental of real estate valued at £12 annual minimum.
1936	EXEC. COUNCIL: Same as above LEGIS. COUNCIL: 2 ex-officio members 3 nominated members 5 elected members (Administrator with casting vote)	Increase in number of elected representatives Balance between elected representatives and other members Reduction in franchise qualifications: £100 in property 15 shillings annual minimum in taxation
1951	EXEC. COUNCIL: Administrator 3 elected members of Legis. Council 4 ex-officio members 1 nominated official member 1 nominated member of Legis. Council LEGIS. COUNCIL: 3 ex-officio members 3 nominated members 8 elected members (Administrator with casting vote)	Universal adult suffrage (21 years and over); elected members enjoy majority in Legis. Council
1955	EXEC. COUNCIL: same as above LEGISLATIVE COUNCIL Composition same as above Divided into 3 committees Elected members of Exec. Council acting as Chairmen	Committee system introduced, allowing elected members of Exec. Council supervisory roles within specific depts. of the civil service. Weakness: Their role was merely advisory
1956	EXEC. COUNCIL 2 official members 1 nominated member of Legis. Council 4 elected members LEGIS. COUNCIL Same as above	Full ministerial system introduced 3 elected members now designated as "Ministers" Nominated officials abolished Elected members could potentially command majority in Exec. Council; Exec. Council to accept collective responsibility and to support all measures of government in the Legis. Council Weakness: All matters of finance and expenditure to remain under the sole authority of the Administrator, acting through the Financial Secretary

1960	EXEC. COUNCIL:	Governor of Windwards abolished
	Administrator	Exec. Council in control of the affairs of the
	1 ex-officio member	state
	4 elected members (including Chief	A Chief Minister, commanding the majority
	Minister)	appointed as head of government
	1 official member of Legis. Council	Ministers and other nonofficials in the Exec.
	LEGIS. COUNCIL:	Council, to be appointed on the advice of the
	10 elected members	Chief Minister
	2 nominated members	Nominated members in the Exec. Council
	Speaker	reduced from 3 to 2
1967	EXEC. COUNCIL:	Associated Statehood introduced
	Premier (Chairman of Cabinet)	Exec. Council now a full-fledged cabinet; Exec.
	Ministers of Government	Council given control over internal affairs
	LEGIS. COUNCIL:	Opposition (thus political parties) officially
	10 elected members	recognized
	Leader of the opposition	Weakness:
	Additional nominated members	Foreign affairs prerogative of British
	Speaker	government
Sources: Adapted from Phillips 1960; C. Harris 1960; and *The Voice*, 18 February 1979.		

An important feature of working-class nationalists was their commitment to a federal framework of decolonization. A number of factors account for this. Throughout the Caribbean, the goal of federation was pursued more vigorously among working-class political movements. The domination of the labor parties throughout the Caribbean in the 1950s and 1960s meant that the working-class forces had little to fear from the West Indian federation, compared to the procolonial groups.[12] Indeed, federation was seen as furthering the objective of full independence. In contrast, the parties of the procolonial groups were reluctant to embrace federation since it threatened to erode their power at the island level.[13] More particularly, the belief in federation by working-class nationalists in St. Lucia reflected the widely held view that the weak economy and small size of St. Lucia were barriers to the island's eventual elevation to full sovereign status. St. Lucia's working-class leadership therefore supported federation to increase the chances of achieving their goals of internal transformation and independence. It is clear that while working-class nationalists favored an interventionist state, they were also cognizant of the fact that a wider, pan-Caribbean notion of sovereignty would be a far more effective sovereign mechanism through which their objectives could be achieved.

Not uncharacteristically, the link between federation and self-government had emanated from the British colonial government itself.[14] The Colonial Office had consistently stressed the view that "political independence is unreal unless it is based on . . . an adequate national income" (see Col. 255 [1950], 12). The notion that "it is clearly impossible in the modern world for the present communities, small and isolated as most of them are, to achieve and maintain full self-government on their own" (Cmnd. 7120 [1947], 6) was held to be a "truism" from which reputable political opinion could not deviate.

These notions dominated the thinking of working-class nationalists in St. Lucia. In the *Workers' Clarion* (9 January 1958, 1), it was declared that the "smaller territories are firmly committed to the Federal ideal which we regard as the only way to economic salvation of these islands." For this reason, George Charles, as leader of the SLP, had expressed support for a federation that would have "a strong centre," that would "have the power and finance to shape the development of the nation," and that would "command a range and volume of revenue sufficient to enable it to make direct contributions to the depressed sectors of the area" (see George Charles in Cmnd. 1417 [1961], 14). This position deviated sharply from those of the leaders of the larger territories such as Jamaica, who were, in the words of Alexander Bustamante, "more than suspicious of the motive behind this federation," viewing it as an attempt by Britain to avoid its developmental responsibilities (W. A. Bustamante in Col. 218 [1948], 21–23).

These features were the outstanding characteristics of working-class nationalism in St. Lucia. The political leadership sought self-government in order to alleviate the economic and social plight of the working-class majority. They saw self-government as allowing the state the freedom to pursue an interventionist strategy that would break sharply with the internal colonial relations. These objectives were perceived as being more attainable within the framework of a federal West Indian state. The actual politics of nationalism in St. Lucia, however, served to frustrate these aims. Instead, the politics of nationalism witnessed a reduced emphasis on the goal of full sovereign statehood, giving rise to the dominance of tentative anticolonialism.

Tentative Anticolonialism in the Politics of Nationalism

The emergence of tentative anticolonialism as ideologically hegemonic within the nationalist movement in St. Lucia was determined by two distinct, yet interrelated, factors. The first was the overwhelming dominance of notions of the economic unviability of St. Lucia, and the second was the determined opposition of the main economic interests to a radical project of internal transformation.

The question of St. Lucia's economic vulnerability significantly influenced the process of anticolonial change. The notion that "the comparative smallness and isolation" of territories such as St. Lucia "make it questionable whether the experiment of responsible government would be practicable" had been raised as an objection to constitutional decolonization as early as the period of the

Wood Commission of the early 1920s (Cmnd. 1679 [1922], 77). While the years between 1924 and 1951 had witnessed significant constitutional advances toward representative government, the view of St. Lucia as economically unviable continued to retard the pace of constitutional change between the 1950s and 1960s (see Table 2.2), when full independence was being contemplated for the larger Caribbean territories.

Despite strong evidence to suggest that the anxiety over economic viability was being used as an ideological justification for the economic hegemony of the planter class,[15] this link between economic development and political democratization was widely and almost unquestioningly accepted by the political class. The underdevelopment of the sugar industry, the absence of mineral resources, the small size of the territory both in terms of geography and population, and the widespread levels of poverty and underdevelopment were all seen as militating against the rapid introduction of constitutional change. Specifically, it was an idea to which members of the propertied class unquestioningly subscribed. For example, during the parliamentary debate on the introduction of the ministerial system, the only member to oppose the resolution, Grace Augustin, presented an economic rationale for her objections. Adhering to the established colonial policy that "the economic resources of dependent areas shall be developed to the point at which responsible government becomes practicable," she accused the British government of being "more liberal with political grants than with monetary." Her central objection was that the territory's economic poverty would render domestic ministerial power ineffectual: "The sergeant dressed up in the General's uniform is sergeant still. . . . I fail to see what advantage there will be in saddling our legislators with trappings suggesting an independence which perhaps does not exist. Backward educationally, what can St. Lucia do in the foreseeable future with our ministerial system? It will be, as I see it, parading in a most expensive political garb" (PRO-CO 1031/1408, 25 February 1955).

While this suggests a demand for greater levels of British financial support, Augustin's objections were also politically motivated. As a French creole member of the Nominated Council, Augustin feared that the ministerial system would erode the economic domination of the local European minority. This is revealed clearly in a later retraction of her criticism. Speaking one year after the inception of the ministerial experiment, Augustin took the opportunity "as the voice that had protested against the ministerial system" to assert that it "was the right move and the right people have been chosen" (*Workers' Clarion*, 26 January 1957, 2). Her belated support for the system was due to the fact that no radical overturning of internal economic relations had occurred. What is discernible, however, was the importance of the economic unviability question as an argument against the process of constitutional change, and as a justification for limiting political possibilities in St. Lucia. This ideological device, it will be seen, was continuously utilized well into the 1970s when full independence was being pursued, severely limiting the population's consciousness in the possibilities of the sovereign statehood.

In the debate on the ministerial system, the more consciously nationalist members of the Legislative Council, such as John Compton, though opposed to the radical labor-oriented ideals, rejected the notion that "bread should come before the vote." Instead, the territory's economic weaknesses were blamed on the absence of local control over the decision-making structure. For Compton, the struggle for political democratization was a struggle for "intimate association with the affairs of the government" as a "first step for the final take over of the affairs of the state" (PRO-CO 1031/1408, 25 February 1955). One of Compton's objections to the 1955 constitutional proposals was the fact that economic decision making was kept under the control of the colonial financial secretary. Compton objected that under the proposals, "You can have Ministers walking about as Ministers with a lot of apparent power, when the final repository of this power is in the Financial Secretary who can tell you what you can do and what you cannot do. . . . If we have a Financial Secretary who is prepared to reduce his office to that of a sausage machine and chop our every legitimate aspiration this constitution would be an empty fraud" (ibid.).

Despite this shift in emphasis, Compton's political commitment to a politics of reformism as distinct from radical transformation resulted in his failure to pursue his argument to its logical conclusion and to fundamentally challenge the notion that economic backwardness should limit the progress toward self-government. While mild reformers like Compton actively pursued local political control, the particular role for the state that they contemplated reflected anxieties about the economic unviability of St. Lucia. This inability to fully unmask the concern over economic backwardness as an ideological fetter tying the hands of radical alternatives to colonialism was seen clearly in Compton's failure to fashion a conception of the postcolonial state that fundamentally challenged the assumptions and parameters of the colonial state.

Thus, for example, one of the earliest expressions of the role of the state envisaged by Compton suggested that the lack of capital demanded an accommodation to the existing internal economic relations of the territory. In an address to the local Chamber of Commerce, Compton, then minister of trade and production, declared that an "umpire" role for the state was the most feasible given the economic underdevelopment of the society:

> Because of the lack of capital, no government whatever its political colour, can at present do more than play a negotiative role [*sic*]—a role allocated

to it in the days of classical capitalism in the nineteenth century, that is, to create conditions conducive to free enterprise, to maintain order, to protect property rights and enforce contracts. It functions in its allotted sphere in the field of education and it attends to the construction of public works, but for a long time to come, at least, no Government will be in a position to substitute public enterprise for that of private. In short, in the game of wealth production, Government will act as an umpire, not as a participant. (*Workers' Clarion*, 20 November 1958, 1)

This marks a significant departure from working-class nationalists' aspirations for direct governmental action in pursuit of rapid social and economic changes to the lives of the majority of the population. Similarly, while working-class nationalists had been ideologically hostile to European economic domination, in Compton's perspective, these political considerations were subordinate to the more urgent task of wealth creation. In these circumstances, the state that emerged reflected a continued sensitivity to the economic vulnerability of the society and the limits of political sovereignty, rather than its possibilities. This substantially meant a continuation of existing economic relations. Compton's ideological understanding of the role of the state was therefore conducive to the emergence of a view in which the sovereign state was consciously subordinate to interests of global capital. It is in this context that Compton's role as the champion of the political forces hostile to working-class nationalism and its version of radical postcolonial transformation was critical in shaping the politics of St. Lucian nationalism.

In direct political terms, Compton emerged as the ideal representative of two main groups that were hostile to the objectives of working-class nationalism. The first were the old beneficiaries of the existing system, and the second were the younger, British-university trained St. Lucian national reformers who emerged in the late 1950s and early 1960s. These reformers had their political origins in the labor movement, but they placed greater emphasis on the "state-building" project than they did on the goal of anticolonial internal transformation. In this sense, they reflected the anxieties about the economic viability of the state. Their opposition was leveled principally at the trade unionist orientation of the working-class nationalists. The reformers pursued the goal of self-government, but were opposed to an economic project of state interventionism, and they identified with the economic aspirations of the propertied class. This identification was formalized with the formation of the United Workers' Party (UWP) in 1964, with Compton as its first leader. The UWP allied the young reformist elements who had broken away from the SLP with members of the Peoples' Progressive Party (PPP), the political organization of the procolonial groups. These groups were in effect supported by British government policy, which aimed to control the pace of constitutional change and foster a "responsible trade unionism" that would leave the internal economic relations of the society largely untouched.

While all the Caribbean territories witnessed the emergence of procolonial political organizations eager to prepare themselves for the looming contestation over the postcolonial state, the influence of these procolonial groups in St. Lucia was far greater than that which can be discerned in similar class groupings in other Caribbean countries. Given the particular circumstances of St. Lucia, and partly as a result of the underdevelopment of the working-class forces themselves, the influence exerted by the old planter class and its "brown-to-white" professional supporters over the politics of nationalism contributed significantly to the politics of tentative anticolonialism. One of the ways in which the influence of this group was manifested was in its direct involvement in the trade unions and political parties of the working class.[16] This reality is captured by F. J. Carasco, who, in an article on the history of trade unionism in St. Lucia, suggests that "the first few years were . . . aimed primarily at getting the union accepted in the community as part of the machinery of industrial relations. Many influential citizens . . . joined the union to give it their support, and the presence of such persons helped to make it acceptable to the employer group" (*The Voice* [Independence Supplement], 19 February 1979). When the historical attitude of these "influential citizens" (including Carasco himself) toward the process of decolonization is considered, the full implications of their control of the early nationalist process for the later role of the state and the limited reading of sovereign possibilities can be better understood.

The legislative record of this group in the 1930s and 1940s, prior to the rise of the working-class challenge, indicates its clear commitment to preserving its own economic interests and its opposition to efforts at improving the conditions of the working people. For example, a British government proposal for a "Labour Ordinance Bill" in response to the 1930s revolts aroused much hostility from the propertied class.[17] One of the proposals in the bill was for the creation of the post of a "Labour Inspector," whose tasks would include the inspection of estate living conditions. In an argument sympathetic to the dominant economic interests, R. G. H. Clarke recommended the postponement of the bill for five years: "for what was the use of making inspections of estate barracks when there were no means of providing such barracks on account of the low prices being obtained for produce." He argued further that "if estate owners were forced to provide suitable housing for their laborers, the laborers would stand the chance of being thrown out of employment because the owners were not at present in a position to supply suitable barracks" (SL Leg. Coun., 14 June 1938, 2).

The narrow political base of this group determined its stance on the question of self-government. Confident in its role as the heir to the "political kingdom," its main concern was to prove its fitness for self-government. It accepted the ideological terms upon which the Colonial Office brought about social and political change: "even if we do make some mistakes at first, we should learn from experience, and ultimately the experiment will be justified" (F. J. Carasco in SL Leg. Coun., 9 September 1948, 6–7). This group consciously saw itself as providing a conservative check to the more antisystemic demands of the working-class leadership. This was clearly expressed by Carasco, who warned his colleagues that "they must no longer take things for granted but . . . must busy themselves and organize themselves" to ensure that "by some organized instruction they may be able to influence and direct the views of the masses" (SL Leg. Coun., 9 September 1948, 6).

With the formation of the SLP in 1949, the promise of universal suffrage, and the growing strength of working-class nationalism, the economically dominant groups formed the PPP in 1950 as a political counterweight to these developments. Indeed, a former leader of the PPP admitted that the party was a "middle-class reactionary thing to the Labour Party" (Francois, interview). The PPP was funded by the plantocracy and commercial elite, run by the professional "brown-to-white" groups, and supported by the urban salaried groups (see PRO-CO 1031/2178, 4 June 1958). The PPP opposed the strong link between the SLP and trade unionism and emphasized that it was the only party in St. Lucia "influenced by no sectional interest" (Kunsman 1963, 613). In its 1950 election manifesto, the party declared that "it would work to promote harmonious relations between all sections of the community in order that our economic security might not be prejudiced by unnecessary strikes or lockouts." While the party did not intend to "set labor's house in order for them," it proposed to bring labor legislation up to date and to guide the formation of labor unions "along proper lines" (PPP 1950). Describing itself as a "free enterprise party strongly opposed to socialism and communism," the PPP wanted to put an end to the "economic disruption" and "unstable investment climate" created by the power of labor under semirepresentative government (Kunsman 1963, 617–618). In its 1957 election manifesto, the PPP described its goals as intended to "maintain the lowest level of government spending, consistent with efficiency, particular attention being paid to reduce the cost of government itself by improvement of the organization of government to eliminate waste." These goals were calculated to achieve "an influx of foreign capital for promoting productive enterprises through which the level of national income can be raised" (PPP 1957, 3).

The response of the planter interests to the 1950s sugar strikes significantly affected the character of St. Lucian nationalism. The planters' main response to the sugar strikes was to assert their value as producers to the viability of the territory. Following the Brown strike, Harold Devaux warned that "the one and only thing which I am not prepared to do is to manage companies which are to be continually hampered by persons intending to use the sugar industry to gain their political ends whatever the economic results may be" (see Malone Commission Report 1952, 45). The planters therefore attempted to limit the impact of nationalism to a realm external to the internal economic relations of the society. This was revealed in the planters' response to the five-week sugar strike of 1957:

> The officers of the trade union and of the St. Lucia Labour Party are the political leaders of this country. . . . They have the control of the economic policy of this country. . . . When I was asked to invest my money in this Public Company, which was sponsored by Government, I was led to believe that it could be operated on sound business lines, that it would be protected by a stable Government. . . . If we are told now that this cannot be . . . I say that we have every justification to demand that they acquire all the shares which they do not already hold and that they operate the Company as a state-owned concern (Sugar Manufacturers Ltd. to Administrator, 6 May 1957).

The propertied class therefore raised the issue of economic stability in an effort to limit the attack against its economic interests and simultaneously to contain the antisystemic objectives of working-class nationalism.

The propertied groups were aided in this objective by the British colonial government. One of the main aims of the colonial administration was to foster a notion of the "appropriate" role of government that would influence the later state forms, particularly given the continued British interests in the region. In the view of the colonial administration, the working-class leadership "had more experience of political agitation than of administration" (see Phillips n.d.). While the British government was committed to a process of political democratization, it was equally intent on ensuring that the process resulted in no radical shift in the internal economic relations. The British government therefore insisted that the working-class leadership abandon its class-based politics. These tendencies informed, for example, the text of an "emergency statement" released by the administrator following the Brown strike:

> Government is an independent party. The sole interests of Government are as follows (i) the preservation of the rule of law; (ii) the security of production, and the prosperity and welfare of all the inhabitants of St. Lucia. Government is not concerned with what share of production is distributed between manufacturers and employees. I must remind all workers and employers that

Government is the trustee of their welfare and property. Accordingly, it is in the interest of Government acting for the good of all that production should not be wantonly interrupted. Without production there is no wealth to be shared at all. In the present impoverished condition of the Colony we cannot afford industrial unrest. We cannot afford the expense of a strike in the sugar valleys. If the expense is incurred and the price is paid, we will all, including workers, and without exception be the poorer. We will create a bad impression abroad, and will frighten away both local and foreign investment capital which is so badly needed in our island home. (*St. Lucia Gazette*, 16 January 1953)

The colonial authorities followed this trend and blamed the 1957 strike on the determination by the trade union–cum–political leadership to win votes at the expense of economic stability. The administrator expressed the hope that "once a new government is in power . . . they will regard the affairs of the sugar industry in a more realistic and sober light—or they can be cajoled or bullied into doing so" (PRO-CO 1031/2809, 17 July 1957, 3). The local colonial government therefore underplayed the role of the state as an agent of anticolonial change and emphasized instead its role as an agent of capital accumulation.

In addition, the British government also contained working-class nationalistists' ambitions through its control of the process of constitutional change in St. Lucia. Adhering to the colonial principle of "colonial tutelage" (Munroe 1972, 29), all advances toward self-government were made dependent upon the demonstration of "responsible leadership" by the working-class nationalists (PRO-CO 1031/2809, 15 May 1957). As a result of their eagerness to accede to a more advanced constitution on the road to self-government, radical leaders were often cowed into obedience through the threat by the British government to withhold further constitutional progress. The use of this strategy was clearly evident in a speech to the legislature by the administrator following the 1957 strike:

It is beyond question that the next five years will probably be the most important phase in the evolution of this area towards nationhood. . . . The Secretary of State has replied that he would like first of all to have a better opportunity for gauging the position regarding the operation of the ministerial system under the present constitution before considering the proposals. . . . Any improvement in our constitutional position will be inevitably linked with the position of our economy. Our economic potential, in turn, is always conditioned by our ability to behave responsibly on all occasions and to generate confidence. (SL Legis. Coun., 6 November 1957, 4)[18]

By the early 1960s, therefore, a number of developments had emerged to ensure a broad consensus on the noninterventionist role of the state and a notion of sovereignty that was less antisystemic than that envisaged by working-class nationalists. In short, the basis for the ideological hegemony of tentative anticolonialism had been well established.

By 1960 the sugar economy had declined, and the subsequent shift from sugar to bananas resulted in a number of socioeconomic transformations, which were viewed as synonymous with "independence." The gradual destruction of the hated sugar economy had defused the main source of anticolonial anger, and the erosion of the economic power of the old planter class in the rural plantation sector and the participation of the peasantry occupying marginal hillside lands in the banana industry led to the view that the "anticolonial" question had been settled. In addition, these tendencies were reinforced by the constitutional advances toward representative government that occurred between 1951 and 1960. A significant step had been taken in 1956 with the introduction of the ministerial system. Under this system, locally elected politicians in the legislature were allowed to function as ministers in the executive council (see Table 2.2). While the "committee system" of the 1955 constitution had allowed elected members to serve only in a supervisory, advisory capacity within various ministries, the ministerial system of 1956 gave these elected members full control over selected ministerial departments. Though significant levels of authority remained in the hands of colonial officials, in the eyes of reformist politicians, these developments represented meaningful advances in the march toward self-government. The 1960 constitution, which allowed for the selection of a local "Chief Minister" who played an advisory role in the selection of ministers and other un-officials, marked a further phase in this process. These constitutional advances led to a reduction in political agitation against the colonial system and created a context in which radical demands on the system were effectively neutralized and silenced.

The rise and eventual fall of the West Indies Federation also nudged the collective consciousness toward tentative anticolonialism. Formed in 1958, the West Indies Federation had been widely viewed as creating the framework for full independence of the West Indian territories. Britain allowed many of the constitutional advances that St. Lucia had made in the late 1940s and the 1950s in order to ensure "constitutional parity" with the other West Indian partners in the union. As a result, the collapse of the West Indies Federation in 1962 proved to be a defeat for the types of sovereign expression envisaged by working-class nationalists (see O'Loughlin 1968, 213–214) and forced upon them, perhaps through sheer political fatigue and frustration, the grudging acceptance of the limited versions of sovereignty to which they were ideologically opposed. The sense of political reversal that pervaded St. Lucian political life following the federation's demise is clearly encapsulated in the claim by Chief Minister George Charles that the territory had been "forced to endure" the "most exasperating episode[s] of nineteenth century colonialism" in the wake of the collapse (Charles, Budget Address 1962).

It is in this economic and constitutional context that one can detect both the formal adoption of the assumptions of tentative anticolonialism and the definitive end of the early nationalist debate in the early period of anticolonial politics culminating in the 1960s. In political terms, its clearest and most consistent articulation was carried by John Compton through the National Labour Movement (NLM) and UWP, the two political parties that he formed with the aim of breaking the hegemony of the SLP over the nationalist process.[19] A significant feature of these organizations was the class basis of the leadership. Collectively referred to as the "Comptonite intellectuals," the leaders of the NLM, formed in 1961, presented themselves as a more modern and professional group, a reality that attracted support from the urban middle class.[20] Similarly, the UWP was formed on 29 March 1964 through a merger of the NLM with the party of the propertied class, the PPP. Given the narrow class basis of the PPP, this alliance allowed the more conservative elements to enhance their chances for election. Compton's British education, his base among the rural agricultural workers, and his movement away from a strict labor platform provided the perfect vehicle for the revival of the political fortunes of the PPP.

The main feature of middle-class reformism that Compton enthusiastically championed was its greater sensitivity to the broader project of "state-construction" than was evident in working-class nationalism. Its anticolonialism was confined, according to a colonial report, to the exploitation of the emotional concepts of colonialism, but did not address the question of economic redistribution (see PRO-CO 1031/3702 [1962]). The main "emotional" plank of middle-class nationalism was a demand for the replacement of British officials with West Indian ones. This was seen in Compton's demand for an administrator of West Indian birth and for the promotion of local police officers to the higher echelons of the police service. This latter demand culminated in a police strike in November 1962, the objective of which was to effect an indigenization of the officer corps of the local police force (see PRO-CO 1031/3702 [1962], 1–2; Hallinan Commission Report 1962, 15).

Middle-class reformist concerns over the economic foundations upon which the self-governing state was to be constructed provided the practical basis for the consolidation of the assumptions of tentative anticolonialism. By the early 1960s the notion of the "umpire" role of the state, which Compton had expressed in 1958, had been reinforced by the more liberal economic and political atmosphere that had been occasioned by the constitutional advances between 1950 and 1960. While in the earlier period the demands for constitutional change were seen as necessary to economic development, by the 1960s the reformers were concerned that demands for greater degrees of constitutional sovereignty would affect economic growth. During the UWP's first year in control of the St. Lucia legislature in 1964,[21] the administrator's speech expressed the government's intention to de-emphasize the question of constitutional change:

> My Government accepts the view that constitutional development is merely the necessary legal framework within which a people work out their own destiny. My Government subscribes to the view that political independence is meaningless without economic viability, and with economic viability political independence is not a law to be observed, but a habit to be acquired. My Government therefore, while striving to remove all political and constitutional obstacles in the way of its economic development, will concentrate its effort in the field of economic development rather than dissipate its energies in the forum of constitutional debate. (SL Leg. Coun., 14 July 1964)

The reformers pursued an internal agenda conducive to the attraction of external capital and were less inclined to identify with labor interests in the manner evident under working-class nationalism. This tactical distancing from the interests of labor was facilitated by the decline of the sugar plantation. The banana industry was more dependent upon small, independent landholders, and this facilitated a decline of the politics of trade union nationalism more suited to the needs of sugar workers (see Barrow-Giles and Soomer 1996), which opened the way for concessions to capital.

An early indication of this shift in emphasis can be gleaned from a meeting between the Colonial Office and Geest. In that meeting, Geest described Compton as the only minister "who appreciated the needs of the St. Lucia economy." Geest's endorsement of Compton had followed from a meeting between the two men in which Geest "had appealed to Compton for support with labour." In response, Compton had expressed his anxiety to "co-operate to the full in order to preserve the sugar industry for the general benefit of the St. Lucia economy."[22] Geest had in turn given Compton the assurance that "so long as satisfactory co-operation could be maintained between him and the local government . . . there was a reasonable chance of success" (PRO-CO 1031/3422, 23 November 1960). It is clear that much of the focus of middle-class reformism involved a de-emphasis on placing limits on international capital and instead shifted to demonstrating its willingness to create conditions conducive to the operations of capital. Subservience to international capital was its dominant instinct.

Given the political domination of the UWP during the 1960s and the 1970s, the dominant view of the state that emerged out of the nationalist period expressed a dependence on external investment. It was opposed to strong expressions of national sovereignty, particularly where such an expression implied setting limits upon the activities of foreign capital. This orientation, coupled with notions of the vulnerability of the St. Lucian state, manifested itself in a reluctance to pursue the trappings of formal sovereignty and to use the available elements of domestic power for economic transformation. The factors of small size (demographic, economic, and territorial), the dependence upon a single export crop in bananas, the domination of middle-class political leaders with a weakened nationalist orientation, and the failure of the federation collectively shaped the emergence of Thorndike's notion of a "politics of inadequacy." According to Thorndike (1979a, 603), this

> could be summed up as a deep-seated feeling that they were simply not viable units in a world of independent states. . . . Elite expectations built up since 1947 had one by one, been dashed. . . . On a popular level in the region and elsewhere, reactions to any possibility of future independence ranged from the contemptuous . . . to prejudice expressed by such phrases as "petty sovereignties" and "Lilliputian exoticism," and expressions of doubt, sometimes in racial terms, in their administrative competence. . . . A qualitatively different factor promoting this inadequacy was that, born out of the labour, rather than any nationalist movement, they had never acted on the question of constitutional development except as a response to events elsewhere in the larger Caribbean area.

It is within this framework that a state-society balance conducive to and sustained by the hegemonic acceptance of a notion of "limited sovereignty" can be identified as the main outcome of St. Lucian nationalism. Through the influence of working-class nationalism, the questions of political democracy and economic redistribution had been placed on the political agenda. The emphasis on universal suffrage and trade unionism had therefore meant that the question of the political participation of the majority and the economic advancement of the mass of the population were critical to notions of independence. At the same time, under the influence of reformist middle-class nationalism and sustained by the guiding hand of the colonial government, greater emphasis was placed on economic development and the avoidance of political options that threatened such development. Central to the thinking of national reformers was the idea that the external economic environment would facilitate the goal of internal economic development.

The fundamental assumptions of tentative anticolonialism therefore gained political ascendancy. In political terms, it was manifested in the constitutional status of Associated Statehood, and in economic terms, in the internal social relations of the banana economy. It was around this state-society balance, which captured the assumptions of tentative anticolonialism, that the future struggle for sovereign statehood would be waged and upon which the later impact of globalization can be assessed. It is therefore necessary to assess the workings of this state-society balance in order to analyze its implications for the later politics of independence under neoliberal globalization.

The State-Society Bargain of "Limited Sovereignty": Associated Statehood and the Banana Economy

The widely perceived limitations in the capacity of St. Lucia for the responsibility of full political sovereignty were formalized in the constitutional status of Associated Statehood, following the failure of the attempted federation of the "Little Eight."[23] The main feature of Associated Statehood was that it offered the territory an opportunity to become a "state in association with Britain." Under this arrangement, the territory was allowed control over its internal affairs while Britain retained responsibility for its external affairs and defense. It was granted the right to "amend its constitution . . . and to declare itself independent" whenever it felt itself ready to do so (see Cmnd. 2865 [1965], 2–4). Similarly, Britain could, with six months notice, unilaterally terminate its association with the territory (Cmnd. 3021 [1966], 9).

Insofar as the particular advance to the internal constitution was concerned, the main feature was the termination of the right of the British government "to reserve bills or disallow laws passed by the territorial legislature" (Cmnd. 2865 [1965], 6). Specific mention was made of the fact that the "general direction and control of the Government of St. Lucia, will rest with the Cabinet consisting of the Premier [previously styled 'Chief Minister'] and other such ministers." This cabinet was held to be "collectively responsible to parliament" (see Cmnd. 3021 [1966], 33). More symbolically, special emphasis was placed on the appointment of governors of local origin to "typify the localization of the Crown which has occurred as a result of internal autonomy" (Broderick 1968, 389).

The crux of the dilemma of Associated Statehood lay in the fluidity of the distinction between the internal and external (see Broderick 1968, 378). While issues such as commercial treaties, trade agreements, civil aviation, shipping, citizenship, and immigration were designated as British responsibilities (see Cmnd. 3021 [1966], 21), such distinctions proved problematic in practice. Particularly troublesome was the notion that "the government will not proceed with or support legislation if the United Kingdom government inform [*sic*] them that its passage would be detrimental" to the discharge of its obligations to the United Kingdom or any other territory with whom it has relations (ibid., 19). The fact that it was the exclusive responsibility and prerogative of Britain to determine when a specific issue held implications for "external affairs" served to negate the "internal sovereignty" promised by Associated Statehood (see Broderick 1968, 372).

Though largely paternalistic in conceptualization (see Hart and Chapman in British HC Sessional Papers, 2 February 1967, 894, 906), there were a number of features of the relationship that suggested that one of Britain's main concerns was to enjoy the economic benefits of a dying colonialism while divesting itself of the responsibilities of government. Significantly, the British government made it clear that constitutional changes "would be irrelevant in the context of development aid, trade and immigration" (Cmnd. 3021 [1966], 6). A major objective of Britain was to remove any responsibility to its Parliament and to immunize itself from criticism in international bodies such as the United Nations for the internal affairs of these territories (see Thomas 1987, 110–124; Cmnd. 3021 [1966], 6–7). The growing demand for universal decolonization meant that Britain was under close scrutiny and was subjected to scathing criticisms within international bodies whenever an economic or political crisis erupted in its remaining colonial possessions. Associated Statehood was therefore designed to show "where British responsibility begins and where it ends" (Thomas 1987, 111).

What is significant for understanding the later accommodations of the St. Lucian state to neoliberal globalization is the fact that despite the restrictive and exploitative nature of Associated Statehood, many of the leading domestic actors were eager to accept it as an "appropriate" solution to the sovereignty question. For example, Garnet Gordon, a founding member of the conservative PPP, responding to a British government publication outlining the minimum requirements for independence, noted that

> it is obvious that the qualifications for independence are very low. Even by these low qualifications it is impracticable for the island of St. Lucia to consider independence on its own. Today it can hardly sustain the standards people demand. . . . This is the case when it has no financial responsibility for external security and foreign representation or the minimum expenses involved in par-

ticipation in the international field. In addition, its economy, now completely
bananas, is completely dependent on the protection it receives in the UK
market. There can be no reasonable entertainment of ideas of independence
in isolation. (Gordon 1966, 4)

Clearly reflected in this statement was an assumption, typical of the political
worldview of middle-class reformers, that Britain would utilize its control of the
territory's external affairs in a benign and "disinterested" manner. There was little
indication that the reformers grasped the full implications of the country's lack
of control over international relations, "the key to legal sovereignty," for its later
economic development (see Thorndike 1979a, 603). Similarly, the dominant
politicians failed to consider the idea that sovereign statehood could facilitate
further economic development. Political thinking was entirely dominated by a
narrow concept of sovereignty, manifested in these leaders' insecurity over the
perceived challenges of external affairs and the fear that the cost of independence would outweigh its benefits. To the reformers, Associated Statehood was
seen as an opportunity to allow Britain to shoulder the costs, freeing St. Lucia
from the economic responsibilities of independence. Quite significantly, when
challenges to Associated Statehood emerged in a later period, the barriers to
economic development formed the basis of that challenge. As will be seen in the
following chapter, this emphasis on economic development was to be the main
determinant of the character of the future project of formal independence.

While the conceptualization, rationale, and operation of Associated
Statehood reveal internal contradictions of tentative anticolonialism, an equally
narrow conception of economic sovereignty was seen in the workings of the
banana economy. Just as Associated Statehood was perceived as the end of colonialism, the total shift from sugar to bananas by the 1960s (see Table 2.3) was
viewed by the reformist politicians as an "emancipation" and as the quintessen-
tial termination point of the nationalist process itself (see Welch 1994, 145). This
positive valuation of the banana economy stemmed from the fact it represented
a "minor social revolution" (Lewis 1968, 149–150) that destroyed the plantation-
based social relations of sugar production.

This theme is evident in most analyses of the political economy of the banana
industry in St. Lucia (see Romalis 1968, 1975; Welch 1994; Acosta and Casimir
1985; Barrow 1992; Williams and Darius 1998). Acosta and Casimir (1985, 43)
estimated that in this period, 50 percent of the banana crop was produced on
farms of less than ten acres. The structure of banana production facilitated the
small peasants as "owners" of the production process, and their participation in
the industry was formalized in the establishment of a statutory organization, the
St. Lucia Banana Growers' Association (SLBGA). Romalis (1975, 225) argues

Table 2.3. Exports of sugar and bananas by quantity and value (EC$)				
	SUGAR		BANANAS	
Period	Quantity (tons)	Value	Quantity (stems)	Value
1950	8,629	$1,137,119	2,258	$4,624
1951	8,017	$1,137,380	20,862	$26,263
1952	7,538	$1,257,032	56,002	$57,135
1953	8,712	$1,598,431	143,262	$198,467
1954	7,301	$1,309,899	306,432	$506,421
1955	9,053	$1,559,090	445,627	$642,778
1956	9,125	$1,598,587	783,950	$1,537,220
1957	5,884	$1,421,526	915,651	$1,884,893
1958	6,270	$1,122,482	1,098,174	$1,906,075
1959	7,000	$997,500	2,513,657	$3,901,000
Source: MacKenzie Commission Report 1960, 3.				

that the change from sugar to bananas "resulted in a very drastic transformation of the impoverished subsistence and wage-bound rural dwellers into a population of small farmers involved in an international export market." She notes that by 1963, the SLBGA had 18,000 registered "members in contrast to 1055 in 1954." She therefore argues that the banana industry "allowed for greater participation by the small grower in island affairs. . . . He finally had an opportunity to express his opinions about and play a major role in an economic undertaking greatly affecting his life, and to acquire political and organizational skills which had previously been the exclusive domain of the island's elite" (ibid., 232–233). Similarly, Acosta and Casimir (1985, 51) argue that the banana economy broke the "traditional linkages between . . . small-scale farming and estate farming." In their view, under the banana economy, "the plantocracy lost its privileged economic position whereby it used to control the only avenue open to small producers . . . on the world market." These social and political transformations accompanied the more obvious improvements in the economic position of the rural population (see Welch 1994, 137; Williams and Darius 1998) and greatly facilitated the legitimacy of the reformist politicians and their attendant stance of tentative anticolonialism.

Upon closer scrutiny, however, it is clear that the optimism of the reformist politicians in the banana economy was misguided and that the identification of bananas with independence was the result either of the political underdevelopment of the reformist leadership or deliberate obfuscation of reality on its part. Indeed, it is clear that the euphoria over the "emancipatory" features of the industry was sustained only by deflecting attention away from the politically debilitating features of the industry. In particular, it ignored the weaknesses resultant from the establishment of a monocrop, export-led economy dependent upon special marketing arrangements established between a foreign multinational corporation and the colonial power.

The very process by which Geest Industries established itself as the sole purchaser of St. Lucian fruit and facilitated the transition of the St. Lucian economy to total dependence on banana production marked a defeat for a more diversified economy envisaged by the working-class nationalists. Indeed, it had been the intention of the George Charles government to facilitate sugar production along co-operative lines alongside the more commercialized banana industry. The government had undertaken a number of steps to realize these objectives. These included the investment of $250,000 in Sugar Manufacturers Ltd., a feasibility study into sugar production (MacKenzie Commission Report 1960), and the imposition of a freeze on the exportation of sugar-manufacturing machinery. The government had also extracted an agreement with Geest to continue sugar production (Charles 1994, 85).

There is much evidence, however, to suggest that Geest had, from the outset, always intended to transform St. Lucia into a banana-producing colony. This intention, hidden from the St. Lucian political authorities, is revealed in a 1960 meeting between Geest and colonial officials over the future of the St. Lucian economy (see PRO-CO 1031/3422, 23 November 1960), where Geest hinted at the futility of sugar production in St. Lucia. Geest rejected the findings of the MacKenzie Commission, which had viewed, favorably, the possibilities for the continuation of "an efficient sugar industry in St. Lucia" (MacKenzie Commission Report 1960, 21), and he overrode concerns about the dangers for a "small territory like St. Lucia [relying] entirely on bananas." The Colonial Office observed that "Geest did not view with any alarm the possibility of dollar bananas being admitted to the United Kingdom market." Geest's confidence was due to the fact that his U.K. marketing contacts had been sufficiently well established to overcome Latin, that is U.S., competition (ibid.). Geest aimed to transform St. Lucia into an exclusively banana-producing territory, despite the expectations of many in government of a more diversified agricultural base. This overturned the development objectives envisaged by the territory's political leadership, then led by George Charles and the SLP.

Quite apart from the implications for internal sovereignty imposed by the overdependence on one main export crop tied to a multinational corporation, there were a number of features of the internal political economy of bananas that contradicted the idea of a "social revolution" championed by the middle-class reformers. According to Barrow (1992, 27–29), the banana industry left untouched the uneven distribution of land in St. Lucia. She notes that during the transition from sugar to bananas, over 40 percent of agricultural land was tied up in large estates that represented only 0.4 percent of the total number of holdings. This uneven distribution belied the egalitarianism associated with the membership and operations of the SLBGA and resulted in the persistence of low-paid wage-labor due to the high incidence of landlessness within the farming community. Moreover, much of the politics of St. Lucia was a reflection of the dictates of the banana economy. This is captured in a later editorial in *The Crusader*, which linked the emergence of the banana economy to the political domination of the UWP and the embrace of external capital:

> The industry and the politics became completely intertwined, and the government saw bananas so much as a UWP-thing that they were less than straight in highlighting the negative possibilities of the industry.... There was a happy corollary to this. John Compton himself saw the banana business as being so closely linked with his political fortunes, that over the past thirty years he has fought indefatigably to preserve the industry from all the vicissitudes which threatened its survival. (Odlum n.d.b, 11)

Central to this was an overwhelming tendency to view the role of government as being largely concerned with creating the internal social and economic conditions favorable to maintaining the "goodwill" of Geest and in maintaining the international trade relations that sustained the banana economy (Slocum 1996, 47–48).

These features of the internal economic relations provide an indication of the outlines of what can be considered a state-society balance that emerged out of the early nationalist period in St. Lucia. The main feature of this state-society settlement was the broad contentment with nonsovereign status as maximizing the economic benefits of the society and as the best that could be hoped for, given St. Lucia's circumstances. Insofar as internal economic relations were concerned, the positive shift in the quality of life of the previously marginalized peasant population brought about by the banana "revolution" was widely accepted as an indication of a process of economic leveling in the society. This was further underpinned by the structural organization of the banana industry, which facilitated political involvement of small peasants in the activities of the SLBGA.

These realities held key implications for the domestic role of the state. The heavy emphasis on economic development meant that the state consciously defined its mission as ensuring the creation of an internal environment conducive to corporate capital. Nationalist concerns about the patterns of external domination and control of the economy, which had been central to working-class nationalism, were conspicuously absent in the St. Lucian definition of sovereign statehood. Similarly, questions of the development and expansion of local cultural expression were underplayed. These developments were underpinned by the assumption that the openness to external capitalist relations was necessary in overcoming the historical condition of economic underdevelopment. This was seen as necessitating a noninterventionist "umpire" role for the state, closely akin to the neoliberal state, which would later gain global hegemony. The alternative view of the interventionist state as a mechanism to rectify the internal imbalances of the colonial past was consciously rejected. That specific understanding of the St. Lucian state that emerged out of the politics of nationalism would hold critical implications for the later movement toward independence in the period of globalization.

The Character of St. Lucian Nationalism: Implications for Decolonization under Globalization

The central notion that emerges from the preceding analysis is the extent to which the view of the role of the state and national sovereignty, shaped by the nationalist experience, approximates the neoliberal assumptions ascendant in the 1980s and beyond. This was evident in a number of instances, such as the limited sovereignty anticipated by the political class, the development of a framework conducive to private capital accumulation, and the reduced emphasis on policies with a strong nationalist content or interventionist outlook. The dominance of these notions in the prenationalist period was critical in shaping how globalization would later impact the independence experience of St. Lucia. The pursuit of formal independence in the period of global economic constraints meant that the St. Lucian experience was devoid of the types of "anticolonial" nationalist development strategies evident in the Caribbean territories that had decolonized in the 1960s. These strategies, as in the case of Barbados, for instance, included the wider provision of secondary and university education; land redistribution, housing, health, and transportation development policies; and the construction of a local industrial base to facilitate the emergence of a local industrial class. Similarly, the emphasis on sports and cultural development identifiable in territories like Jamaica, Barbados, and Trinidad found little expression in St. Lucia. The differences in nationalist expression were evident not only between St. Lucia and states that had overtly embraced a "socialist" or noncapitalist path but also in relation to states like Barbados and Trinidad and Tobago, which had pursued mild nationalist reforms. While compromises born of economic dependency can be identified in all the Caribbean states, St. Lucia was one of the few states in which an accommodation to the colonial framework was elevated to a principle and defended as a desirable condition.

The impact of the mid-1970s environment resulted in two contradictory tendencies insofar as the question of the nature of St. Lucian nationalist project was concerned. The first was a legitimation of limited sovereignty. The uncertain economic condition of the mid-1970s revived the question of economic vulnerability that had featured prominently in the early nationalist period, and it continued to be used as an argument for moderation by John Compton and the reformist leadership. The struggling economies resulted in a widespread notion of a "crisis of independence" throughout the Caribbean, and because of the relative absence of radical nationalist approaches, St. Lucia was widely proclaimed by domestic politicians and international financial institutions as a model of success (for example, in *The Voice* [Independence Supplement], 19 February 1979). Its experience contrasted sharply with countries such as Jamaica and Guyana, where policies with a strong nationalist and socialist content had resulted in economic and political crises. In those countries, the policies sustained by the global environment of the 1960s required adjustment to the economic conditions of the mid-1970s, at tremendous social and political costs. In contrast, the minimalist conceptions of national independence in St. Lucia proved compatible with the global economic and political conditions of the mid-1970s, validating and legitimizing the tentative anticolonialism that had pervaded its early nationalist discourse.

At the same time, an opposite tendency can also be identified. The greater economic challenges of the mid-1970s environment gave rise to the idea that more could be gained from full sovereign status. The oil price increases, the devaluation of the British pound, the increases in the price of manufactured goods, and the reduction in the levels of aid led to a rethinking of the assumptions of Associated Statehood. As will be seen in the next chapter, one of the central arguments by which Compton rationalized his move toward independence was that under Associated Statehood, "matters will be affecting us in which we have no voice" and that "areas of assistance will exist to which we have no access" (in *The Voice*, 22 April 1976, 1). Far from providing a safeguard against economic vulnerability, Associated Statehood exacerbated these vulnerabilities by denying the territory access to trade arrangements and sources of financial and development aid, and the general capacity to manipulate the external environment to its economic benefit. In short, the new global conditions challenged the fundamental ideological basis of Associated Statehood.

Two issues can be seen as particularly relevant in the study of the independence project in St. Lucia under neoliberal globalization. First, the push toward formal decolonization was undertaken in a context where the political consequences of such an objective were widely acknowledged to be limited. Thus St. Lucian independent statehood was seen as implying no qualitative shift in the role, philosophy, and function of the state (SLU Government "Green paper" on Independence 1978). The second issue is the fact that the main justification for independence was economic. According to Thorndike (1979b, 161), "so far as external affairs were concerned, it was not so much a case of 'seeking first the political kingdom' as utilizing any political advancement to increase and diversify sources of aid and markets of goods and services." Clearly absent was a view of the independent state as a mechanism to transcend the internal colonial relations of the society, as was done in other Caribbean territories in the 1960s and 1970s. The prevailing tendency to accommodate and adjust to the demands of global capital continued to be dominant in the period when full independence was being pursued.

Quite significantly, however, the 1970s witnessed the emergence of a socialist interpretation of the possibilities offered by the global environment. Under this orientation, formal independence was seen as incompatible with the limited role for the state. The socialist independence project was motivated by increasing popular discontent over the economic, political, and cultural marginalization of the mass of the population. The socialists saw this as a consequence of the absence of a culture of political interventionism in St. Lucia and viewed sovereignty as a tool to further complete the project of internal transformation identified in the early nationalist period. The contestation between these various tendencies was the central political conflict in St. Lucia in the period leading to formal independence, culminating in the 1979 electoral victory of the SLP, three months after independence. The episode is critical in understanding the impact of the newly emergent global political economy on the independence project in St. Lucia.

CHAPTER 3

The Politics of St. Lucian Decolonization, 1970-1982

The Global Political-Economic Context and the Movement toward Formal Independence

Contrary to popular and academic notions that see small size and economic underdevelopment as arguments against the demand for formal sovereignty (see Jackson 1990; Hintjens 1995), it was the prospects for economic development that underpinned the movement toward formal independence in St. Lucia. While in the late 1960s Associated Statehood was seen as the final resting place of the country's sovereign aspirations and as being compatible with the territory's economic development aspirations, by the early 1970s it was seen as inhibiting such development. When the case was made for formal independence, the key to economic development was identified in the once-dreaded sphere of global economic relations (Thorndike 1979a, 1979b). The urgency for independence also explains why the federal aspiration was abandoned and why miniaturized nationalism was embraced as a last and desperate option.[1]

A major justification for independence was that under Associated Statehood, Britain's international obligations conflicted with its obligations to St. Lucia. Particularly ominous was Britain's involvement in the European Union (EU). Indeed, this was the most pertinent issue raised by Compton when he formally broached the issue of independence at an annual convention of the United Workers' Party (UWP): "The British who in the past protected our banana exports from unfair competition from some African countries can no longer do so, as the treaty of Association to the European Economic Community demands free trade between member states.... The British cannot speak for us. Who then must put St. Lucia's case?" (*The Voice*, 22 April 1976, 1). Compton also lamented the fact that while the British dependent territories possessed 62 percent of the population of all overseas dependent territories in the EU, the monies for dependent territories from the European Development Fund (EDF) were distributed equally among the colonial powers. In Compton's view, the British regions received less than their due share, "because . . . Britain was not ready to fight our case" (ibid.).

Particularly galling to Compton was the stipulation that the Associated States could not pursue external relations that could undermine British interests. This severely limited St. Lucia's ability to further its economic development. This was felt most acutely in the tourism industry, which suffered from an "inadequacy of airline flights" due to British reluctance to negotiate air route rights with Canadian and North American carriers (Compton, Budget Address 1975, 14; Thorndike 1979b, 14), thus denying St. Lucia full access to the more lucrative North American tourist market. The limitations on external affairs also meant that St. Lucia was compromised in the formative stages of the Caribbean Free Trade Area (CARIFTA) and the Caribbean Community (CARICOM) and during EU-CARICOM negotiations.[2] The special provisions for EU membership that were extended to the Associated States "implied that a part of the CARIFTA countries would be associated with the European Community under the Lomé Convention and other CARIFTA countries would be associated with the Council Decision on Overseas Countries and Territories" (Thomas 1987, 162–163).[3] Despite the fact that in 1974, "entrustment" powers were granted to St. Lucia to sign the CARICOM treaty, this was subject to a number of conditions pertaining to the protection of British interests (ibid., 160). Therefore, St. Lucia could not partake in, and benefit from, CARICOM agreements where the U.K. government thought that British interests were threatened (ibid., 162–163; Broderick 1968, 378). The constitutional gaps between St. Lucia and its CARICOM partners provided both psychological and economic reasons for abandoning colonial status (see Compton in *The Voice*, 10 January 1976, 4).

In addition, it had become clear that a number of development agencies and international financial institutions were refusing St. Lucia aid and development assistance on account of its nonsovereign status (see Thomas 1987, 160; Compton in *West Indies Chronicle*, August/September 1978, 20). These economic limitations made the achievement of full sovereign status an immediate necessity: "Matters will be affecting us in which we have no voice. Areas of assistance will exist to which we have no access and we will continue like helpless flotsam, left behind by the ebbing tide of Empire. This is a fate which I cannot recommend that we endure much longer" (Compton in *The Voice*, 22 April 1976, 1). In Compton's view, formal independence was necessary in order to allow the St. Lucian leadership "to interface with the international community . . . which you could not have access to because of your constitutional limitation" (Compton, interview).

However, in the very process of signaling St. Lucia's intention to move toward independence, it was not the possibilities for economic growth that were emphasized, but the fact that the existing environment left "little room for manoeuvre" (Compton, Budget Address 1974; Compton, Budget Address 1975, 4). Thus, while dissatisfaction with the economic limitations of the relationship with Britain spurred the movement toward independence, the global economic environment of the early 1970s was seen as severely constraining the economic options of the state (*Financial Times*, 29 April 1974, 32). This shaped the nature of the expected character of the independence project.

The limiting features of the global environment highlighted by the premier in the 1974 budget address included the "twin problems of world inflation and the energy crisis," which he claimed had "completely altered" the priorities of economic expansion, the construction of physical infrastructure to support the expanding economy, and the improvement in the quality of life, which had shaped the developmental assumptions of the 1960s (Compton, Budget Address 1974, 1). Specifically, the rise in oil prices had increased prices for petroleum-based products such as chemical fertilizers and synthetic fibers used in banana production as well as for imported manufactured consumer goods. The oil price increase also led to shortfalls in tourism revenue due to increases in the price of tourist-oriented services (ibid., 2). These problems were exacerbated by the "worsening economic position in the United Kingdom" and the instability of the pound sterling, which, by 1975, following its flotation in 1972, had declined in value by 29 percent in relation to the U.S. dollar, resulting in corresponding increases in the cost of non-U.K. imports (Compton, Budget Address 1975, 3).[4]

Compounding the economic plight of the territory was a decline in banana production, resulting in sharp reductions in export earnings. As a consequence of a prolonged drought between 1970 and 1975, banana production declined from a peak of 87,000 tons in 1969 to a low of 32,000 tons in 1975 (World Bank 1979, 2). In the period when formal independence was being pursued, the St. Lucian economy was "caught in a vice of soaring costs on one hand, and declining production on the other," and had to contend with the related problem of rising unemployment (Compton, Budget Address 1975, 3). The impact of the precarious global economic context was reflected in the government's economic policy, foreign policy, and the constitutional framework of Compton's independence project.

The main feature of the government's economic development policy was its dependence on foreign capital within the context of an export-driven economy (Compton in *West Indies Chronicle*, May/June 1975, 4). While the government was expected to be the "prime mover of economic and social activity," it was committed to extending the "greatest degree of encouragement" to private foreign capital "as one of the tools employed to solve the social and economic problems of the state" (Allen Lewis, Throne Speech 1978). Offering St. Lucia's "historical structural deficit conditions in its balance of payments" as an explanation for this economic orientation, Barrow-Giles (1992b, 62, 108) saw economic dependency as the characteristic feature of the St. Lucian economy in this period. This was evidenced in the "degree of foreign ownership of the local economy, the importance of foreign trade to the GDP, trade deficits, the major role played by foreign investment in stimulating economic activity, and a reliance on foreign aid for survival" (ibid.).

Economic dependency was most clearly reflected in the degree of foreign ownership of the economy. A 1979 study by Kenny Anthony under the auspices of a group called the Rural Transformation Collective (RTC) revealed the dominance of external capital in the agricultural sector. The study showed that all land in excess of 500 acres per owner was owned by seventeen persons or corporate entities, of which six were of U.S. or British origin (Anthony 1978, 4). It identified a process of "deepening capitalist penetration and organization in the agricultural sector" and noted that "as many as 55 joint stock companies, and corporations own land in the big estate sector." These investments were "largely for speculative purposes in real estate, or as collateral to finance loans for other business activity" (ibid., 7). A related study observed that only two of the eight estates over 2,000 acres in 1972/1973 were owned by St. Lucians. One of the leading foreign owners was Geest Industries, which, by 1983, owned 40,000 acres of land (Demacque in Thomson 1987, 67). Foreign ownership of land was facilitated by the Aliens Landholding Act, which was widely recognized as being among the most liberal throughout the Caribbean. The premier's own description of a "national" as "one who has commitments to St. Lucia" reflected this accommodation to external capital (see Chen-Young 1973, 34).

Similar patterns obtained in the tourist and manufacturing sectors, exacerbated by the underdeveloped nature of these sectors and local capital's aversion to these activities (see GOSL National Development Strategy 1977, 29).[5] The two major industrial enterprises established between 1971 and 1974, Heineken Brewery and WINERA (a cardboard and paper product manufacturing plant), were of German and Venezuelan ownership respectively. The seven major hotels in the territory were all foreign-owned. In 1973 the Courtline Company was the major tourism investor, owning 34 percent of the existing bed capacity (ibid., 31). Similarly, the commercial banking sector was, as late as 1977, dominated by five foreign banks. These banks operated within a context where "exchange controls were not stringent" and where their policies were directed "not to the economic needs of the country" but rather to what "the local and foreign market would allow" (see Dolly Committee Report 1977, 86).

The domination of external capital was facilitated by a number of government incentives throughout the 1970s (see National Development Corporation 1973). In 1969 an "investment guarantee" was signed between the St. Lucia and U.S. governments providing protection against expropriation for U.S. enterprises. Similarly, the Fiscal Incentives Act of 1974 offered a wide range of concessions to foreign enterprises. This act granted fifteen-year exemptions from the payment of income taxes and customs duties on plant and machinery related to industry (ibid., 8). The St. Lucia government also provided relief from double taxation through agreements with the United States, Canada, Great Britain, New Zealand, Switzerland, Norway, Sweden, and Denmark (ibid., 11). As late as 1979, in the context of a pending election, the prime minister reiterated the theme of appeasing external capital in an attempt to neutralize his political opponents: "good name and goodwill are very fragile things. . . . At this stage of our economic and political development, St. Lucia needs friends internationally in both the diplomatic and commercial communities. We therefore cannot afford to gratuitously insult and abuse those whose goodwill our country needs, be they individuals, corporations or governments" (Compton, Budget Address 1979, 12).

One episode that highlights Compton's dependence on external capital was the wide range of concessions under which a U.S. multinational oil company, Amerada-Hess, was allowed to establish a U.S.$135 million operation in St. Lucia. These concessions were enshrined in the Oil Refinery Act of 1977. Section 3 of the act gave the company "an irrevocable right and license to own, construct and operate the project site and to do all things necessary or appropriate in connection therewith" for an initial period of fifty years from the production date. The act also allowed the company to "extend the said right and license for a further period or periods of twenty-five years each . . . upon such terms as the parties . . . shall mutually agree" (Oil Refinery Act 1977, section 3, 52).

Section 5 of the act, which was concerned with the government's obligations to Amerada-Hess, went even further. Article 3 of that section gave the company the right, without charge, "to conduct and maintain such navigation channels, turning basins, docks, piers . . . and any and all ancillary facilities in the Cul-de-sac Bay and the harbour as Hess may consider necessary for the proper operation of the project" and conceded that "Hess and the officials shall have and enjoy exclusive control" of these facilities. Article 6 of section 5 further gave the company the right to reclaim land from waters adjacent to the Queen's Chain or seashore. These reclaimed lands were sold to Amerada-Hess at a cost of EC$300 per acre, while the Queen's Chain itself was sold to Amerada-Hess at a cost of EC$1,000 per acre. The government, on receiving such payments, agreed to convey and vest these lands to Amerada-Hess "free and clear of all liens, encumbrances, rights-of-way, easements or restrictions" (Oil Refinery Act, section 5, article 6).

The tax exemptions to the company were listed under article 12 of section 5. The act held that Amerada-Hess and its affiliates and their non–St. Lucian sub-contractors would be exempt, for a period of twenty years, "from the payment of all rates, taxes, excises, stamp duties, imposts and exactions" (Oil Refinery Act 1977, section 5, article 12a). These included income or profit taxes, sales, use, and gross receipt taxes; all property and franchise taxes; and all annual or specific license fees (except vehicle licenses) (ibid., section 5, article 12b). At the same time, all building materials, furnishings, and equipment related to the Amerada-Hess project were exempt from import duties. The company was further exempt from all harbor, "pilotage, wharfage, quay and tonnage dues for vessels discharging or loading into or from the terminal, the refinery or related facilities" (ibid., section 5, article 14). The government also undertook to waive all foreign exchange restrictions on Amerada-Hess, its affiliates, and its foreign contractors or subcontractors (ibid., section 3, article 15).

Three specific features of the Amerada-Hess agreement reflected the degree to which the UWP government was willing to accommodate the company. First, it required an affirmative vote from all seventeen members of the Lower House, government and opposition alike (Oil Refinery Act, section 2, article 2). Second, it stipulated that all disputes arising in connection with the agreement should be settled in Paris in accordance with the rules of the International Chamber of Commerce (ibid., section 10) rather than in the domestic courts of St. Lucia, according to domestic laws as the opposition preferred. Third, it allowed for lower throughput charges than had been anticipated by the opposition, which had demanded charges based on an "escalator clause" tied to the movement in world oil prices. The act, however, set fixed rates: two U.S. cents per barrel for incoming crude oil, and four U.S. cents for outgoing refined oil (ibid., section 4, articles 2 and 3).

Apart from the terms of the agreement itself, the general tenor of the government's defense of the agreement served to reinforce the territory's dependence. During the debate Compton asserted that "when an investor offers to St. Lucia such an opportunity, the red carpet should have been laid out for him" and that "such an agreement should have been met not with misgivings but with jubilation" (*St. Lucia Hansard*, 27 June 1977, 2; see also Barrow-Giles 1992b, 122). Compton defended the agreement on the grounds that more favorable terms were evident elsewhere in the Caribbean region, and St. Lucia should not let the opportunity slip by. He also argued that free trade zones and tax holidays had become established features of the economic policies of territories far more developed than St. Lucia (*St. Lucia Hansard*, 27 June 1977, 19, 28–33).

Compton's development strategy received strong support from international financial institutions. A 1979 World Bank report observed approvingly that a "dynamic approach to changing market conditions" had been adopted for the tourism industry since "much of the larger hotel stock is under foreign ownership, which is directly linked to tour operators in their respective countries" (World Bank 1979, 15). Similarly, the bank noted that of "all the Caribbean LDCs, St. Lucia appears the most firmly committed to attracting external, mainly US, investments in manufacturing industry" (ibid., 23). This validation was an important basis upon which the UWP government defended its economic approach against demands for more radical policies (Compton, Budget Address 1979, 3–4).

The emphasis on attracting foreign direct investment as distinct from borrowing from the private capital markets was a result of both Compton's personal political approach and the limiting structural context. While private loans had become more readily available to developing countries in the 1970s, on generally favorable terms, the strong influence of the Lewis model of development reflected itself in fiscal conservatism where the maintenance of a surplus in current account was a high priority.[5] Foreign direct investment was preferred because it meant that the state avoided fixed payments. Second, St. Lucia's semi-independent status limited its ability to borrow from the capital markets. Not only did Britain provide the territory with budgetary support, but St. Lucia also had access to soft loans from the European Development Bank and other donor agencies to fund capital expenditure and other social programs. These factors, coupled with Compton's generally antistatist approach, led to a preference for foreign direct investment.

The impact of the external economic environment was also reflected in the constitutional changes that were pursued. Though desirous of formal sovereignty, the government was equally concerned about pursuing a notion of independence that was compatible with the preferred economic orientation. Constitutional decolonization was characterized by a deliberate attempt to limit the changes to the legal and political minimum required to transcend Associated Statehood. Compton outlined this policy during the debate on the draft constitution, which he declared "breaks no new ground, and that is deliberately so." He insisted that "independence is not an emotional issue. . . . In fact there is quite a song and dance about the terminology of independence. What we are doing is extending our constitution to include two matters of vital importance to us: matters relating to Foreign Affairs . . . and the matter of Defence" (*St. Lucia*

Hansard, 21 July 1978, 9). The inconsistencies in this orientation were identified by the main opposition party, the St. Lucia Labour Party (SLP), and elements of the labor movement, who insisted that the independence constitution should have as its aim the abolition of the features of the old colonial relation. The St. Lucia Teachers' Union (SLTU), for example, argued that "the former constitution served the needs of a semi-colonial society operating with direct links to Britain. Independence should, therefore, be a complete reversion of the colonial links as far as immediately possible" (*The Crusader*, 15 July 1978, 5–6, 22 July 1978, 8).[7]

The union criticized the decision to retain a local governor-general to serve as the representative of the British Crown and argued that "the ideological and psychological outlook which accepts the office of Governor General is essentially colonial." It therefore demanded that "our people should be liberated from the myths which surround that office" (*The Crusader*, 15 July 1978, 5). Similarly, the SLTU was critical of the decision to retain a nominated upper chamber since this preserved the position of unelected "powerful sectional interests" (ibid., 6).

In defense of its position, the SLTU argued that Compton was promoting a constitutional structure that had been found wanting elsewhere in the Caribbean, due to inadequacies in the inherited independence constitutions. The union pointed to Trinidad and Tobago as an example of a state that had adopted a republican constitution in the early 1970s as a result of the inadequacies of the inherited independence constitution (*The Crusader*, 15 July 1978, 6). According to the union, Compton seemed to "accept the colonial and ultra conservative logic of a step by step approach to constitutional decolonization." In contrast, the SLTU claimed that "St. Lucia can advance its constitutional evolution by several years if we are prepared to make effective use of the concrete experiences of the other territories" (ibid., 5).

The government was also criticized for failing to link constitutional development with local economic control. Accusing the Compton administration of being "the local concubine of the white expatriate exploiter," Peter Josie, a leading member of the St. Lucian Left, highlighted the economic limitations of Compton's constitutional approach:

> Can we in St. Lucia today say that if this government ever got constitutional or political independence that we will at the same time evolve automatically into economic independence and cultural liberation, can we say that? When we look at the history of this government, no intelligent and sane person can ever say this. . . . We see St. Lucia being sold out every day to foreigners, we see our island, the only thing we have—apart from our people—is our soil, we

see that being scooped away from our hands everyday in the name of progress. (*St. Lucia Hansard*, 20 October 1978, 29, 30)

Among the features of the constitution that Josie challenged was the high priority placed on the entrenchment of property rights in the preamble of the constitution (see ibid.). The leading opposition forces sought to point out the contradictions inherent in Compton's idea of independence, which placed emphasis on limiting sovereignty, rather than facilitating its expansion. This was more particularly the case since the government's claim that the existing constitution was "a sound document which has generally served us well" conflicted with the government's own position in its "Green Paper" on independence, "that the present constitution had outlived its usefulness and was inadequate for a modern state" (see *The Crusader*, 18 March 1978, 10; see also St. Hill in *The Crusader*, 21 January 1978, 9).

While the government had described "defense" and "foreign affairs" as two significant departures from the colonial framework, its approach to these areas also sought to preserve the economic and political relations of the colonial past. The government advocated a "limited foreign policy" as the chosen framework for independent St. Lucia. This "limited foreign policy" orientation was leveled as a critique of radical economic nationalism and "third world" politics pursued elsewhere in the Caribbean. Compton accused radical Caribbean leaders of "posturing on the world stage and dabbling in third world politics while neglecting pressing domestic issues facing the region." In contrast, he argued that his foreign policy would be shaped by the fact that "our total history has been bound up with the West" and by "what could provide the island with the best thrust for its economic advancement" (in *The Voice* [Independence Supplement], 19 February 1979, 21). This involved "membership of the United Nations and its many agencies, the Commonwealth, the European Economic Community and the OAS" (ibid.) and a concern to

so conduct our affairs as not to introduce into this region of peace and tranquillity the conflicts of the "cold war" ideology with all its grievous consequences. While recognising that we are part of the developing world whose problems may be similar to our own, and whose experiences can assist us in providing appropriate solutions, our human resources are too slender and our material needs too great to permit us to expend these in the barren wasteland of posturing and polemics. . . . We must accept that there exist [*sic*] now in our country a chronic shortage of both capital and technology. Where these are lacking they must be brought in as long as we ensure that they are employed not only to make a profit, but more important that in doing so they contribute to the quality of life of our people and respect the sovereignty of our government. (Compton 1979b)

These assurances were also intended to neutralize the demands for a greater degree of economic nationalism emanating from the radical nationalists.[8]

The government's stance on defense reinforced this position. The government saw no dilemma in an accommodation to U.S. military domination in the wake of British political withdrawal. Arguing that the question of defense "is quite absolutely academic . . . in this nuclear age" (*St. Lucia Hansard*, 21 July 1978, 9), Compton welcomed the growing U.S. military presence in the region: "The United States, which has always considered the Caribbean as its 'sphere of interest' and has referred to it as a 'closed sea' in respect of military/naval activities, is expected to be more intimately involved in the defence of the area, and as a consequence, the deterrence factor at present resides, not in the UK, but in the US, hence membership in the OAS is the clear answer" (GOSL, Independence for St. Lucia [1978], 8). Independence and national sovereignty were defined as limited given the narrow degree of "permissibility" of the post-1973 environment. This definition reflected the political position of Compton himself, but was also shaped by the historical considerations of economic vulnerability and the need for economic development.

Independence and the Radical Nationalist Challenge

Much of the politics of St. Lucian decolonization in the 1970s was shaped by the fact that the St. Lucian Left, growing in popularity and influence as a result of developments in the region and the wider globe, proposed radically different options for independent St. Lucia. In contrast to Compton, who saw the 1970s environment as demanding a "limited sovereignty" for St. Lucia, the St. Lucian Left saw this environment facilitating a more radical internal and external role for the state. The Left's challenge was based on the fact that Compton himself had argued that the existing global environment was supportive of the independence aspirations of small states (Compton in *The Voice*, 22 April 1976, 2). It saw the resurgence of radical nationalist movements and the strength of third world positions in the United Nations as indicating a more permissive global environment and argued that the ruling regime had underestimated the importance of this factor.

The first organized expression of a radical nationalist alternative to Compton in the 1970s emerged from the "Forum." This was largely a group of educated, urban-based civil servants engaged in popular political education. Among the leading "Forumites" were George Odlum (an Oxford graduate), Calixte George, Hilford Deterville, and Peter Josie. Though constrained in its political activities by the large number of civil servants in its membership, the Forum gradually evolved into an overtly political group concerned with themes of "nationalism, black pride, and the dangers of foreign control of the island's land and economy" (Midgett 1983, 142). The Forumites were influenced by the New World Group of Caribbean social scientists at the University of the West Indies, who were critical of the degree of foreign control of Caribbean economies (George, Williams, and Deterville, interviews). The Forum was also heavily influenced by the "Black Power" discourse of the 1960s, which was critical of the state's failure to challenge the racially based patterns of economic and cultural domination of the European minority over the black majority (see Odlum n.d.a; Rodney 1990; Odlum in Dabreo 1981).

In 1972 the Forum became a full-fledged political organization and was renamed the St. Lucia Action Movement (SLAM). This transformation from a popular education group to a political party occurred in response to official harassment of the Forum. The Public Order Act had been strengthened to prevent civil servants from appearing on public platforms, and a series of bans was placed on political meetings (Frederick Clarke, Throne Speech 1970, 4–5; Odlum in Dabreo 1981, 176–177; Midgett 1983, 143).[9] These measures "depleted the reserves and the skills available in the Forum" (Odlum in Dabreo 1981, 177; see Wayne 1986, 34) but at the same time created the context for a further radicalization of the movement. By 1973 the radical members of SLAM, such as George Odlum, Peter Josie, and Hilford Deterville, had joined the SLP, shifting the SLP farther to the left.

Another important radical nationalist group was the Workers' Revolutionary Movement (WRM), which emerged in the mid-1970s. This group was more overtly socialist than the SLP and justified its existence on the need to create a "political party identified to the fullest extent with working class politics" (Anthony 1978, 12). One of the leading figures of the WRM, Kenny Anthony, was closely linked to and heavily influenced by Jamaica's Marxist Workers Liberation League (WLL), led by the Caribbean's leading Marxist thinker, Trevor Munroe, of the University of the West Indies Mona Jamaica Campus (Anthony, interview). The WRM was, however, more consciously influenced by the theories of noncapitalist development that shaped the politics of other Caribbean states such as Jamaica, Guyana, and Grenada, as distinct from the orthodox Soviet Marxism of the WLL.

These examples of radical nationalism in neighboring Caribbean territories heavily influenced political developments in St. Lucia. This was particularly true of Grenada, where the challenge by the New Jewel Movement (NJM) of Maurice Bishop against the regime of Eric Gairy had produced both a tactical and philosophical model that attracted St. Lucian radicals. In the early 1970s Bishop met Odlum and other Forumites at a secret meeting on Rat Island, a small islet off the coast of St. Lucia, from which a close political relationship was forged (see Wayne 1986, 26–27). Similarly, the political questions raised in Grenada reflected themselves in St. Lucia. Thus questions of economic empowerment through a process of land reform and public participation in the process of budget formation, as well as the issue of overcoming the limits of the inherited Westminster parliamentary democratic system (which Bishop described as "two second democracy"), which were central to the Grenadian experience, emerged as important political questions in St. Lucia. The NJM also represented a broad-based alliance of all the forces in Grenada opposed to the political repression and economic corruption of the Eric Gairy regime and had adopted the tactic of armed struggle. All of these developments were reflected in varying degrees in the politics of St. Lucia in this period. By the mid-1970s, therefore, a distinct political counter-current had emerged that saw the global environment of the late 1970s as offering greater possibilities for radical change than that envisaged by Compton.

A principal feature of radical nationalism was its concern with ensuring a greater degree of domestic control over the limited resources of the state. The radicals criticized Compton for ignoring the extent to which the instrument of sovereign statehood could be used to alleviate the racial and economic legacies of the colonial past. Similarly, the embrace of external private capital was seen as conflicting with the objective of black economic empowerment and ownership. George Odlum, for example, expressed a notion of national sovereignty that attempted to strike a balance between the dependence on external capital and the need to address the issues of race and foreign economic domination. He argued that

> the investment policy of a territory is one of the keen indicators of the desire to protect the people from exploitation. Additionally, this is one of the most subtle and delicate areas of government since there is need to balance the attraction of scarce capital against the sell-out to foreign interests. However, there is a chronic danger in postcolonial societies and postslave societies to underestimate the value of their assets and to over-estimate the value of foreign injections of capital and expertise. (Odlum n.d.a, 6–9)

Odlum maintained that while foreign ownership of land may be tolerated, "it should never be easy to pick up large areas of land in St. Lucia." As a countermeasure to this "concentration of capital in white hands," Odlum stressed the need to "open every possible avenue to encourage black participation in entrepreneurship and investment" (ibid.).

Local (largely black) economic ownership and participation in the economy were central to radical nationalism. This general theme of local economic control was expressed forcefully by a St. Lucia youth delegation to the XI World Festival of Youth and Students held in Cuba in 1978. The delegation charged that St. Lucia was "seeking political independence from Britain only to clear the way for US imperialism to further penetrate our country's economy and to exploit our people in the typical neocolonial manner" (Earl Bousquet in *The Crusader*, 26 August 1978, 8). They also criticized the domination by British, Canadian, and U.S. firms in the banking and tourism sectors. The terms upon which the Amerada-Hess operations were established in St. Lucia received particular criticism. The delegation's main argument was that the high level of U.S. investments limited the state in its pursuit of independent policies and opened it to U.S. military domination (ibid.).

The SLP's 1979 election manifesto provides an important indication of the radicals' approach to independence. Written largely by George Odlum, with a contribution on education by Kenny Anthony, the manifesto advocated greater levels of government intervention in the economy and a reorientation of economic priorities to reflect domestic needs. It criticized the fact that "St. Lucia's agriculture program was . . . eighty percent export-oriented" and resulted in a situation in which "the foreign exchange earned from exported crops was frittered away on high-priced foreign food." The SLP's agricultural program placed a "strong emphasis on the production of food for domestic use, co-operatives . . . and land reform," to rectify a situation in which "5,000 landless agricultural workers were forced to squat, rent and sharecrop—while 32,000 acres of agricultural lands were owned by some 17 individuals" (Wayne 1986, 59).

To increase local participation in the economy, the SLP promised to establish a national bank to "introduce and maintain programs designed to encourage thrift, provide avenues for St. Lucians abroad to invest savings and credit resources at home, tap external financial institutions, and generally assist capital formation in St. Lucia" (Wayne 1986, 60). It also proposed to utilize "the necessary apparatus of state power and influence . . . in putting together incentives, safeguards and concessions necessary to raise the share of St. Lucians in the economy." In order to achieve greater local participation in the tourism industry, the party planned to promote a "cottage-type tourism" centered on the construction of guesthouses preferably owned by local investors and to purchase hotel stock facing financial difficulties, such as the Halcyon Days Hotel, which had fallen into receivership (ibid., 61). The radicals also criticized Compton's "limited foreign policy" because it ignored the growing strength of national liberation movements and the ways in which these movements could strengthen the internal sovereignty of the state. Kenny Anthony, for example, argued that the Non-Aligned Movement could provide a basis for support in the event that St. Lucia wanted to pursue an economic policy that was contrary to that desired by the dominant Western powers (*The Crusader*, 22 September 1978, 2, 9). The Left therefore saw the growing nationalist movements and the increasing leverage of the third world in international forums as facilitating a more radical orientation.

This notion of independence gained tremendous support in the 1970s, culminating in the defeat of the UWP in the general election of July 1979. The fact of Compton's defeat itself indicates the growing legitimacy and popular basis of the radical alternative to Comptonism and the shifting internal dynamics of the politics of St. Lucia in the period leading to independence.

A resurgence in industrial unrest among agricultural labor for the first time since the 1950s (Stoby Commission Report 1973, 4) was the first indication of growing popular disillusionment with the Compton regime in the 1970s. An early manifestation of this discontent was a series of strikes in the 1973/1974 period involving, in one case, as many as 700 workers on the Geest-owned banana estates of Roseau and Cul-de-sac. While the earliest of these strikes erupted spontaneously among banana workers, much of the blame was placed on Odlum and Josie for fomenting "Black Power" agitation among banana workers (see ibid., 12, 14, 21–25). Odlum and Josie were also involved in a later wave of strikes over the nonrecognition of their union, the National Organization of Workers (NOW), formed to challenge the low wages on the Geest estates.[10] A further wave of strikes occurred in 1976, this time led by Odlum's Farmers and Farm Workers' Union (*The Voice of St. Lucia*, 1976).[11] One such strike was estimated to have cost the Dennery estates EC$224,181 and the Roseau and Cul-de-sac estates a production shortfall of EC$35,493 (*The Voice*, 15 August 1976, 12).

The link between radical nationalists and the working population was an important feature of the politics of St. Lucia in this period.[12] The image of the Forum and SLAM as organizations of the university-trained urban middle class had previously worked against the radicals. With their takeover of the trade union movement, leaders such as George Odlum, Peter Josie, Calixte George, and Hilford Deterville became closely identified with labor interests and the aspirations of agricultural laborers (Carasco 1979, 10). This served to erode the perception of Compton as the main defender of the economic interests of the rural population. The growing popularity of the radicals also served to increase their weight within the SLP, thus marking a distinctive leftward shift in the main opposition party. This was further heightened by the links established between Odlum and the Caribbean Left, particularly with Bishop and the NJM.

The challenge to Compton was not confined to the organized elements of the agro-proletariat, but also encompassed the unionized sections of the urban salariat as well. A pay dispute between the government and the urban middle class represented by the Civil Service Association and the SLTU was one of the main sources of political conflict between 1973 and 1979. The degree of economic and political instability occasioned by this dispute is discernible in a number of reports between 1973 and 1979 (Stoby Commission Report 1973; Dolly Committee Report 1977; Hewlett Commission Report 1979), which suggest a strong link between the economic conditions of the mid-1970s and the political militancy of the population. Despite salary increases for the civil service of between 50 and 70 percent of their salaries in 1973, public-sector workers continued to strike intermittently well up to the independence period and before the general election of July 1979 (Compton in *Government Information Service-St. Lucia News*, 21 March 1979). While the strikers attributed their actions to inadequate pay and to increases in the rate of inflation, their protest also reflected the high degree of politicization of the union movement, whose ultimate objective was the political defeat of the UWP.

In addition to these industrial disturbances, a political conflict between the SLP and the UWP over the issue of independence formed a significant part of the political challenge to the postcolonial order that Compton was seeking to establish. Ironically, a number of leading radicals in the SLP thought it prudent to oppose independence, largely due to their opposition to Compton.[13] In Odlum's view, "the position was that independence under Compton was not going to be independence, but would be the colonial thing re-worked. And that it was an independence that we should not help to organize. It was a device. It was not that we were ever against independence. We felt that it would be tactically wrong to put independence in their hands before an election" (Odlum, interview).

The SLP argued that Compton had disregarded the recognized constitutional procedures for pursuing independence and that he intended to use the instrument of sovereign statehood to increase internal repression. The SLP's argument was that section 10(1) of the West Indies Act, which dealt with the independence procedure, had stipulated that independence could be pursued either by a referendum or by a change in the constitution, which required a two-thirds majority in the House of Parliament (*The Voice*, 26 August 1976; SLP 1978). Since Compton had decided to pursue independence by inviting the British government to terminate its association with the territory (*The Voice* [Independence Supplement], 19 February 1979, 27–29), the SLP responded by demanding elec-

tions before independence. At several points in the debate the SLP came peril-
ously close to defending the colonial status of the territory (SLP 1978, 5; Cmnd.
7328 [1978], 14–15). In its "Red Paper"—the answer to the government's "Green
Paper" on independence—the SLP claimed that "the overwhelming majority
of the people of St. Lucia DO NOT WANT St. Lucia to go into independence
at this time" (SLP 1978, 3). Odlum later qualified this position by suggesting
that the people were "suspicious" of independence (see *The Crusader*, 1 April
1978, 10). The SLP also argued that "St. Lucia is not too big to maintain ties of
association with the United Kingdom" as in the "case of St. Lucia's Caribbean
neighbors—Martinique, Guadeloupe and Puerto Rico—and other countries
further [*sic*] afield which in size, population and wealth, far outstrip St. Lucia
but yet maintain ties with metropolitan countries" (SLP 1978, 5). During the
independence constitutional conference, the SLP declared that its position was
one of "nonparticipation" unless a "process of consultation had been activated
or machinery established" to ascertain the wishes of the people (Cmnd. 7328
[1978], 16). The SLP also boycotted the independence celebrations.

However, the SLP position was not fully reflective of the full spectrum of
radical nationalist opinion on independence. The WRM, by contrast, saw independence as a "necessary step in the development and furthering of the struggle
of the people and the working class in particular against imperialism." According
to the WRM, "with independence, and free of colonial political domination,
our working people, assisted by their revolutionary organizations, will be able
to move one small step further in their struggle against the local and foreign
exploiters. With British political domination out of the way, our working people
will have one enemy less to deal with at [a] direct political level" (Earl Bousquet
in *The Crusader* 28 October 1978, 3).

The SLP's challenge to the independence procedure was marked by the reality and threat of political violence. One of the more dramatic of such episodes
occurred at a local hotel, where Odlum led a group of supporters to confront a
British government representative for the "betrayal" of the St. Lucian people.
Odlum later declared that "he could guarantee the safety of no one during the
independence celebrations" (see *Keesing's Contemporary Archives*, 11 May 1979,
29591). The entire period was marked by increasing levels of violence at political
meetings, the quasi-militarization of armed gangs of Odlum supporters, and
a general atmosphere in which the likelihood of an armed coup d'état was a
strong possibility (*The Crusader*, 1 July 1974, 1; *The Voice*, 20 December 1975, 1).
Odlum's political meetings in this period normally entailed the screening of a
video recording demonstrating the mechanics of an armed takeover.[14]

In response to these political challenges, the government increased the level
of repression by legislative means, which contributed to political instability. In

March 1976 the Public Order Act was amended to place restrictions on the holding of public meetings and demonstrations (Public Order Act 1976, Part II, section 4). The amendment outlawed quasi-military organization, military training and drills for nonceremonial purposes, wearing uniforms, and oaths relating to seditious or subversive enterprises (Public Order Act 1976, Part IV). The act also included clauses rendering persons inciting racial hatred or inducing the public "to commit assault or to destroy or do damage to property" or to "cause disaffection amongst the police force" liable to punishment (*The Voice*, 25 March 1976, 6). Similarly, an Essential Services Act was introduced to restrict the activities of the union movement (SLP 1978), by making it illegal for certain categories of the workforce, such as the police and fire officers, to engage in industrial action.

The government also resorted to the use of force, and between 1974 and 1979 the use of guns and tear gas to break up political meetings became commonplace (SLP 1978; *The Voice*, 20 December 1975, 1; *The Crusader*, 13 July 1974, 2). The period also witnessed an increase in police action against opposition politicians. Both Odlum and Josie faced criminal charges for violating the terms of the Public Order Act (*The Crusader*, 1 July 1974, 1). There was also an increase in dismissals of the opponents of the UWP from the public service (SLP 1978, 3–5).[15] These repressive measures were likened to the techniques used by other repressive regimes in the Caribbean such as those of Grenada's Eric Gairy and Guyana's Forbes Burnham (see Francois 1977).

These instances of UWP repression served to intensify the challenges to the Compton regime and to legitimize the activities and ideas of the radicals. Compton consequently led St. Lucia into independence on 22 February 1979, but the stage had been set for the defeat of the UWP. Facing an increasingly militant and youthful electorate, confronted by a vigorous campaign from populist SLP leaders, beleaguered by strikes and demands for pay increases, and delegitimized by charges of corruption, political victimization, and electoral corruption, the UWP was replaced by the SLP in the general election of July 1979.

The Limits of Radical Nationalism

Despite its victory over the UWP, the experience of the SLP in government demonstrated in concrete terms the limitations of radical nationalism in a recently decolonized postcolonial state at the cusp of the establishment of neoliberalism as a globally hegemonic force. These limitations were highlighted first in its relationship to international capital, best illustrated by its conflict with the Amerada-Hess Oil Company. Second, the SLP had overestimated the extent to which the global political environment was supportive of a radical foreign policy. Finally, the SLP underestimated the potential for domestic resistance to its internal economic and social policies.

The conflict between the SLP and the U.S. multinational oil company Amerada-Hess highlighted the limitations of the radical nationalist project. One writer described it as demonstrating "too clearly the classic situation which prevails when a multi-national corporation confronts a small highly dependent country seeking to improve its material conditions" (Barrow-Giles 1992b, 118–119). The SLP, while in opposition, had viewed the operations of Amerada-Hess as a glaring example of the subservience of the UWP administration to international capital and had challenged a number of the company's demands. It had been particularly hostile to Amerada-Hess's demand that the entire lower house should vote in favor of the Oil Refinery Act. The SLP had also insisted that throughput charges should be linked to the movement in world oil prices and that disputes with the company should be settled in accordance with local laws.

The response of the SLP in opposition had provided an early indication of the limits to its radicalism. Though its lawyers had argued that the company's demand for a "fundamental term" was a violation of the rules of parliamentary government (see Calderon in *St. Lucia Hansard*, 25 June 1977, 9), the entire opposition voted in favor of the bill. It did so claiming that its action safeguarded the economic livelihood of the people of St. Lucia and reflected the fact that Amerada-Hess had promised to employ about 3,000 St. Lucians (see Louisy in *St. Lucia Hansard*, 28 June 1977, 40; Koester 1986; Barrow-Giles 1992b, 122–123).

Once the SLP was in power, the opportunity was open for it to renegotiate the Oil Refinery Act, and it was widely anticipated that the SLP would do so (see *Caribbean Insight*, August 1979, 2). However, it failed to do so. Despite rhetorical claims to the contrary, the SLP clearly recognized the weaknesses of the St. Lucian state in relation to international corporate capital. It was therefore not surprising that six months into the SLP administration, *Caribbean Insight* (December 1979, 5) reported that the government had "shed much of the radicalism it exuded while in opposition" and suggested that this was "an indication that it may be finding the whole business of government and meeting the needs of the country, its people and international community very much different from what it perceived them to be while John Compton was in power."

Two separate but related developments served to accentuate the weakness of the government in relation to the U.S. multinational. The first was Hurricane Allen in August 1980, which damaged EC$250 million of the country's infrastructure, ravaged 100 percent of the territory's banana crop, and left sixteen people dead and about 6,000 homeless (see *Caribbean Insight*, September 1980,

7; Thomson 1987, 10). The second development was a wildcat strike on the Amerada-Hess construction site in mid-1981, during which the site experienced a forty-one-day closure.

The dire economic straits of the state following Hurricane Allen deepened the government's dependency on the company. Amerada-Hess, as a "goodwill" gesture, had agreed to rebuild a large number of schools that had suffered damage. It is within this context that the widely anticipated review of the Oil Refinery Act was shelved, and the government was forced to adopt a more accommodating stance to the company. According to one writer, "during this period, Hess provided much assistance to the Government and on the basis of such assistance and the promise of further employment, Hess consistently demanded the non-unionization of its workers" (Barrow-Giles 1992b, 123–124).

This issue of the non-unionization of workers and Amerada-Hess's response to the wildcat strike in mid-1981 revealed further aspects of the government's dependency. According to *Caribbean Insight* (August 1981), Amerada-Hess "on more than one occasion directly snubbed the St. Lucia government and flouted industrial relations practice by refusing official requests to re-open the construction site before settlement talks could take place. The Company also attempted to apply a form of 'blackmail' on the government by ceasing work on the rehabilitation of scores of the island's schools."

Equally reflective of the state's dependency was the government's response to the company during the wildcat strikes. The government's initial response was to consider categorizing employment in the oil sector as an essential service (Barrow-Giles 1992b, 124; Duncan 1980). This move was reversed following a hostile reaction from the island's unions, but the government settled instead for an amendment to the Oil Refinery Act. One provision of this amendment gave the responsible minister the right, in the event of a stoppage of work, to "take all lawful measures to ensure that supervisory staff are permitted to enter and to leave the construction site" (see Barrow-Giles 1992b, 124). The limits to economic nationalism were also reflected in Odlum's attempt to rationalize the approach adopted toward the company (see Duncan 1980, 12).[16] Odlum presented the level of Amerada-Hess's commitments in the country, the degree of "defenselessness" of the state after Hurricane Allen, and the fear that an Amerada-Hess pullout might "have had a cyclical effect on some other investors in the pipeline" as the reasons for the SLP's new conciliatory stance (Duncan 1980, 12–13). In a climb down from his earlier position, Odlum viewed an anticipated throughput charge of U.S.$6,000 a day as being "not a bad projection" when measured against the "failing banana industry." Similarly, Odlum attributed the large number of dismissals on the Amerada-Hess project to the government's failure to produce "the sort of guarantee that they want" (ibid., 13). Therefore, while Hurricane Allen had indeed reinforced the territory's vulnerability, the government's U-turn was also the result of the dependence of the state on external capital.

The weaknesses of the St. Lucian state are further highlighted when the global dimensions of the Amerada-Hess investment are considered. Koester (1981, 1986) argues that the Amerada-Hess investment in St. Lucia was designed to strengthen the company's hand in relation to a dispute with the U.S. Virgin Islands over the renegotiation of a 1965 contract (*Multinational Monitor* 1981, 11). In his view, the Amerada-Hess–St. Lucia agreement allowed the corporation to threaten the Virgin Islands government with the closure of its St. Croix refinery, in the absence of a satisfactory agreement.[17] Further, the St. Lucia agreement allowed Amerada-Hess to increase its profits by a process of "transfer pricing" and to avoid U.S. tax laws by declaring the cost of utilities in St. Lucia as opposed to St. Croix or even the U.S. itself (see Koester 1986, 193; 1990, 12). The truth of these assertions is partly confirmed by the fact that the levels of investment promised did not, and to date have not, materialized. Thus, according to Koester (1986, 198):

> Although the trans-shipment terminal at Cul-de-sac Bay has been operational since 1982 and the Oil Refinery Act stipulates that once it is completed the corporation will begin refinery construction, no such work has begun. . . . Even without the refinery, the terminal in St. Lucia provides the corporation with a subsidiary for transfer pricing. The St. Lucia subsidiary can overprice crude oil that it sells to St. Croix so that the profits are made in St. Lucia where there is no tax, instead of St. Croix where the company's new contract stipulates that it will pay its entire federal corporate income tax without a subsidy.[18]

The fact was that the St. Lucia operations were "more valuable as a threat to the Virgin Islands than as an operating refining unit" (Koester 1981, 11), and consequently, the promised levels of employment anticipated in the Amerada-Hess investment have failed to materialize. Indeed, the number of people employed at the Amerada-Hess site has never exceeded 300 (ibid., 11). A later study observed that the Amerada-Hess payroll covered only forty employees (Barry et al. 1984, 357).

Given the familiarity of the radical wing of the SLP with these aspects of the Amerada-Hess operations (see Josie in *St. Lucia Hansard*, 29 June 1977, 46–47), its inability to revise the Amerada-Hess agreement demonstrates that the party's approach to economic development, despite protestations to the contrary, was defined in terms of the injection of external capital into the economy, the very foundation upon which Compton's approach had been built. This militated against the SLP's notion of nationalism. Similar limitations can be identified in the pursuit of the "independent foreign policy" that the SLP had defined for itself.

The main features of the SLP's radical foreign policy intended to reflect a new direction in the expression of national independence were outlined by Odlum before Parliament in September 1979. The new foreign policy approach was rationalized on the basis of a more optimistic interpretation of the possibilities for the pursuit of radical policies offered by the global environment. Odlum argued that the global environment both demanded and facilitated a more active role for new states in international affairs. In contrast to the years between 1940 and 1970, when the international community "was seized with the consolidation of peace" and with "efforts to regularize world trade and commerce in a legal form," he saw the post-1979 period as offering wider possibilities. This was so because, prior to the 1970s, "new developing states did not . . . present a numerical pressure group . . . within the International Community" (*St. Lucia Hansard*, 14 September 1979, 3).

Odlum believed that a radical stance in international politics was essential for widening economic development options. This lay in opposition to Compton's ideological attachment to the territory's historical economic relations. In Odlum's view, St. Lucia's limited economy and size made it necessary to pursue the widest possible range of international relations. While a radical economic stance does not necessarily give rise to a radical stance in international politics, St. Lucia's geopolitical proximity to the United States in the Cold War context was seen as limiting the territory's ability to establish international economic alliances of its own choosing. Odlum's "radical" foreign policy was therefore articulated in an attempt to signal his willingness to overcome U.S. economic, political, and military domination as a necessary step in furthering the economic development of the territory.

Odlum pledged not to entertain foreign military bases within the territory. He further declared that the state would "never be used for, or form a part of, any plan to mount hostilities against third states." Relatedly, he declared that St. Lucia would not "support groupings that are hostile to or threaten the territorial sovereignty of third states." Most important, the foreign policy statement expressed intolerance toward attempts by third states to interfere in the internal affairs of St. Lucia. This applied not only to direct military confrontations but also to the political conditions attached to economic aid (*St. Lucia Hansard*, 14 September 1979, 5).

An important feature of Odlum's radical foreign policy was the overt support for third world and nationalist movements globally. In his declaration,

Odlum gave notice of St. Lucia's intention to join the Non-Aligned Movement (*St. Lucia Hansard*, 14 September 1979, 6). In addition, Odlum took the opportunity to reiterate his government's commitment to the principles expressed in the "Declaration of St. Georges." This declaration was a joint statement of objectives and aspirations outlined by Dominica (under Oliver Seraphine), Grenada (under the Peoples' Revolutionary Government of Maurice Bishop), and St. Lucia (led by Allan Louisy but guided by Odlum, his deputy), all of which had embraced a socialist-oriented path. In this declaration, a number of initiatives suggesting a more radical orientation were expressed. These included "an independent and nonaligned foreign policy, opposition to colonialism in the region and internationally, [and] support for liberation movements in Southern Africa" (*Caribbean Insight*, August 1979, 2).

As can be gleaned from the Declaration of St. Georges, St. Lucia's radical foreign policy was heavily influenced by the seizure of power by the Peoples' Revolutionary Army in Grenada on 13 March 1979, a few months before the SLP's rise to power in St. Lucia. Dominica's participation in the Declaration of St. Georges also reflects a decisive shift to the left in the politics of all the newly independent states of the Windward Islands under the influence of Grenada. The timing of these developments, following closely upon St. Lucia's independence, had reinforced Odlum's optimism in the possibilities for radical change in St. Lucia. An important feature of the Grenada experience was a deepening of political relations with Cuba and other socialist states, and this served as a model for the St. Lucian radicals. Thus Odlum declared a commitment to deepen ties with Cuba. Odlum defended this in terms of "establishing Cuba's proper role and place within the concept of a Caribbean community" (see *Caribbean and West Indies Chronicle*, October/November 1979, 1) and as a basis for improving the economic and social condition of St. Lucia. In this regard, Cuba's social achievements made it an attractive model and presented the opportunity for St. Lucia to tap into Cuban technical assistance.

The Declaration of St. Georges also expressed a commitment to put forward a "revised concept of the Organization of Eastern Caribbean States (OECS)" (*Caribbean Insight*, August 1979, 1–2).[19] The major factor for this revision lay in the three territories' opposition to the conservative ideological orientation of the OECS. In particular, earlier efforts at the establishment of a regional defense force were viewed as unsatisfactory.[20] The Declaration of St. Georges expressed support for a regional defense force that would serve not as a device "to prop up any shaky regimes or to help keep a dictator in power . . . but would be concerned with resisting external aggression" (ibid., 1).

St. Lucia's foreign policy orientation assumed a permissive global political environment, which reflected a decline in U.S. global power. To the St. Lucian

Table 3.1. Revolutionary upheavals in the third world, 1974–1980		
Country	Event	Date
Ethiopia	Deposition of Haile Selassie	12 September 1974
Cambodia	Khmer Rouge take Phnom Penh	17 April 1975
Vietnam	NLF takes Saigon	30 April 1975
Laos	Pathet Lao take over state	9 May 1975
Guinea-Bissau	Independence from Portugal	9 September 1974
Mozambique	Independence from Portugal	25 June 1975
Cape Verde	Independence from Portugal	5 July 1975
São Tome	Independence from Portugal	12 July 1975
Angola	Independence from Portugal	11 July 1975
Afghanistan	PDPA military coup	27 April 1978
Iran	Khomeni installed	11 February 1979
Grenada	NJM takes power	13 March 1979
Nicaragua	FSLN takes power	19 July 1979
Zimbabwe	Independence from Britain	17 April 1980

Source: Halliday 1986, 92.
Note: NLF = National Liberation Front; PDPA = People's Democratic Party of Afghanistan; NJM = New Jewel Movement; FSLN = Sandinista National Liberation Front.

Left, the U.S. president Jimmy Carter's notion of "ideological pluralism" was symptomatic of this decline. This assumption of U.S. decline was also sustained by the increasing political success of a wave of radical national liberation movements throughout the third world from the mid to late 1970s, as seen in Table 3.1.

The post-1979 environment, however, was far less permissive of radical stances in economic and political affairs than had been anticipated by the St. Lucian Left. In an influential study, Halliday (1986, 81–104) sought to identify three "waves" of revolutions in the postwar period. Each of these waves, in Halliday's view, indicated a degree of permissiveness within the international system for structural realignment. The period of Halliday's third wave coincides with the period in which the assumptions of St. Lucia's radical foreign policy were being framed (see Table 3.1).[21] Halliday's central argument is that the decade of the 1980s witnessed a termination of the global context that had sustained this process of change. When applied to the St. Lucian experience, Halliday's formulation suggests that the radical foreign policy was frustrated by the fact that it had emerged in a period in which the permissive global political context was coming to a close. Indeed, the decade of the 1980s is widely accepted as the period in which the ideology and practice of global neoliberalism gained ascendancy (Harvey 2005).

There are a number of features of the international system that, by 1979/1980, challenged the St. Lucian Left's assumption of the existence of an environment favorable to socialism and radical nationalism. In the first instance, the notion of "ideological pluralism," which had lent ideological validation to the socialist direction, was being shelved during the latter years of the Carter presidency. Thus on 1 October 1979 Carter used the pretext of the presence of a Soviet brigade in Cuba to outline a more hostile policy toward the Caribbean (see *Caribbean and West Indies Chronicle*, October/November 1979, 3). While the new policy combined military coercion with economic assistance, the reversals in U.S. policy were most apparent in the increased level of military aggression. This reality was intensified under the Reagan administration. The pattern of U.S. reassertion of a military presence in the region is captured in the following account by the Collective for Caribbean Project for Justice and Peace (1982, 3):

> From 1980 onwards, a series of large-scale military manoeuvres were held aimed at increasing direct intervention capacity in the region; *Solid Shield 80* and *Readex 80* which included landing of marines in Guantanamo and naval practices off Puerto Rico. The Caribbean section of *Ocean Venture 81*, defined as the largest manoeuvres held since World War II, included mock invasions of Cuba and Grenada. *Falcon Vista*, carried out together with the Honduras navy, was against Nicaragua. . . . In 1982 *Safepass 82* took place, north of Cuba involving 30 warships from six Western nations.

Subsequently, in April 1982 *Readex2-82*, which involved all the U.S. military branches, the Royal Netherlands navy, and 45,000 sailors, sixty ships, and two aircraft carriers, took place (ibid.).

This heightened U.S. military presence was also reflected in an increase in U.S. arms sales to the Caribbean and Latin America, which between 1979 and 1980 grew from U.S.$4.7 million to U.S.$31.8 million (Collective for Caribbean Project for Justice and Peace 1982, 3). Equally spectacular was a 145 percent increase in military aid for the Eastern Caribbean between 1983 and 1984, independent of the military expenditure for the Grenada invasion (see Resource Center 1984, 24; see also Sim and Anderson 1980). (Table 3.2 shows the level of U.S. military spending in St. Lucia and the Anglophone Caribbean between 1980 and 1982.)

While the U.S. invasion of Grenada in October 1983 was the decisive turning point in the reversal of the anti-imperialist project in the Anglophone Caribbean, the pattern was repeated less spectacularly in St. Lucia and the other Caribbean territories. Odlum's relationship to Grenada, Cuba, and Libya, and his plans to reorganize St. Lucia's security forces, had been viewed as "ominous" by U.S. secu-

Table 3.2. U.S. security and economic assistance in selected Anglophone Caribbean territories, 1980–1982 (in thousands of U.S. dollars)						
Country	1980		1981		1982	
	Security	Economic	Security	Economic	Security	Economic
Bahamas	--	--	40	--	1,060	--
Barbados	58	--	5,084	--	2,100	--
Dominica	--	--	30	--	33	
Guyana	--	4,695	25	6,803	40	7,313
Jamaica	--	14,408	42,587	19,500	41,075	21,335
St. Lucia*	3,307	--	4,310	--	60	--
St. Vincent	--	--	58	--	60	--
Trinidad	--	--	--	--	--	--

Source: Collective for Caribbean Project for Justice and Peace 1982.
*Two significant factors are identifiable in the St. Lucian case. The first is the relatively large amount of military aid in relation to the size of the territory and in relation to other OECS territories such as Dominica and St. Vincent in the years 1980 and 1981. The second is the sharp drop in spending in 1982. This was because of the early collapse of the SLP government in 1982.

rity analysts (Sim and Anderson 1980, 12; *News Analysis*, 1 February 1982, 1–2). Prior to the Grenada events, a series of political changes in the Caribbean, themselves a consequence of heightened U.S. involvement, limited the effectiveness of radical nationalism in St. Lucia. The Seraphine government of Dominica, following the economic destruction of Hurricane David in 1979, had distanced itself from the Caribbean Left under pressure from the United States (see *Caribbean Insight*, November 1979, 1); in 1980 Michael Manley of Jamaica was replaced by the U.S.-backed Edward Seaga (see Belle 1984, 17); and the victory that year of Eugenia Charles of Dominica saw the emergence of a staunch and "enthusiastic supporter of the Reagan administration and of US regional interests" (Thomson 1987, 7). In addition, the period witnessed a counteroffensive against radicalism by the traditionally conservative leaders of the Caribbean such as Tom Adams of Barbados, Milton Cato of St. Vincent, and Vere Bird of Antigua.[22] These leaders were later to play a key role in facilitating the U.S. invasion of Grenada. This shifting global and regional context led to the defeat of the internal social and economic policies of the SLP and to the collapse of the government itself.

The Internal Economic Order and the Limits of Radical Nationalism

The internal economic agenda of the SLP was spelled out in the first budget presented by the new government on 24 March 1980. Odlum described it as a

"Robin Hood" budget since it was designed to "take from the privileged sector of the society who 'have' and lighten the load of the poor" (*Caribbean Insight*, May 1980, 6). It signaled a sharp deviation from the foreign investment policy pursued by the previous government. The SLP placed a high level of taxation on the corporate sector and rationalized the policy on the basis that the "present scourge of unemployment and the apparent inertia in the economy" required an alteration in government's expenditure commitments (see ibid.). Among the more dramatic increases in taxation was a 500 percent increase in licenses on commercial banks from EC$4,000 annually to EC$20,000. These increases were not "considered to be prohibitive by any means" and were implemented in an effort to bring bank license fees "in line with those of our sister CARICOM states" (Louisy, Budget Address 1980, 31). Other segments of the domestic commercial sector were also subjected to increased taxation. For example, license fees on all insurance companies were raised by 100 percent (*Caribbean Insight*, May 1980, 6). Increases in hotel occupancy taxes from 5 to 7 percent were announced to "assist rather than militate against the development of the tourist industry as it will largely be channelled into tourism promotion" (Louisy, Budget Address 1980, 31–32). The government also introduced measures to bring the expatriate managerial sector, previously exempt from taxation, under the purview of its taxation policy (see ibid., 31–33).

New economic policies were also pursued within the agricultural sector. The government's main goal was to give the small producer a greater degree of control in the banana industry. To this end, the government proposed to act upon the recommendations of the Commission of Enquiry into the banana industry, which had identified a number of barriers to the participation of small farmers. This commission, chaired by the New World Group agricultural economist George Beckford, had recommended the need to increase the size of the board of directors of the SLBGA as a means of dismantling "the wall of frustration which prevents 90 per cent of the membership from entering the decision making arena, which sacrifices participation for expediency, which insulates management from the general membership" (Thomson 1987, 71). One of the commission's important findings was the strong influence of Geest Industries, in its capacity as a "grower," over the SLBGA.[23] The commission concluded that "there was a fundamental conflict of interest for Geest to be both 'marketing agent' and 'buyer' of Windward fruit. This conflict must inevitably work to the advantage of Geest Industries and the disadvantage of the producers and their association" (ibid.).

The SLP government therefore resolved to break the monopoly of the large landowners over the directorship of the SLBGA, to exert greater control over the activities of Geest within the local industry, and to reduce the dependence of the territory on banana production. The government expressed a commitment to increase local food production in an effort to reduce the food import bill (Louisy, Budget Address 1980, 15).

The SLP government also sought to participate directly in the economy, in violation of the "umpire" state form championed by Compton. Three months after taking office, the government announced its purchase of the Halcyon Days Hotel. While Odlum offered reassurances that there was no official plan to take over other hotels, he viewed this as an opportunity "to explode the 'capitalist myth' that the state cannot compare with private investors when it came to operating a business profitably" (Wayne 1986, 120–121). The government also founded the National Commercial Bank (NCB), which it described as a mechanism to break the near monopoly of foreign-owned banks over the commercial banking sector, whose "lending criteria" were "out of tune with the developmental needs of an emerging nation" (Louisy, Budget Address 1980, 22). One of the NCB's main goals was to assist in the promotion of investment opportunities among local entrepreneurs.

However, the response to the interventionist orientation of the SLP was decidedly hostile. The challenge to the government came from two fronts. On the one hand, the local capitalist class, in league with the UWP, waged a vigorous challenge to the policies of the SLP. Second, the more conservative elements of the SLP leadership mounted strong opposition to the socialism of the left wing of the government. These developments defeated the radical nationalist orientation of the SLP.

The event that crystallized the hostility of the local capitalist class toward the SLP was Odlum's decision to regulate the importation and sale of a number of goods previously imported by the private sector. This decision to place price controls on building materials such as lumber and cement and essential foods such as flour was ostensibly taken in response to Hurricane Allen. It was opposed, however, by the St. Lucia Chamber of Commerce on the basis that Odlum was pushing the "socialist line." According to the Chamber's president, Ornan Monplaisir, Odlum's actions marked "the commencement of the erosion of the private sector locally" and would result in "a hesitancy on the part of foreign investors and entrepreneurs to participate even in the most generous development opportunities" (*Caribbean Insight*, November 1980, 6). Indeed, a series of business closures during this period was perceived as indicating the private sector's growing unease with the government's policies. Thus in the latter half of 1980 the British Booker-McConnell investment group decided to close down the largest department store in the Windward Islands, putting 150 people out of work. While the reasons for the company's decision were unrelated to the government's actions, it was widely perceived by the opponents of the government as an indication of private-sector unease over the local investment climate (see Compton 1980; *Caribbean Insight*, October 1980, 6).

The challenge by the local business sector coincided with an ideological split within the government. The background to this ideological split lay in a dispute over an informal "leadership agreement" that had been worked out between the leader of the SLP, Allan Louisy, and his deputy, George Odlum. Essentially, the agreement involved Louisy vacating the prime minister post after six months in office and having Odlum succeed him. The rationale for the agreement was that Louisy, a retired judge from the Appeal Court of the West Indies Associated States, would present a conservative face to the electorate, thus neutralizing fears of Odlum's "Communism." Once the party had won office, Odlum would then have assumed, in the eyes of many, his rightful place as prime minister. The crisis broke out over Louisy's refusal to honor the agreement, forcing Odlum into a popular campaign to oust the official leader. This leadership struggle played a critical role in shaping the performance of the SLP, in contributing to political instability, and in further retarding economic development.

The first phase of the leadership struggle culminated in a vote of no confidence in Louisy during the 1981/1982 budget debate, with the Odlum faction voting with the UWP members against the government (see Midgett 1998, 3–5). Following the defeat of the Louisy budget, Odlum, along with his leading supporters, such as his brother Jon Odlum and Mikey Pilgrim, formed the overtly left-wing Progressive Labour Party (PLP). The PLP immediately embarked on a popular campaign to overthrow the minority SLP government of Winston Cenac, who had replaced Louisy as prime minister. The eventual overthrow of the SLP occurred with the collapse of the Cenac government in mid-January 1982, following a period of industrial unrest and business shutdowns by the island's labor movement and the business community, which received political support from the PLP and UWP (see James n.d.).

The local private sector during this period clearly indicated its intention to return to the UWP economic approach of accommodation to capital, both domestic and foreign. This can be seen in a number of ways. In the first place, the imposition of a wide-ranging consumption tax led the Chamber of Commerce to increase pressure on the Cenac government. The tax was considered damaging to business interests, who resented the fact that the decision was taken "without prior consultation with the . . . private sector" (see James n.d., 35–38). Local business interests supported calls for the government's resignation and announced a national shutdown to emphasize the continuing deterioration in the economy and the economic mismanagement by the government (see Press Releases: St. Lucia Chamber of Commerce, 13 January 1982; St. Lucia Manufacturers' Association, 13 January 1982; St. Lucia Small Business Association, 12 January 1982).

Protest against the government received support across a wide section of society, particularly the trade union movement, though the business sector was the most vocal in calls for the resignation of the government. Significantly, the business closures, spearheaded by the private sector, were stepped up long after the left-wing element of the SLP had been expelled from the cabinet and had formed the PLP. There was also a clear dichotomy in motives between the union movement and business sector with respect to the protest action. The initial protest had ostensibly been mounted to force the government to withdraw a piece of legislation that was designed to protect a member of the SLP government, Evans Calderon, from disqualification from the House. Calderon was charged with undertaking private legal work involving a contract between the government and a local firm, thus constituting a conflict of interest (see James n.d., 24–25). The government, in response, sought to introduce a bill to repeal the existing laws governing the awarding of contracts to members of government. The most offensive feature of the bill was its retroactive application, as it was "deemed to have come into operation" on 23 February 1979, thus negating all attempts to effect Calderon's disqualification (ibid., 26–28). What is interesting, however, is that the Chamber of Commerce continued with the national shutdown long after the prime minister, Winston Cenac, had agreed to withdraw the legislation.

In contrast, the trade union movement expressed reservations over the calls for the government's resignation. A letter to the prime minister from the unions noted that their position was "in no way linked to the stance taken by the Chamber of Commerce" and acknowledged the "good intentions of government . . . at meeting the economic demands of workers." The unions also registered awareness of the "involvement of internal and external forces in sowing confusion and contributing significantly to a crisis which will inevitably lead to a catastrophe" (SLTU et al. to Cenac, 14 January 1982). Evidence of a conflict of motives between radicals and the private sector existed as early as 1981, when the WRM warned of the danger of the return of the "most rabid anti-people elements" who "are attempting to manipulate the situation so that anti-worker elements may again be established in positions of political power" (WRM 1981).

Increasing tension between the state and private investors also prompted ideological and political conflict within the SLP. Contrary to popular perceptions, which reduce the episode to a Machiavellian grab for power by Odlum (see

James n.d), a close analysis of these developments reveals that economic policy was central to the leadership crisis. The "ideological split" within the SLP was caused by the party's conservative wing's commitment to the economic dependency model of development. This wing of the party resisted radical nationalism on the basis of its incompatibility with the development needs of St. Lucia. Louisy would later admit that he reneged on the leadership agreement because of Odlum's ties with Cuba (Louisy in Dabreo 1981, 151). Similarly, following a North American tour in August 1981, Cenac identified the threat of "extreme leftist-oriented ideology" as "crippling" the country's economic activity. He saw the need to contain the "fear of such an ideology" as "one of the greatest tasks facing his government" (*Caribbean Insight*, August 1981, 8). In the tourism sector, it was observed that hotel occupancy rates had fallen from a record average of almost 88 percent in 1978 to a low of 45 percent in 1982. The industrial sector was described as being at a standstill. This theme was echoed by the chairman of the National Development Corporation—the arm of the government concerned with investment promotion—who claimed that the corporation's overseas investment promotion efforts had been "blunted by recession, entrepreneurial pessimism and a pervading sense of uncertainty about the island's recent political problems" (ibid.). The conservative wing of the SLP was therefore instrumental in promoting a concept of national independence that was consistent with economic dependence and avoided strategies that would threaten the development approach pursued by Compton (*Caribbean Insight*, September 1981, 9).

Neoliberal Globalization and the Defeat of Radical Nationalism

The leadership struggle within the SLP was therefore a consequence of the adjustment of the newly independent state to the reality of global-capitalist economic power. Consequently, the fall of the SLP government in 1982 can be seen as a defeat of the radical independence project, which had its roots in the global environment of the early 1970s. The radical project was designed primarily to facilitate a greater degree of participation of the state in the economy, to reduce the degree of foreign ownership and control of the economic sector, and to protect the mass of the population from the economic domination of the local business class. It was premised on the notion of the role of the state that prioritized nationally determined political choices over the interests of global capital. The success of the business sector in facilitating the collapse of the government reflected a resistance to a notion of national independence, which threatened the interests of global capital with which it closely identified.

While the defeat of the radical independence project can be blamed on Odlum's unnecessarily inflammatory rhetoric and the destabilization of the local business class, the shifting global environment provided the overarching structural framework that made the SLP's defeat possible. The assumed favorability of the post-1973 global political environment, which had underpinned the pursuit of the radical nationalist project, proved misguided given the political transformations ushered in by the end of the decade. These political transformations manifested themselves most spectacularly in a shift to the right within the dominant states of the world economy and in the overt hostility to the national liberation project in the Caribbean region. Thus the U.S. invasion of Grenada on 25 October 1983 represented a watershed insofar as the pursuit of radical economic and foreign policies within the postindependence states of the Anglophone Caribbean is concerned. More generally, however, the economic shifts associated with the erosion of the Bretton Woods order and the oil shocks of the mid-1970s also militated against the pursuit of radicalism. The implications of these developments were seen most clearly in the difficult economic circumstances under which the political leadership of St. Lucia had been called upon to navigate the early period of independence.

Compton's economic and political policies had been consciously tailored to respond to the dire economic conditions ushered in by the rise in oil prices and the currency fluctuations of the mid-1970s. He therefore pursued an accommodationist stance to global capital in order to attract foreign direct investment in St. Lucia. While the radical nationalist project pursued by the SLP received wide support from the majority of the population and while it formed an essential element in the process of decolonization, it was constrained by the weakness of the state in relation to global capital. Further, the global environment of the early 1980s militated against its realization. Far from suggesting the weakness of multinational capital, the crisis of the post-1973 period revealed the weaknesses of small states dependent on capital to meet their development objectives. The elements that had sustained radical nationalism, such as the demands for a new international economic order, had been replaced by structures that increased the capacity of global capital to influence the internal development objectives of nominally independent states. It is within this context that the SLP was defeated in the general election of 3 May 1982, won by Compton's UWP with a 14-3 majority in Parliament. This brought to an end radical resistance to integration into the norms of global capitalism.

CHAPTER 4

St. Lucia under Global Neoliberal Hegemony, 1982-1990

The Global Political-Economic Context and the Establishment of Neoliberalism in St. Lucia

Perhaps the most critical feature of the political economy of St. Lucia in the years immediately following the return of Compton to office in 1982, and following the collapse of the Grenada revolution at the wider regional level, was the emergence of local and global realities that sustained Compton's ideas on the role of the state in its relation to global capital. In short, the global political economy validated Compton's brand of limited sovereignty, coincidental with the interest of ideological neoliberalism. Thus, while the precarious global economy of the post-1973 period had been used to justify a narrow independence framework, the global economic crisis of the 1980s provided a rationale for the further embrace of neoliberalism. In the 1983 budget Compton (Budget Address 1983, 3) identified the "wounds" and "scars" of the "longest and deepest recession since World War II" as limiting the development options of small states. These "wounds" and "scars" referred to the high unemployment levels of 32 million in the European Community and 10 million in the United States. Similarly, a decline in the value of the pound sterling against the U.S. dollar reduced the value of St. Lucian exports by 25 percent, resulting in a loss of more than $12 million per annum. It also significantly reduced the value of the £10 million aid package that Britain promised to St. Lucia as part of the independence "golden handshake." Mirroring the concerns of the mid-1970s, Compton identified the negative impact of the global environment on tourism: "The recession and high unemployment in North America and Europe and the devaluation of currencies of Mexico one of our leading competitors for North America traffic, and of Britain and some other European tourist markets, have had the pincer effect of reducing demand for our products while making those of our main competitors cheaper and more attractive.' Further, the global economic crisis also reduced the level of aid from sources such as Canada and Venezuela (Compton, Budget Address 1983, 4).

The government's view of the constraints that these realities posed on its policy options were eagerly expressed by Compton in a speech further reinforcing the historical pattern of dependency: "as our economic problems have their root-cause in the world economic recession, so too must our search for solutions harmonize with those of the international community." This would "permit the country to survive this long and difficult period of adjustment of the world economic order" (Compton, Budget Address 1983, 7). Compton was therefore issuing a clear call for the rejection of any response that might have envisaged a process of resistance to global capitalism.

A central feature of the process of global neoliberal adjustment was a rethinking of the economic relationships between developed states and the formerly colonized territories. Vaughan Lewis (1993, 109–110) has argued persuasively that this process of global adjustment fundamentally challenged the "traditional modus operandi" of the small states of the Organization of Eastern Caribbean States (OECS). Among the more prominent of these developments was the rethinking of the aid and trade packages that had hitherto defined European-Caribbean relations. This was seen, for example, in the alterations to the Lomé Convention. Thus, while the first Lomé Convention of 1975 was widely regarded as "a unique model in the political economy of North-South relations" (Long 1980, ix), these "economic buffers" to political sovereignty came under increasing attack as the demands of liberalization and globalization intensified.[1]

Another critical factor shaping the embrace of the neoliberal model in St. Lucia was the experience of economic crisis within the more developed countries (MDCs) of CARICOM in the decade of the 1980s.[2] Ramsaran (1993, 239–240) describes the decade of the 1980s as a "disastrous one for the Commonwealth Caribbean" and summarizes the experience of the MDCs:

> In the case of Jamaica, though the economy grew by an average annual rate of 3.5 per cent between 1986 and 1989, real gross domestic product in 1989 was still only about 5 per cent above that of 1976. In 1977 the Guyanese economy entered a phase of such continuous decline that, by the early 1980s, real gross domestic product had fallen below the levels of the early 1970s. In the case of Trinidad and Tobago, the economy experienced seven consecutive years (1983–89) of negative growth. This followed an average growth rate of almost

7 per cent in 1976–82. Following a period of buoyant growth between 1976 and 1980, the Barbadian economy also entered a period of stagnation. Real gross domestic product in 1988 is estimated to have been less than 10 per cent above that of 1980.

This experience of economic contraction within the Caribbean MDCs influenced the development of neoliberalism in St. Lucia in a number of ways. First, the crises of the MDCs confirmed the failure of the socialist model since the territories that had been most committed to the noncapitalist path, such as Guyana and Jamaica, faced the deepest crises. Further, the crises in the MDCs led to a shortfall in earnings from regional manufacturing trade accruing to St. Lucia. Also, while St. Lucia and the other small economies of the Eastern Caribbean continued to perform better than the MDCs, the economic crises in the larger states continued to reinforce the notion of economic marginalization among the smaller countries that formed the OECS. Ramsaran (1993, 240) observes that in the difficult economic period of the 1980s, "smaller islands such as St. Lucia and St. Kitts came to enjoy per capita incomes three to four times that of Guyana." He argues that this superior economic performance was an indication of the emphasis on "foreign investment, monetary policy and exchange control." In his view also, "tourism seems to have been a crucial factor in helping the smaller islands deal with the foreign exchange problems that bedevilled the more developed countries. The pooling of reserves and the discipline inherent in a common central banking arrangement also helped maintain an atmosphere conducive to growth."[3] Similarly, Harker (1993, 20) observes that the banana producers reaped windfall gains due to the change in relative parities between the sterling and the U.S. dollar. (See Table 4.1 for an indication of the performance of the St. Lucian economy in the 1980s.)

Despite the economic successes of these less developed countries (LDCs), the impact of the economic failure of the MDCs reinforced the notion of economic marginalization among the OECS and further pushed St. Lucia toward a stance of conservatism and a limited role for the state. This was partly due to the fact that the expectations of the smaller territories in the benefits of independence had historically been shaped by the experience of the larger territories. The crises in the larger states were therefore seen as holding negative consequences for the smaller territories. Thus, according to Lewis (1993, 118), by the end of the 1980s "all governments and policy analysts within the region had their sense of the smallness, fragility, and dependency of the countries' economies, and of the regional economy as a whole, reinforced as they saw both trade and growth decline in the area for much of the time."

Table 4.1. A comparative view of St. Lucia's GDP growth rate in the 1980s	
Country	1980–1990
Antigua and Barbuda	5.3
Dominica	4.4
Monsterrat	5.0
St. Kitts and Nevis	5.9
St. Lucia	7.0
St. Vincent and the Grenadines	6.0
OECS Region	5.8
CARICOM Region	0.1
Source: Thomas 2000, 63.	

Conversely, the economic stability of the smaller countries of the OECS resulted in a validation of the neoliberal model in St. Lucia. The strong performance of the OECS was attributed to the embrace of a policy of export-led growth and the emphasis placed on foreign investment and private capital in the development process (Lewis 1993, 118–119; Ramsaran 1993, 240). The overall result of these developments in St. Lucia was to reinforce the notion of the absence of alternative policy options to what was championed by the dominant capitalist states in the world economy. The precarious global economy was used as a source of ideological justification for an overt dependence on global capital, and for reinforcing notions of a limited role for the sovereign state in St. Lucia.

The emergence of neoliberalism in St. Lucia and the Caribbean was also the result of key regional political actors deliberately pursuing it as an ideal. The passage in the United States of the Caribbean Basin Economic Recovery Act in 1983 marked the earliest indication of the deliberate implementation of the neoliberal model of development in the region. This legislation was first promulgated by Ronald Reagan in February 1982 as the Caribbean Basin Initiative (CBI) (Griffith 1990, 33). While the CBI was officially announced as a one-way free trade arrangement allowing duty-free access of selected Caribbean products into the U.S. market, one of its main aims was to consolidate U.S. economic and political power in the region. A number of studies have described the CBI as an economic "carrot" intended to complement the military "stick" of the United States. This was particularly important in a context where the containment of Caribbean nationalist and socialist movements was high on the U.S. foreign policy agenda (Ramsaran 1982; Wiltshire-Brodber 1983; Feinberg and Newfarmer 1984; Midgett 1985; Polanyi-Levitt 1985; Deere et al. 1990, 153–186; Griffith 1990).

A central feature of the CBI was its intent to replace the anticapitalist orientation of the 1970s with free-market norms. This was seen most clearly in the conditions for eligibility to CBI benefits. A country could be denied access to CBI concessions if it was a Communist country; if it failed to protect U.S. property from expropriation; or if it failed to observe U.S. copyright laws (Barbados Export Promotion Division 1985, 8). Another key reflection of the neoliberalism of the CBI was the emphasis on technical support to the regional private sector. The CBI was explicitly advertised as "a private-sector driven programme" whose success depended on "the extent to which Caribbean businesses and entrepreneurs take advantage of the opportunity given them by the United States" (Kemp 1985, 2). Also, one of the CBI's goals was to foster regional institutional development among private-sector organizations.[4] This was reflected primarily in a more central role given to the private sector "in fostering the approval of decisions at the top level" of the Caribbean Community (CARICOM) (Giacalone 1993, 3). Among these decisions were the "Common External Tariff (CET), changed rules of added value, and the organization of a sub-regional stock market" (ibid.). Significantly, the implementation of these measures required the reversal of some of these states' earlier nationalist-driven policies. For example, in order to lay the "groundwork for the sub-regional stock market," the Aliens Landholding Act of Trinidad and Tobago, which prevented foreigners from owning real estate, had to be abolished (ibid., 4).

The influence of the CBI in championing neoliberalism was clearly discernible in St. Lucia. Its major impact lay in the provision of ideological support to the neoliberal model in the postsocialist context. While Compton enthusiastically embraced the CBI, he saw it as demanding of the state a further degree of restructuring in order to fully maximize its benefits. Thus, on the one hand, Compton boasted that with the "passage of the Caribbean Basin Initiative there has been a substantial interest by companies wanting to locate in the Caribbean area." On the other hand, however, he was forced to concede that St. Lucia was "not the only pebble on the beach," and "must get her act together if she wants to enter the race" (Compton, Budget Address 1984, 15). This placed the appeasement of external capital high on the St. Lucian political agenda. This was reflected in the emphasis on factors such as maintaining good labor relations and ensuring a cheap and skilled workforce.[5] The government also emphasized providing good transport and communications infrastructure and suitable real estate and offering financial aid and other incentives to foreign investors (ibid., 16).

In addition to the U.S. influence, there was also an increasing identification by the Caribbean political leadership with the objectives of global neoliberalism. This embrace of neoliberalism coincided very closely with the reemergence of a hegemonic organic bloc of conservative leaders throughout the region, many of whom had been strongly opposed to the socialist Left in the 1970s.[6] The clearest indication of their commitment to neoliberal ideology was the declaration known as the "Nassau Understanding" at the CARICOM heads of government meeting of 1984 (see CARICOM 1984).

The Nassau Understanding expressed a commitment to structural adjustment as "an integral part of the development process" and as a logical adaptation to "major external or internal shocks to the economic system." Central to this process of adjustment was a recognition of the "very important role for the private sector within a socially just market economy" (CARICOM 1984, 2). To overcome economic vulnerability, the leaders pledged to engage in an "unrelenting drive . . . to enforce operating efficiency in all public sector activity." This drive was to be pursued through "an upgrading of the management and functioning of existing state enterprises and public utilities, including giving them the autonomy and responsibility to operate on strictly commercial lines within broad policy guidelines clearly laid down by the government" (ibid., 3). The CARICOM heads also emphasized "income restraint." Regional companies were urged to limit dividend distribution and freeze executive salaries and benefits, while trade unions were encouraged to play their part in "limiting and moderating claims for increases in remuneration packages." The governments, in turn, pledged to "exercise strict economy in public expenditure on wages and salaries and on consumption." While the leaders recognized that the process of structural adjustment would result in "short-term dislocation," they believed that the "failure to adjust structurally" would have "the consequence of the even more serious problem of large scale unemployment" (ibid.).

This wholesale acceptance of neoliberalism was also a consequence of an increasing dependence upon international financial institutions for economic support (McAffee 1991; Barry et al. 1984; Deere et al. 1990). It was also indicative of a real shift in the underlying ideological assumptions shaping the political consciousness of the post-1983 leadership of the CARICOM states. Given the fact that the St. Lucian economy was relatively untouched by the conditions that had necessitated direct International Monetary Fund (IMF) intervention in other CARICOM states, the influence of the multilateral institutions was seen largely in the presentation of an ideological justification for the path of development preferred by Compton.

This was expressed in two ways. First, the "blessing" of these institutions was heavily relied upon as proof of the "correctness" of the path being pursued by the St. Lucia government. Every major economic speech was punctuated by supportive World Bank and IMF reports, provided as evidence of good and effective government in St. Lucia (Compton, Budget Addresses 1982–1989). Ideological approval from the external multilaterals was seen as critical in gaining the internal support of the electorate.

Complementing this process was a tendency to rely on the development targets of these multilaterals as a basis for formulating domestic economic policy. For example, the 1985 budget, which Compton described as "the most difficult financial instrument that I ever had the task of preparing," was heavily influenced by the IMF's concern about the size of the public sector and the rate of expenditure on public services (Compton, Budget Address 1985, 10). The absence of opposition to the increased influence of the multilateral institutions on the strategies pursued by the St. Lucian state was a result of the fact that these policies complemented the ideological orientation of the ruling United Workers' Party (UWP). However, while the neoliberal agenda represented a return to the preindependence economic policy framework of the UWP, it was expressed at a greater level of ideological dominance than in the earlier period. Indeed, it was facilitated by the fact that similar shifts were identifiable throughout the world system, both in terms of the retreat of radical nationalism and the dominance of neoliberal ideology. This orientation largely determined the role of the St. Lucian state in the 1980s.

The Role of the St. Lucian State under Hegemonic Neoliberalism

The broad economic, political, and ideological realities of the 1980s global environment reduced the St. Lucian state to the management of adjustment to global economic realities as its defining feature. A number of developments characterized this process. There was a series of internal adjustments in state policy in order to accommodate the demands of global neoliberalism. Among the strategies employed was a reversing of the dirigiste policies of the previous St. Lucia Labour Party (SLP) regime. There was also an attempt to contain the demands of labor, in particular, and to reduce the reliance of the broader society upon the state. The government also reasserted the reliance of the state upon external capital and made a commitment to protect private-sector activity from governmental interference. These strategies were sustained through the development of an ideological rationale that sought to delegitimize the previous link between anticapitalism and anticolonialism. There was also an attempt to strengthen state viability, as seen in an attempt to create a unified Windward Islands government. This strategy emerged in the late 1980s and early 1990s when a number of international developments reinforced the notion of Caribbean marginalization.

The dismantling of the state structure erected by the SLP was one of the principal goals of the UWP upon its return to office in 1982. While a large and robustly interventionist state had been historically absent in St. Lucia, the 1980s witnessed a heightened attack against interventionism. This was well illustrated by the 1984 budget, in which Compton advocated the need for a "thorough scrutiny . . . to see what dead branches must be pruned from the tree of our economy to ensure that it recovers, flowers, and bears fruit." This "pruning" was largely aimed at the modest advances in social services that had been attempted by the SLP. Compton asked the country to consider whether the state could afford to "provide a free health service and expensive drugs to all and sundry, citizens and noncitizens, regardless of their ability to pay . . . and whether we must pay thirty cents for every dollars' worth of milk we distribute to poor children under the World Food Programme" (Compton, Budget Address 1984, 12).

The government also began to reduce the size of the public sector, since the "increasing demand on revenues to maintain a costly administrative structure" was seen as one of the main constraints to economic growth (Compton, Budget Address 1984, 13). The government's antidirigiste stance was also manifested through an emphasis on "efficiency" in the public sector. While this notion of efficiency was formulated as an attack against wastage in the public sector, it also encompassed a "restructuring" of the public sector with specific emphasis on "pruning" of that sector (Compton, Budget Address 1983, 16–17). This policy was pursued, with the approval of the World Bank, through an imposition of a freeze on new hiring in the public sector (World Bank 1985, 6).

Far more controversial, however, was a series of responses designed to achieve "downsizing." *Combat*, an organ of the National Workers' Union (NWU), one of the island's largest collective bargaining organizations, reported in June 1985 the laying off of 150 community health aides within the Ministry of Health, as part of the government's drive toward "cutting the bulgs [*sic*] in various ministries" (*Combat*, 29 June 1985, 1). Equally controversial, was the laying-off of unmarried pregnant teachers (ibid., 3). While the government presented moralistic arguments to support its action, the decision was motivated less by morality than by neoliberalism. The St. Lucia Teachers Union saw this decision as blatant sexual discrimination, and presented it as a violation of a government agreement, signed in 1984, that guaranteed paid maternity leave to all permanent and temporary employees whose appointment exceeded two years (ibid.).

Given St. Lucia's weak state sector, the antidirigism of the UWP was not particularly marked by a significant process of privatization. Privatization, as will be seen in a later chapter, gathered pace, tellingly, with the return of the SLP to political office in 1997. One clear instance of UWP divestment, however, was the privatization of the Government Funding Scheme (GFS), as a result of which more than 150 workers were threatened with being laid off (*Combat*, 12 October 1985, 1).[7] This embrace of the privatization option in preference to other strategies to revitalize the GFS evoked a scathing response from the NWU: "In true UWP style . . . there seems to be favour for the privatization option which would only complete what has been going on almost since the inception of the Funding Scheme. Everything would now be in the hands of certain select and favoured party hacks" (ibid.). The NWU was alluding to a pattern of corruption, which the union suggested could be viewed as an alternative explanation for the inefficiency of the scheme.

Another important feature of the St. Lucian state was its role in the containment of labor's demands. In the period following the fall of the SLP, a report from the International Labour Organization listed St. Lucia as one of the countries in the world "that has an above average loss of working time due to strikes" (Barry et al. 1984, 356). As a result, the UWP sought to tactically distance itself from the aspirations of labor. This development marked one of the sharpest breaks in the pattern that had been established from the earliest manifestations of St. Lucian nationalism. The main feature of the government's strategy was the pursuit of wage restraints to maintain fiscal discipline. This policy of wage restraints within the public sector was intended to serve "as a guide to wage level awards in the private sector" (Bowen 1992, 20). Central to this policy was an attempt to delegitimize the union's pay demands. This was clearly seen in the government's response to the demands for pay increases by the island's trade unions in the 1983 budget: "Some people continue to make demands knowing full well that these demands cannot, in present circumstances, be met. How in heaven's name can there be new demands for higher salaries in 1983 when the increases awarded in 1982 cannot, even now, be fully met? How can there be demands for increases in personal income when the national income has been declining?" (Compton, Budget Address 1983, 6).

A scathing critique was launched at the level of public-sector labor costs. It was argued that while the "public sector workers comprise a mere 19 percent of the labor force, they receive 51 percent or 55.56 million of Government recurrent expenditure. While the average per capita income in St. Lucia is $EC 1562, the per capita in the public sector is $EC 7685" (ibid., 6). An attack on public servants as a "labor aristocracy" therefore formed a central part of the government's attempt to delegitimize the demands of the trade unions.

While this suggests an openly hostile stance toward labor, the government's attack was also expressed through more subtle approaches. One indication of a more sophisticated approach was a strategy of "consensus" building. This was pursued largely in the form of tripartism, which was described as "one of the most critical elements of economic policy in the state" (Compton, Budget Address 1982, 8). Under tripartism, government, business, and labor agreed to a set of policies designed to ensure economic stability. Central to this notion was

a "standing Commission on wages, prices, productivity, and investment," out of
which emerged a prices and wages agreement in which the unions were required
to "accept wage increases of no more than 5 to 10 per cent per annum, whilst the
commercial sector was supposed to guarantee price movements of no more than
9 to 12 per cent" (*Combat*, 1 May 1986, 1).

While tripartism was never formally established, the formulation of the concept suggests that the need to "tame" labor was central to the process. This strategy sought to induce labor into accepting the neoliberal path as the only possible
means of development. According to Compton (Budget Address 1982, 8–9),

> The elements of our Incomes and Prices policy have to encompass Productivity
> and Employment. The Government, the Trade Unions and the Private Sector
> have to co-operate in this most vital area of our economy. The trade unions
> must accept moderate increases which come out of increased productivity,
> they must also seek to motivate their workers to accept their responsibility to
> create employment and maintain prices at reasonable levels. The Government,
> for its part will seek to give incentives to both parties. The trade unions will
> receive from the Government the undertaking to establish proper procedures
> for the protection of workers and their rights. Incentives will be given to the
> private sector for productivity gains through appropriate technology and for
> the creation of additional employment opportunities.

This project emphasized the need for wage restraint on the part of labor.
Similarly, trade unions were invited to make increased productivity a central feature of their functions. Correspondingly, the traditional trade union functions
of wage bargaining and protecting labor were de-emphasized and ideologically
delegitimized.

The state's strategy toward labor was clearly influenced by the multilateral
financial institutions. Compton (Budget Address 1982, 5) linked the need for
a tripartite commission to a World Bank report of 21 April 1982, which saw
the need for the "improvement in the investment climate" as an essential "pre-
requisite for private-sector investment." This insistence on greater restraint on
the part of labor was typical of the World Bank throughout the 1980s. Though
a 1985 World Bank report accused private companies of being more concerned
about shareholder profitability than the community at large, it sought to blame
the failure of tripartism largely on the trade unions. Trade unions were accused
of taking "a narrow view of their responsibility, limiting it to their membership
and not the society at large," and were urged to "re-examine their role in development and to devote some attention to increasing productivity." They were
also reminded of their "responsibility to the unemployed and underemployed"

through the creation of "an atmosphere conducive to the new job opportunities" (World Bank 1985, 7). The World Bank saw unemployment and underinvestment as a consequence of labor's wage demands (ibid., 6), and following its lead, Compton warned that any increase in salaries would be met by an increase in taxation on the entire population or through phased layoffs and early retirement: "These are social costs which I am sure that few in our community will advocate and I am sure no union leader will deserve our thanks if the results of his efforts lead to greater hardship and higher unemployment in this country" (Compton, Budget Address 1983, 6–7).

As proof of the "irresponsibility" of St. Lucian trade unionism, he argued that their wage demands were "counter to everything that is happening elsewhere" where "not only there has been [*sic*] a general reduction in wage demands, but in many instances unions have proposed wage freeze [*sic*] and even wage cuts to save jobs." St. Lucia's unions were warned therefore that they "cannot continue to act as though we are in another world of economic conditions or that we write the rules for the rest of the world" (Compton, Budget Address 1983, 6–7).

This attack against labor, however, sprang from the increased need to create a sociopolitical context favorable to international capital. In his first budget address following his return to office in mid-1982, Compton had identified "improvement in the investment climate" as the greatest challenge facing his government. In fulfillment of this objective, two policy initiatives, both of which had been outlined by the World Bank, had been declared as being absolutely necessary: "the existence of good, smooth industrial relations and a wage policy based on productivity" and "a sympathetic attitude of Government towards the private sector" (Compton, Budget Address 1982, 5). This reemphasis on the role of private and foreign capital in national development marked a conscious break with the ideological stance that had characterized the nationalist impulse of the immediate postindependence period under the SLP.

Commitment to external capital was expressed largely through the promotion of export-led manufacturing, a policy supported by the World Bank, which saw "export-led growth" as critical "given the small size of the local market" (World Bank 1985, 19). The government therefore provided a wide range of incentives to foreign capital (see Barrow-Giles 1992b, 110–111; World Bank 1985, 34–35). Describing St. Lucia's foreign investment policy as "flexible," a 1985 World Bank report noted approvingly the range of concessions offered outside the framework of the Fiscal Incentives Act. Among these was a treaty designed to cover investment promotion and protection for U.K. companies. Its provisions bound the St. Lucia and U.K. governments to "accord 'fair and equitable' treatment to investments in their countries by nationals and companies of the other" and to allow for "compensation after expropriation, free transfer of capital and earnings, and settlement of disputes by international arbitration." Compensation was also to be provided for losses incurred through "war or armed conflict, revolution, a state of national emergency, revolt, insurrection or riot." The treaty also prohibited the "nationalization or expropriation of investment" (World Bank 1985, 34–35). These developments indicate the success of international corporate capital in reclaiming the political space that had been eroded during the radical nationalist period.

One of the main strategies pursued by the government to facilitate foreign investment and export-led manufacturing was the establishment of export-processing zones (EPZs). These were to serve as low-cost, cheap labor, duty-free manufacturing enclaves geared primarily toward the North American market. In the mid-1980s these developments were largely designed to take advantage of the U.S. CBI program (see Kelly 1986, 823). Accounts of the success of these strategies vary, but the 1980s certainly saw an increase in manufacturing in St. Lucia, particularly in the electronics industry, a development that continued well into the 1990s. Klak and Rulli (1993, 130) observe that St. Lucia's electronics exports climbed from U.S.$977,000 in 1977 to about U.S.$3.6 million in 1986. Ferguson, writing in 1997, observed that "a full 14% of national employment [derived] from factories located in export processing zones" (Klak 1998b, 78). Relying on National Development Corporation (NDC) records, Klak (ibid., 75) noted that "St. Lucia's formal sector workforce in 1997 included 3,565 manufacturing employees" representing "nine per cent of the formal sector work force, or an average of 51 workers per factory." Elsewhere, Goss and Conway (1992, 310) suggested that in 1988, nontraditional industries employed about 7 percent of the working population. They noted that, rivaled only by St. Kitts and Nevis, "St. Lucia has been one of the leading OECS countries able to attract FDI [foreign direct investment] in the nontraditional manufacturing sector" (see Table 4.2).

Table 4.2. OECS nontraditional exports to the United States				
Country	1983	1985	1987	1989
Antigua and Barbuda	6,565	24,638	8,601	4,746
Dominica	235	13,468	10,290	7,453
Grenada	211	1,204	2,861	6,768
Montserrat	920	2,875	2,244	2,221
St. Kitts and Nevis	10 612	13,876	21,028	17,518
St. Lucia	4,655	13,322	17,670	23,920
St. Vincent and the Grenadines	4,176	9,638	8,493	9,050
Source: Goss and Conway 1992, 313.				
Note: All figures in thousands of U.S. (1987) dollars.				

The strategies promoting export-led manufacturing nevertheless illustrate some of the key tensions inherent in the role of the postcolonial state under neoliberalism. In particular, the state's role as a facilitator of the needs of external capital conflicted with its responsibilities to the populace. The state facilitated, for example, a heightened degree of economic exploitation of the working population within the export-manufacturing enclaves and advertised a cheap, exploitable female workforce as one of the attractions of St. Lucia. Government investment brochures typically stressed factors such as "a large adaptable labor pool of high manual dexterity" and an "extremely modest" wage structure as being among St. Lucia's advantages (see Kelly 1987, 89; see also Klak and Myers 1998).

The exploitative nature of labor conditions in the EPZs was demonstrated in a study conducted by Kelly on female labor (Kelly 1986, 1987). She found that the "number one problem, cited by over sixty per cent of the women [surveyed], was low pay," with workers complaining that they "did not earn enough to raise themselves above a bare subsistence level" (Kelly 1986, 826).[8] Given these realities Kelly (1987, 93–94) concluded elsewhere that

> if low wages . . . are St. Lucia's prime attraction for foreign investors, then perhaps the entire strategy for industrialization should be re-thought. Companies that leave whenever wages rise above rock-bottom levels cannot be in the long run benefit [*sic*] workers or St. Lucia in general. . . . Exhorting workers to "accept the disciplines of our Far Eastern competitors" seems misguided. . . . This sort of "discipline" is incongruous with the St. Lucian political culture, valuing as it does a democratic form of government and respect for civil rights.

Further, the fact that the success of the export-led model depended on the ability to outperform neighboring territories made the need to respond to the demands of external capital a permanent feature of government policy. Government priorities therefore shifted from a commitment to the needs of the domestic population to a commitment to creating conditions to attract foreign investment. Indeed, by the mid-1980s the ability to attract foreign capital had become the essential base upon which government success was measured (Compton, Budget Address 1984, 16). The power of external capital increased at the expense of internally driven national priorities and exposed St. Lucia to continuous pressure to adopt more neoliberal measures.

The World Bank, for example, while describing St. Lucia's regulatory environment as "adequate," lamented that St. Lucia "has not moved towards increased trade liberalization" (World Bank 1992, 9). The bank was pleased that St. Lucia had not introduced the CARICOM CET but complained of import licensing arrangements designed to protect certain CARICOM products and the existence of import monopolies for some goods. The bank argued that "rather than introducing the CET, the narrowing of tariff rates to the 5–20% range and the elimination of the non-tariff barriers should . . . be actively pursued" (ibid.). This also shows the manner in which the regional integration objectives were being swallowed up by the neoliberal thrust of global institutions.

This subordination to the dictates of external capital placed a tremendous ideological burden upon the shoulders of the domestic state. Paradoxically, the government ideologically defended its neoliberalism on the basis that it safeguarded the sovereignty of St. Lucia. While Compton identified neoliberal economic policies as the solution to St. Lucia's developmental needs, he also described his policies as an attempt to resist the "colonialist" control of the IMF. In the 1984 budget address, he argued that

> as the Minister of Finance who in 1964 presented the first Budget which freed us from [U.K.] Treasury control, I am not prepared to be the Minister who presents St. Lucia back to the International Treasury control of the I.M.F. I have said repeatedly that there is no room for both of us. If they must come then I must go. But my work is not over yet and it will not be over until every child in this country can get a place in school and a teacher to learn from, and on leaving school can be assured of a job to employ his knowledge and his talents in the land of his birth. These are the goals I set myself and these goals are not compatible with those of the IMF. (Compton, Budget Address 1984, 11–12)

The pursuit of the neoliberal model of development was justified simultaneously on the basis of what was demanded by the international multilateral institutions and on the need to safeguard the sovereignty of the state from the dominance of multilateral institutions.

An important ideological goal of the government was to redefine the state's responsibilities to its citizenry (see Joseph 1997, 54–61). One way in which this was manifested was through the separation of "politics" from "administration." Compton thus presented the "management" of the economy as being above "politics." Previously contested social and economic questions were presented as having been "settled" and consequently removed from the political agenda. Compton clearly articulated this in the 1984 budget, which celebrated the achievements of his party over the twenty-year period from 1964. After outlining the social and economic achievements of his "management," Compton (Budget Address 1984, 5–6) sought to delegitimize the "politics" of the Left:

Too often in the euphoria of our apparent successes great expectations have been aroused—expectations far in excess of the economic growth rate and the availability of the nation's resources to meet them. This leads to the type of frustration which can encourage the destructive politics of the type culminating in the disaster of 1979. If we are to set our country back on course we must first raise our sights. . . . We must raise our standards, particularly the standards of our politics. . . . This everlasting "roro"[9] climate cannot be productive for us as a people.

Consistent with the emphasis on managerialism was the need to lower the expectations of the citizenry in order to minimize domestic resistance to the redefinition of the state's role. This was done through an emphasis on "efficiency" as the main justification for the new role of the state, thus suggesting "nonpolitical" motives. Consequently, any attempt to challenge these priorities was labeled antidevelopmental. This, however, represented a tactical abandonment by the state of its historical responsibilities to its population and reflected an attempt to reduce the expectations of the population in the state's "delivery" capacity (Riviere 1990, 2; Bgoya and Hyden 1987).

While these strategies reflected what the government hoped to achieve by way of harmonizing state-society relations with the demands of neoliberalism, very little was actually done to bring about such a harmonization in the 1980s. It was not until the early 1990s that the Social and Economic Consultative Council was established. Its aim was to integrate the broad spectrum of social, economic, youth, and religious organizations into a semiformal policy discussion group. In the 1980s the attempt to create such a consultative group was limited to the pronouncements on tripartism. This absence of clearly defined political and economic structures through which state-society relations could be readjusted was partly a reflection of the government's electoral stability and also a result, as will be seen later, of the absence of grassroots resistance to the government's neoliberalism. Indeed, it was not until the early 1990s, when neither of these conditions held—that is, when resistance began to emerge and when the government's electoral strength was tested—that a more concrete attempt to formalize the social partnership was pursued.

Regional Political Unification—State Response to Neoliberalism

While the government was tardy in creating institutional mechanisms to manage state-society relations in a context of neoliberal dominance, a far greater effort was expended on pursuing a project of political and economic integration within the OECS in order to strengthen state viability. This pursuit of Windwards Island political unification was a direct response to the rude awakening encountered by these newly independent states when confronted with the actual reality of their marginalization and smallness, despite their historical perceptions of weakness, limited sovereignty, and structural insignificance.

While the economies of the members of the OECS had performed well throughout much of the 1980s, this renewed quest for regional political integration was the result of a heightened sense of Caribbean marginalization in the late 1980s and early 1990s. This perception of marginalization was shaped by a number of global developments in the period. Ironically, the very strength of some regional economies threatened to deny them access to concessionary financing from international donors (Lewis 1988b, 21). Many of the Eastern Caribbean leaders were aware, however, that the performance of their economies was the result of the wide range of international concessions, rather than due to the inherent strength of their economies themselves. According to Lewis-Meeks (1991, 85), their success reflected their heavy reliance "on grants and concessionary loans from other countries, net private transfers from abroad, and protected prices for bananas and sugar from the EC, which together the World Bank estimated to amount to 25% of total GDP." It is on this basis that Compton described the OECS nations as "countries of subvention . . . not independent countries" (ibid., 167). These insecurities were compounded by the impending formation of the Single European Market (SEM) in 1992, widely viewed as sounding the death knell for the preferential trading arrangements for Caribbean products like rum, sugar, and bananas.

This sense of economic marginalization was also compounded by the political developments in the Soviet Union and Eastern Europe in the mid-to-late 1980s, associated with Mikhail Gorbachev's attempts to reform socialism and to bring to an end the global political relations of the Cold War. These developments eventually resulted in the collapse of Communism in Eastern Europe and the Soviet Union. Remarking on the shifting geopolitics of the period, Compton described the 1990 budget as having opened "against the background of extraordinary happenings in the world outside." These were seen as "events which we cannot influence, but which can have far reaching effects upon the future of our country and the daily lives of our citizens" (Compton, Budget Address 1990, 1). One clear consequence of the fall of Communism was a reduction of development aid to the Caribbean due to a shifting geopolitical agenda among the dominant Western capitalist states. One of the early signs of such a reduction in aid was a cutback in a U.S. support fund for Latin America and the Caribbean from U.S.$545 million to U.S.$350 million "in order to provide emergency funds to Eastern Europe" (Barrow-Giles 1992a, 16–17). This loss of development aid was the result of a general reduction in the strategic significance of the Caribbean region due to "improved super power relations" (*Caribbean Insight*, March 1991, 1). In the view of Timothy Ashby, a former official in the U.S. Department of Commerce, Washington now increasingly saw the Caribbean "as a group of small, self-interested countries which speak with many voices when they should be speaking with one" and concluded that the region "was no longer a priority area for US investment and aid" (ibid.).

This downgrading of the strategic importance of the Caribbean region was also reflected in the new U.S. economic initiatives for the region, such as the Enterprise for the Americas Initiative (EAI) of President George H. W. Bush. In contrast to Reagan's CBI, which had offered one-way free trade for Caribbean products to the U.S. market, the EAI stressed the need for Caribbean states to "balance obligations and benefits" and viewed "special treatment for the Caribbean region" as "contrary to US policy on liberalization" (*Caribbean Insight*, July 1991, 6). Among the demands placed upon regional governments was the "removal of impediments to increased trade and investment, as well as co-operation on the Uruguay Round of the GATT trade talks" (*Caribbean Insight*, August 1991, 1). One of the "impediments" identified by the promoters of the EAI was the CARICOM CET. While the eventual EAI-CARICOM agreement did not affect the CET, it was widely acknowledged within CARICOM that the EAI marked the end of the special treatment of the Caribbean by the United States (ibid.).

In St. Lucia, the shifting geopolitical context also challenged the "limited foreign policy" framework that Compton had pursued. This foreign policy, as has been seen, had expressed a complete dependence on the so-called traditional partners of Britain and North America. Similarly, Compton's foreign policy had expressed an unquestioning identification with Western Cold War aspirations as a basis for improving the economic condition of St. Lucia. With the political realignments of the post–Cold War period, such a framework of economic development was rendered obsolete. This has been captured in a study on the implications of the collapse of the Soviet Union on the foreign policy of St. Lucia by Barrow-Giles (1992a). She argued that the central view of St. Lucia in the postsocialist period was of a "struggling 'Third World' country trying to survive in the international arena" (ibid., 16).

These developments served to reinforce the economic and political vulnerability of the states of the OECS, and it is against this background that initiatives for Windward Islands political unification can be understood. According to Lewis-Meeks (1991, 65), "underlying the OECS integration movement was a view of the world by OECS politicians as a place threatening to countries as small as themselves." In Compton's view, "the OECS territories could not exist financially as independent countries nor were they able to fulfill their obligations to the international community, having neither the money nor the expertise to man both their civil services at home and their offices overseas, which were vital to procuring financial assistance" (ibid., 167; see Lewis 1988b, 12–13). Political unification of the small territories of the Eastern Caribbean was therefore pursued as an additional "adjustment" to the changes in the global economy.

The first indication of the thrust to OECS unification emerged from a May 1987 communiqué from the heads of government, which declared the intention of the various governments to embark on a program of public sensitization toward the goal of political and economic integration (see OECS 1988, 2). The initiative for this process of integration had come from the prime minister of St. Vincent, James Mitchell. In Mitchell's view, the various states of the OECS had "exhausted the possibilities of separate independence and the time had now come for them to pursue their development by pooling resources to combat common problems" (Lewis-Meeks 1991, 3). While this early declaration had envisaged an OECS-wide union, by the early 1990s the initiative remained alive only among the four Windward Islands of Dominica, Grenada, St. Lucia, and St. Vincent. The withdrawal of Antigua and other Leeward Islands had reduced the size of the embryonic political entity, but it strengthened the commitment of the four remaining territories to political unification. Between 1991 and 1992 four Regional Constituent Assemblies (RCAs) (with a fifth concluding session) were held to explore the issue of Windward Islands political union (see OECS n.d., 12–13). The RCAs received submissions from regional interest and political groups on the type of political union that should be created. Among the questions debated within the RCAs were the issues of citizenship, immigration, and electoral machinery; fiscal and financial arrangements; the structure and functioning of a unified administration and civil service; external representation; defense and security; and the harmonization of economic development policies (Lewis 1988b, 18–19).[10]

This emphasis on regional political integration reflected the Eastern Caribbean states' perceived need to overcome the miniaturized nationalism that had taken root with the dissolution of the Associated Statehood constitutions. The Windward Islands' leaders had been resolute in pursuing a unitary state as the preferred mechanism of integration. This had been clearly articulated by James Mitchell, who had declared his willingness to "work under any other leader" (*Caribbean Insight*, July 1987, 12), and by 1991 legislation for the referendum on Windward Islands political unification had been introduced in the St. Lucian parliament, and similar legislation was tabled in the other countries (*Caribbean Insight*, October 1990, 11). The timing of the initiative, and the urgency with which it was being pursued, was also rooted in local political considerations by the various heads of government. This was particularly true of Compton, James Mitchell, and Eugenia Charles of Dominica, who had enjoyed a close ideological affinity under the banner of the Caribbean Democratic Union in the period when the reversal of Caribbean socialism had been their chief concern shared with their northern ally, the United States (see P. Lewis 1999, 42).

However, the widely anticipated political unification never materialized. Indeed, in St. Lucia the political unification initiative had taken place against a background of growing public discontent with the government's neoliberalism. This challenge to the development assumptions of neoliberalism suggested the government's failure to adjust society's expectations to the realities of global neoliberalism. This discontent, as will be seen later, was also reflected in the resistance by the various civic groups in the Windward Islands to the control of Compton, Charles, and Mitchell over the unification initiative.

In the main, however, the general thrust of the government in this period was an attempt to harmonize its internal sociopolitical relations with that demanded by the imperatives of the external economic environment, and it did so with success. The economic challenges the Caribbean region faced in the 1980s vindicated the historical antidirigiste philosophy of the Compton administration. The "power struggle" that had wrecked the SLP also served to strengthen Compton, and the neoliberal ideological framework was embraced because of its association with "stability." The earlier experience of the SLP, in contrast, was largely equated with "instability." This was true not only because of the internal ideological squabbles of the SLP but also because of the hostility that its policies had aroused from the dominant capitalist interests, both internal and external.

Compton's economic strategy also benefited from the retreat of the Caribbean Left in the wake of the collapse of the Grenada revolution. This was reflected in the political marginalization of George Odlum and the Progressive Labour Party (PLP) and in the emergence of Julian Hunte as leader of the SLP in 1984. Hunte, a self-made Castries businessman, was a former member of the UWP and had had little association with the SLP's socialism in the preceding decade. Consequently, in this period the philosophy of the SLP became more closely attuned to that of the UWP, and became removed from the anticolonial socialist nationalism of the 1970s.

By the late 1980s, however, there was perceptible erosion in support for the neoliberal model, presenting a fundamental ideological dilemma for the St. Lucian state. Central to this dilemma was the reemergence of the social and economic questions that had been critical to the rise of nationalism, thereby indicating a failure by the state to shift popular consciousness to accepting neoliberal adjustments.

The Domestic Challenge to Neoliberalism

By the mid to late 1980s stresses were beginning to emerge within the relatively harmonious domestic political scene that had existed since the collapse of the SLP. One of the earliest signs of this shift was seen in the rejection by the trade union movement of tripartism, through which the government had hoped to build domestic consensus around the neoliberal model. An article that appeared in *Combat*, entitled "Tripartite Revisited," indicated the union movement's growing unease with the neoliberal model. It rejected the notion that the crisis of the St. Lucian economy was a consequence of the demands of labor. In contrast, it claimed that "recession in our economy, like inflation before it, was due almost exclusively to the fact that the economy operates as a mere adjunct, a dependent extension, of the international capitalist economy." The impending economic threats of the late 1980s consequently were seen as being "largely the result of the level, distribution and character of investment in the preceding economic periods of the 60s and 70s" (*Combat*, 1 May 1986, 7).

The *Combat* article reversed the government's critique of labor and attributed the territory's economic weaknesses to the backwardness of the St. Lucian entrepreneurial class and the government's foreign investment policies. The paper complained that the local capitalists "displayed an unwillingness to invest in the productive sectors of the economy," and while such investment "would not have prevented recession," it was argued that "an adequate level, and rational distribution of investment in the productive sector of the economy could have . . . ameliorated the effects of recession" (*Combat*, 1 May 1986, 7). Similarly, the government was accused of ignoring the historically risk-averse patterns of investment of the local business class and was blamed for the shortage of investment capital through its overreliance on the "industrialization by invitation" model. This model was seen to encourage a siphoning of investment capital "by means of a complex of concessions ranging from low wages . . . to ten years plus tax holidays" (ibid.). As a consequence, the union argued that "wage movements are not the causal factor of our economic plight and their suppression will not move St. Lucia out of its economic lag" (ibid., 9).

This assessment challenged both the practical and ideological terms of tripartism. On the practical side, *Combat* argued that the restriction of price movements to no more than 9 to 12 percent was "in fact no concession at all, [since] in a period of recession, with demand lagging, prices would not continue to spiral as they had done for the better part of the 70s" (*Combat*, 1 May 1986, 7). On a more ideological level, it asserted that "we do not allow bourgeois theorists to determine our position on crucial economic and labour questions" and denounced those elements of the union movement that "succumb to the UWP call for an incomes policy." Instead, labor activists were encouraged to persist in demystifying "theories and propositions that have their roots in the drive of the capitalist class to maximize profits, whether in or out of crisis period [*sic*] at the expense of the producers of all wealth—the workers" (ibid., 9).

This tendency led to the gradual return of conflict between the government and the union movement. Among the points of conflict between the public service unions and the government were the layoffs of the community health aides in August 1985 (*Combat*, 28 September 1985, 1); the dismissal of workers in the GFS (*Combat*, 29 June 1985, 1); layoffs in the Ministry of Agriculture (*Combat*, 28 September 1985, 1); the dismissal of pregnant unmarried teachers (*Combat*, 29 June 1985, 3); and layoffs at the state-owned Halcyon Days hotel and the Dennery Farm Company (Farmco). These dismissals were blamed "on the indifference of government to the right of every citizen to work, and on their lack of any conviction that there is a dynamic role for the state sector in the economy" (*Combat*, 28 September 1985, 1). The conflict between the unions and the government was reflected clearly in a letter by the president of the NWU, Tyronne Maynard, in which he warned Compton that his actions to "rob [the] workers of an opportunity to earn an income will be in the long run seen as a crime against humanity." The letter warned that

> any politician in office who does not recognize that St. Lucia is becoming tense day by day, and that the present situation requires dialogue at all levels so as to find the right solution to get our people out of its [*sic*] painful mire would be digging his political grave. . . . It is all well and good for a few IMF fanatics to remain in Washington, eat well, enjoy a reasonable standard of living, send their children to university and then dispatch a prescription that bears no relevance to our situation. . . . Please remember that you are the one who will have to face a desperate and emotional electorate come the next general election. (*The Voice*, 12 June 1985, 1)

Despite these indications of conflict, there was no major outburst of open industrial unrest in the period. The union movement was unable to mount a concerted political challenge to the neoliberal project comparable to what it had achieved in the 1970s. The retreat of the St. Lucian Left had deprived the labor movement of an organizational and ideological center around which to mount such a challenge. While criticizing neoliberalism, the trade union movement continued to operate within the assumptions of the dominant ideological paradigm. The minister of labor, Clendon Mason, in a December 1986 Christmas message to the unions, praised the NWU for never imposing a "burden that would break

the camel's back" and for not attempting to "kill the goose which lay the golden
egg of wages for the workers." He noted that the "salubrious national climate of
industrial relations during 1986" was "carefully cultivated and motivated by a
small band of vigilant and dedicated individuals in the informal *tripartite* setting
representing the workers, the employers and government" (*Combat* [Christmas
Issue] 1986, 8). The union movement's verbal critique, however, suggested that
a challenge to the Compton regime was taking shape for the first time since the
collapse of the SLP in 1982. This was to find greater expression, as will be seen
later, when a process of "deepening globalization" further eroded the economic
fabric of the St. Lucian state.

A far more significant indication of opposition to the UWP in the latter half
of the 1980s was a conflict between banana growers and the government. Much
of the political support for Compton in the 1980s had come from the banana
growers of the northeastern sections of St. Lucia. Relatedly, the economic performance of St. Lucia in the 1980s was largely attributable to the strong showing of the banana industry. Thus the 1987 budget had noted that the St. Lucia
economy grew by 6 percent over the one-year period from 1986, "the highest
since 1979 and one of the highest in the entire CARICOM region" (Compton,
Budget Address 1987). The banana industry was reported to attain record levels
of production in 1986, producing 112,000 tonnes valued at EC$137.171 million.
In the 1988 budget, it was noted that since 1982, the industry "had contributed
$488 million and in 1987 alone, the contribution was $EC 114.5 million or an
increase of 300% over 1982" (Compton, Budget Address 1988, 6).

By 1988, however, the industry was beginning to suffer from the need for
adjustment to the demands of the shifting global environment, resulting in a
challenge by banana producers to the UWP government. The first signs of conflict between the government and the banana producers occurred in the latter
half of 1988 following the dissolution of the entire board of the St. Lucia Banana
Growers' Association (SLBGA) by an act of Parliament on 25 October. On one
level, this decision was rooted in considerations of local political advantage. It
was argued both by Compton and the minister of agriculture, Ferdinand Henry,
that the decision was taken because of the political ambitions of key members of
the SLBGA board (see *Caribbean Insight*, November 1988, 4).

Nonetheless, growing global pressures on the banana industry was a key factor shaping the decision. Central to the conflict between the SLBGA board and
the UWP government was the board's criticism of the government's decision to
introduce a 5 percent levy on banana profits for the construction of roads in the
banana-producing areas. Resistance by the SLBGA board to what was perceived
by the government as a necessary structural requirement in the face of growing
international pressures on Caribbean bananas was seen as requiring the sharpest

response by the state. The minister of agriculture argued that "the board had entered into a direct confrontation with the government at a critical time for the industry with the approach of the European Single Market." This was viewed as "a state of affairs which could not be allowed to continue in the country's main industry" (*Caribbean Insight*, November 1988, 4).

While existing conflicts between the St. Lucia government and banana producers were to be intensified in the 1990s, this early confrontation between the government and the SLBGA board reveals a number of features that illustrate the difficulty of the state in sustaining harmonious domestic state-society relations while simultaneously operating within a neoliberal framework. One of the ways in which this tension was reflected was in the government's need to undermine the democratic basis of the SLBGA as a consequence of the pressures from the global environment. Indeed, not only did the dissolution of the SLBGA board undermine democracy within the industry, but, as argued by one commentator, it also contravened the laws of St. Lucia (see Francois 1996, 94–97).[11] This early SLBGA-government conflict therefore was illustrative of the pressures on the state to embrace undemocratic norms in fulfillment of the needs demanded by the economic environment. The implications of this are particularly significant given the fact that Caribbean nationalism had been concerned with deepening the democratic fabric of the society, and had been premised and fought for on the promise of such democratization.

Another important indication of resistance to Compton's neoliberalism was domestic opposition to his project of political unification. There was an overwhelming suspicion that the Windward Islands unification initiative had been an attempt to consolidate the power of the neoliberal leaders at the regional level. This consideration shaped the response of the SLP leader, Julian Hunte, to the proposal. Acting in his capacity as the chairman of Standing Committee of Opposition Parties of East Caribbean States (SCOPE),[12] Hunte announced a boycott by regional opposition parties of the first RCA on the grounds that the "whole initiative" was "being placed in a particular direction for the convenience of the governments in office" (*Caribbean Insight*, December 1990, 16).[13] In order to break the control of the governments over the process, SCOPE demanded that the constituent assembly be "completely independent with its own chairman regulating its own business and having clear terms of reference" (ibid.). Further indications of Hunte's opposition to the Windward Islands unification initiative was seen in a boycott by the SLP of the following two RCAs.

By the time of the third RCA, there were growing signs of waning enthusiasm for Windward Islands political unification. The central feature of the third RCA was a rejection of the unitary state model, which had been preferred by the Windward Islands' governments, and the emergence of a "clear consensus" for the federal form (*Caribbean Insight*, October 1991, 12). This shift from the type of union envisaged by the Windward Islands' leadership had also emerged in a period when changes in the respective local political contexts that had facilitated unification were widely anticipated. Of particular significance in this regard was the 1990 election in Dominica, which saw Eugenia Charles retain political office by a one-seat majority (see Emmanuel 1992, 32). The approaching 1992 election in St. Lucia also contributed to a growing sense that the narrow window of political and ideological consensus that had existed within the Windward Islands was coming to a close. The move to unification therefore came to a standstill. The rejection of the unitary state approach in the third RCA led James Mitchell to declare that the "trend seems to be that we are incapable of creating a new country" (*Caribbean Insight*, October 1991, 5). Although it had been widely anticipated that referenda in the various territories would quickly follow the fourth RCA, no such test of public sentiment ever occurred due to anxieties that "the public was not yet ready to vote for it" (ibid., 7).

Similarly, although the UWP won an 11-6 parliamentary majority in the 1992 election, no further steps were taken to formally debate the issue of Windward Islands unification in the St. Lucian parliament. Hunter Francois, who was closely involved in nonpartisan public discussions on the OECS, places much of the blame for the failure of Windward Islands unification on the government of St. Lucia: "St. Lucia never brought it to the House of Assembly. I went all over the islands, speaking on OECS unity. In Grenada the different parties were all there, and they were all in favor. St. Vincent no question. Dominica had some difficult fellows . . . , I must admit, but it was only St. Lucia that failed to carry out its undertaking to bring the matter to the House of Assembly" (Francois, interview).

Earl Huntley, a former permanent secretary in St. Lucia's Ministry of Foreign Affairs and ambassador to the United Nations, concurs with this view. He argues that Compton's historical record would suggest that "he has not been as pro-integration as it would appear," since "at key moments in the last thirty years, when some form of union could have been achieved, he was the one who pulled back." He sees Compton's failure to bring the issue to the St. Lucia Parliament as a continuation of this tendency: "It was passed in Grenada. All the parties voted for it. In St. Vincent there was only one party in Parliament. In any case the opposition had . . . been supporting it. In Dominica, the UWP voted against it, but the Labour Party and Freedom Party voted for it. In St. Lucia, it just never got to the House" (Huntley, interview).

However, there is evidence to suggest that Compton was aware of shifting political circumstances that threatened to erode political support for the Windward Islands leaders. In a conversation with Huntley, he rationalized his decision on the basis that "Eugenia [Charles] was having problems . . . and when they looked at the popular vote in Dominica it appeared that she would not have gotten the majority required in the referendum." Huntley, however, notes that it is significant that "Dominica took it to parliament. . . . But [Compton] did nothing" (Huntley, interview).

The attempts at regional political integration reflected the manner in which anxieties over the prospect of economic marginalization had reinforced the limitations of miniaturized nationalism. While Compton's project of political integration had failed, these anxieties played a critical role in sustaining his political domination of St. Lucia into the 1992 election. It represented a continued reflection of the harmony between Compton's domestic neoliberal approach and the external economic environment. However, the general elections in St. Lucia between 1982 and 1992 indicate a simultaneous resistance to neoliberalism and an underlying fear of economic marginalization, and provide a poignant indication of the impact of global neoliberalism on the internal politics of St. Lucia in the 1980s.

Neoliberalism and General Elections, 1982–1992

As early as the 1982 election, evidence suggests that the UWP had failed to fully win over the mass of the population to its project. It was swept into office on a 14-3 landslide of seats in Parliament in that year, but failed to improve significantly on the percentage of the national vote that it had won in the 1979 election, where it had suffered a 12-5 defeat (see Table 4.3). The election reflected the UWP's failure to capture the voters who had withheld their support from the SLP and reflected disillusionment with the ideological split within the SLP rather than a positive affirmation of the UWP's neoliberalism. This point was ably argued in a Workers' Revolutionary Movement (WRM) analysis of the 1982 election:

> The low turn-out at the polls is itself an indication of the genuine disappointment and frustration of the people over the corruption, in-fighting and mismanagement of the last two and a half years. Torn between the PLP and the SLP, undecided and frustrated, more than 4,000 people who voted labour in 79 did not vote this time. The swing to the UWP was precisely 13.6 per cent. In other words the difference between their popular support in 1979 and in 1982 is 13.6 per cent. This tells us that although the UWP victory appears to be a landslide . . . they have still not won over a large slice of new support. St. Lucia today is as divided as before. (WRM 1982d)

Table 4.3. Distribution of votes and seats, 1979–1987			
Election	SLP	UWP	PLP
1979	Votes: 25,294 (56.2)	19,706 (43.8)	——
	Seats: 12 (70.6)	5 (29.4)	
1982	Votes: 8,122 (16.7)	27,252 (56.2)	13,133 (27.1)
	Seats: 2 (12)	14 (82)	1 (6)
1987 1	Votes: 18,889 (38.3)	25,892 (52.5)	4,572 (9.3)
	Seats: 8 (47.1)	9 (52.9)	0
1987 2	Votes: 21,515 (40.8)	28,046 (53. 2)	3,176 (6 0)
	Seats: 8 (47. 1).	9 (52.9)	

Sources: Emmanuel 1992, 40; Barrow-Giles n.d., 18. Emmanuel (1992) provides an erroneous record of the seat distribution of the 1982 election. The figures presented here come from the corrected version of Barrow-Giles (n.d.).
Note: The figures in parentheses show the percentages of total votes and the number of total seats.

The continued adherence on the part of the electorate to the ideas of the Left was also demonstrated by the strong support shown in the 1982 election for the most leftward of the parties, the PLP. Formed less than one year before the election was called, the PLP was able to attract more than 25 percent of the national vote. In contrast, the older and more established SLP, which boasted within its ranks the conservative elements who had opposed Odlum's socialism, recorded the poorest performance in the 1982 election. While the UWP had pursued its election on the basis of a return to an accommodation to international capital, it failed to significantly adjust the consciousness of the St. Lucian electorate to the need for such an accommodation.

Although the 1982 election indicated a withholding of support from the UWP, the two general elections held in April 1987 indicated a political comeback for the SLP.[14] The most significant feature of these elections was the remarkable recovery of the SLP from its 1982 debacle, coming to within one seat of winning the government. While both the SLP and the UWP improved their performances in the election of 30 April, and while the number of seats per party remained unchanged (see Table 4.3), the SLP's strong performance suggested an unwillingness by voters to provide Compton with the mandate he needed for his economic agenda.[15] To justify his call for the second 1987 election, Compton had insisted that he required a more substantial majority in order to allow him the political space required to run the country (see *Caribbean Insight*, May 1987, 1). Arguing that the one-seat deficit would allow the SLP to "get by treachery what it did not get in free and fair elections," Compton described a 59 percent turnout in the election as resulting in "a distortion of the will of the people." Predicting a 12-5 parliamentary majority in the second election, Compton called on the people to make their voices heard "loud and clear" (ibid.). The failure to gain the anticipated majority therefore suggests a failure on the part of Compton to substantially shift domestic political opinion toward his political and economic approach.

Compton's desire for a larger electoral mandate must also be understood against the background of the objective of OECS political integration. While this process gained momentum in the early 1990s, the idea had first been publicly articulated, as stated earlier, in May 1987, when member governments agreed to "engage in a process of comprehensive consultation within their countries, including a referendum on this matter before deciding on further appropriate steps" (OECS 1988, 2).[16] Although the issue of regional integration had not been fully articulated during the 1987 elections, it had been "mooted" by Compton, who served as chairman of the OECS in the period leading up to the election (*Caribbean Insight*, July 1987, 12). It is in this context that his determination to win a 12-5 majority in Parliament can be understood. What is critical, however, is that the result of the second election of 1987 reflected a failure by Compton to decisively rally the mass of the St. Lucian populace behind his political and economic objectives. While a number of factors can account for the political recovery of the SLP, the election results provide a continuing indication of the resistance of the St. Lucia electorate to the neoliberal model.[17] The high levels of layoffs in the mid-1980s, growing unemployment, and the continuing failure of the state to meet the expectations of the populace accounted for this.

By the 1990s, however, growing concerns over Caribbean economic marginalization had served to weaken the opposition's challenge to Compton. This was reflected in the strong preference for the UWP in the 1992 election. The main issue over which the 1992 election was contested was the question of the economic management of St. Lucia. A central theme of the UWP election campaign was the need to "keep St. Lucia in good hands," with much emphasis placed on the management skills of John Compton. The UWP campaign centered around the strong performance of the St. Lucian economy in the 1980s, a decade in which many other Caribbean territories had witnessed sharp economic reversals (see *Caribbean Insight*, May 1992, 1). The strategy adopted by the UWP therefore reflected a continued reliance on the ideological assumptions of neoliberalism that had been employed throughout the 1980s.

This reliance on external neoliberal validation as a basis for winning domestic political support was clearly revealed in the UWP's 1992 election manifesto. Entitled "A Secure Future for St. Lucia," the manifesto described Compton as "a shining star in the region" (UWP 1992, 3). Major sections of the manifesto were devoted to quotations from the World Bank expressing satisfaction with Compton's management. The section of the manifesto on the economy, for ex-

ample, opened with a World Bank declaration that "St. Lucia is an example of
a well-managed economy which has been relatively successful in implementing
an outward-looking growth strategy" (ibid., 6). Similarly, an entire section of
the following page was taken up with World Bank reviews on St. Lucia's fiscal
performance (ibid., 7). On the basis of these positive endorsements from the
World Bank, the manifesto's central argument was that it was necessary that the
country "continues to enjoy the international respect which it currently does, so
that it can preserve its record of success in attracting the international financial
assistance and investment which is currently required to fuel the process of economic and social development" (ibid., 2).

It can be safely argued that the UWP's strong economic performance in the
1980s was a critical factor in shaping the party's victory in the 1992 election. A
closely related factor was the emphasis that had been placed on the threats to
the economic survival of St. Lucia in the early 1990s. On this basis the UWP
recouped its losses from the 1987 election and won eleven seats to the SLP's
six. The population's endorsement of Compton's neoliberal economic strategy
was largely due to the fact that the external economic environment served to
complement his internal economic approach. In this context, opposition concerns about the overreliance on bananas and tourism, and the concerns about
the economic dependency of the state, failed to resonate with voters. According
to a local trade unionist, the UWP victory represented a "fear of the unknown"
(George Goddard in *Caribbean Insight*, May 1992, 1). At the same time, the SLP
had also suffered from a loss of public confidence in Hunte due to two highly
publicized incidents of violence in the period leading up to the general election.
Political doubts over Hunte's suitability were to remain a fixture of the politics
of St. Lucia into the 1990s, during which time he was to face a number of challenges to his leadership. Indeed, prior to the 1992 election the leader of the PLP,
George Odlum, had publicly expressed greater confidence in the leadership of
Compton over that of Hunte. Odlum's appeal to PLP supporters to vote for the
UWP, though motivated by political opportunism, was widely viewed as contributing to the UWP victory (see *Caribbean Insight*, May 1992, 2) and ensured
its continuation in office into the mid-1990s.

The politics of St. Lucia in the 1980s therefore reflected tensions between
the pursuit of neoliberalism, dictated by globalization, and the fulfillment of
domestic aspirations that had found their expression in the nationalist movement. The St. Lucia government was obligated to adjust existing state-society
relations to achieve a situation that freed the state from its historical obligations
to its citizenry. The continued failure of its efforts was perhaps the clearest short-
coming of the UWP in the period. The expectations of the population reflected
a continued identification with the aspirations of egalitarianism, economic en-

franchisement, and, most pointedly, the advancement and protection of labor that had emerged in the nationalist period. However, the neoliberal model resuscitated the economic relations of the colonial condition as an appropriate model of development. The pursuit of foreign private capital, the exploitation of cheap domestic labor, and the creation of the conditions conducive to private capital accumulation were policies that had characterized the policies of the colonial state.

There was, however, one feature of the St. Lucian state that marked a sharp break with the assumptions of colonialism. This was the emphasis on infrastructural and industrial development. Indeed, one of the motives for independence was that the colonial condition had militated against the full industrial and economic development of St. Lucia. Not surprisingly, it was the establishment of physical infrastructure such as roads, airports, seaports, and industrial zones, and the development of utilities such as water, electricity, and telecommunications services that Compton recognized as his main contribution to anticolonialism (Compton, Budget Address 1984). Also, a common defense by Compton of his neoliberal model was that it had kept St. Lucia out of the clutches of the IMF. Thus Compton (Budget Address 1989, 2) was able to boast, though with much exaggeration, that

> the government of St. Lucia decided . . . , whatever the financial disciplines were necessary [*sic*], these must be self-imposed and there was no place for the International Monetary Fund. There could not be "two male crabs in the same hole." The wisdom of this decision is now evident to all. We have been able to carry out our own restructuring without tears; without massive lay-offs or any lay-offs for that matter; without increases in the prices of basic commodities; without resultant riots in the streets; without cuts in our social services. Not only did we not reduce wages and salaries, but we have in fact increased them, however modestly, but increased them above the rate of inflation, so that in fact everyone is better off.

Given the universalization of neoliberal ideology, Compton's electoral successes reflected the population's acceptance of the importance of "living within its means" as a necessary adjunct to "economic development." It also reflected the illegitimacy of the international financial institutions of global neoliberalism in the eyes of the populace. Thus, while neoliberalism presented a number of challenges to the assumptions of anticolonial national development, the strong performance of the St. Lucian economy was a key factor in sustaining Compton's electoral dominance.

While the external economic environment of the 1980s had largely complemented Compton's economic approach, the process of global neoliberal reform
from 1992 onward proved less compatible to his internal economic strategy.
Central to Compton's economic success in the 1980s had been the special arrangements that had protected Windward Islands' bananas on the European
market. Much of Compton's domination of the political life of St. Lucia had in
fact been sustained by this economic reality. With the changes associated with
the intensifying globalization process in the post-1992 period, a fundamental
internal challenge to Compton's neoliberalism was to emerge. Global changes
had a profound effect on the internal politics of St. Lucia, producing an open
revolt of the banana producers against the Compton regime in October 1992
and culminating in the defeat of the UWP by the SLP in 1997.

CHAPTER 5

Deepening Globalization and the Unmaking of the Postcolonial Order, 1990-1997

Global Change, Adjustment, and the Political Economy of Bananas

A series of global shifts in the 1990s signaled the "emergence of a new world order characterized by the globalization of production and consumption, [and] the liberalization and regionalization of the rule of economic law" (Nurse 1995, 2–3). These changes held far-reaching implications for the St. Lucia banana industry, leading to a process of adjustment that made the question of globalization, in a very direct sense, a "localized" issue for St. Lucians (Slocum 1996). The adjustments included privatization of the St. Lucia Banana Growers Association, the purchase by the Windward Islands governments of Geest Industries' banana interests in the United Kingdom, and the increased fragmentation of the banana industry structure through privatization, which replaced co-operative production with private competition. The common feature of these developments was the reduction in the level of control of small producers over the industry as a result of the growing influence of "commercial considerations" in running the industry.

Developments from 1992 onward saw the steady erosion of the guarantees given to Caribbean fruit under the first Lomé Convention of 1975. A special protocol under this treaty had guaranteed that "in respect of its banana exports to the Community markets, no African, Caribbean, and Pacific [ACP] state shall be placed, as regards access to its traditional markets and its advantages on these markets in a less favourable position than in the past or present" (CBEA 1994, 1). This guarantee was a consistent feature of the first three Lomé conventions, while in the fourth it was qualified by the assertion of the right of the European Community (EC) to establish a common regime for bananas. This assertion clearly indicates the manner in which the external economy had provided a context in which the internal economic project of the independent state could be sustained. Indeed, Lomé had shaped much of the economic fabric of the St. Lucia banana industry and, by extension, much of its wider political economy.

The first blow to the St. Lucia banana industry was struck by the introduction of a new European Union (EU) banana import regime (NBR) in 1993 as a consequence of the formation of the Single European Market (SEM). The main implication of the NBR was the increased access to the U.K. market for lower-cost "dollar bananas" from Latin America (GOSL Strategy Paper 1999, 7). Indeed, well before the SEM had come into effect, Latin American producers had begun to increase banana exports to Europe to corner the opening European market. Between 1988 and 1992 banana shipments to Europe from the "big three" Latin American multinational banana producers—Chiquita, Del Monte, and Dole—increased by 46 percent (Grossman 1998, 53).

The NBR, however, contained a number of features beneficial to Caribbean producers. First, it continued to offer a measure of protection for Caribbean bananas through the application of tariff quotas to non-EU/ACP banana suppliers (Nurse 1995, 2).[1] Relatedly, ACP producers were allowed duty-free quotas, which in the case of St. Lucia amounted to 127,000 tonnes (GOSL Strategy Paper 1999, 7). Another beneficial feature of the NBR was the allocation of 30 percent of dollar licenses to importers of ACP and EU fruit. This allowed the Windward Islands to register as official importers of their bananas and to exploit a useful source of revenue. It also gave the Windward Islands increased leverage in relation to Geest Industries since "that Company now depended on shipping Windwards fruit to gain access to profitable dollar licenses" (Grossman 1998, 55).

However, the continued process of globalization of world trade brought these special arrangements under attack. One of the earliest challenges to the NBR of 1993 came from within the EU itself from states such as Germany, which had little historical attachment to ACP states. This reality led to the fear that the fate of the Caribbean region would be decided by "those EC member governments with more interest in resolving global trade issues than in the special relationships enshrined in the Lomé Convention" (*Caribbean Insight*, November 1992, 4). Compton (Budget Address 1993, 3) echoed this fear in the St. Lucia House of Assembly: "As far as St. Lucia is concerned, our trading relationships are no longer determined by our former ties with the United Kingdom which, for historical reasons, we could influence, but rather the faceless bureaucrats of Brussels who are known by such numbers as DGVI and DGVII."

Further challenges to the special arrangements for Caribbean bananas were made by the General Agreement on Tariffs and Trade (GATT). Given the general commitment of GATT to the liberalization of world trade, its first response was to impose a seven-year limit on the NBR (*Caribbean Insight*, March 1992, 1). More serious for the St. Lucia banana industry, however, was the challenge mounted within GATT by a number of Latin American states who saw the NBR as being against the principles of free trade.[2] These challenges were upheld in 1993 when a GATT panel ruled that the features of the NBR that "provide tariff and other preferences for ACP countries" were incompatible with GATT (see CBEA 1994, 2, 1997, para. 12). A major implication of the ruling was that in one stroke, it rendered illegal "a wide range of other preferences enshrined in the Lomé Convention" (CBEA 1994, 3, 1997, para. 12).

The formation of the World Trade Organization (WTO) in January 1995 intensified these challenges. Having replaced GATT as the global regulator of world trade, the WTO "significantly altered the rules of engagement, scope and legal enforceability of trade and trade-related agreements at the international level" (see Andrew 1999, 81). Among the major differences between GATT and the WTO was the fact that the latter created a "permanent legal framework" and "rules on procedure . . . and dispute settlement mechanisms." Similarly, the WTO was marked by the additional jurisdiction over services and intellectual property as distinct from the trade in goods (Andrew 1999, 82). Of greatest significance, however, was the WTO's transcendence of GATT's "á la carte" system, where contracting parties could choose whether they wanted to adhere to the various agreements (Petersman 1997, 54). In short, the WTO represented a formal institutionalization of the objectives and principles of global neoliberalism.

Within the auspices of the WTO, a further challenge to the EU banana import regime was mounted by the United States, Ecuador, Guatemala, Honduras, and Mexico in May 1996. The WTO upheld this challenge in mid-1997 (see WTO 1999, 82). To many Caribbean observers, the WTO ruling reflected the extent to which the new global trade order further facilitated the domination of powerful states and multinationals. This perception is clearly reflected in an account by the Caribbean Banana Exporters Association (CBEA) of the treatment of the Caribbean states during the dispute:

> Although the case was brought by the USA and its co-complainants against the EU, the Caribbean and other ACP banana exporting states had more at stake than any other party. . . . For this reason the Caribbean sought full rights of participation in the hearings. This was refused, primarily because the USA opposed it. In contrast to proceedings under the GATT, the Caribbean and other ACP states were limited to the restricted rights of attendance and inter-

vention of a third country with no direct interest. Worse still, at the insistence of the complainants, the Caribbean legal advisers were expelled from the hearings on the grounds that they were not permanent Government officials, even though they were fully accredited members of the delegation of St. Lucia....[3] It is also disturbing that the panel made a definite interpretation of the obligations of the EU and the ACP states under the Lomé Convention which was fundamentally in conflict with the understanding of the Agreement by the parties to it, namely the EU and ACP states, and without fully hearing the arguments of the ACP states thereon. (CBEA 1997, paras. 14–17)

Several aspects of the U.S. challenge to the EU banana-importing regime lend support to the notion that the structures of world trade redound largely to the benefit of large multinational corporations. An article entitled "How US Politics Smashed Caribbean Bananas" (*Outlet*, 25 February, 3, 10 March 2000) shows the close connection between political financial contributions by Chiquita—and the related interests of its director, Carl Linder—and the vigor with which the United States pursued its "banana war" against the EU and, in particular, its imposition of punitive sanctions against the EU. In a well-documented account of Linder's political lobbying activities, the authors highlight a number of features of the U.S. challenge to the EU banana regime, which they attribute to the political influence of Chiquita. They observe that punitive actions were taken against the EU in a context where Chiquita's share of the EU banana market was as high as 20 percent. In contrast, "the USTR has negotiated with Japan to allow American companies a 3% share of the Japanese market for rice" (*Outlet*, 3, 10 March 2000, 13; *Newsweek*, 28 April 1997, 18–21).

On this basis, heightened U.S. pressure against the EU banana regime in 1999 can be understood. Dissatisfied that a new WTO-compliant banana regime had not emerged by the promised January 1999 date, the United States threatened unilateral trade sanctions against specified EU products. In response to these threats, the EU's trade representative, Leon Brittan, requested arbitration "on the level of suspension of concessions requested by the United States" (WTO 1999, 82, 83; see also *Caribbean Insight*, January 1999, 1). The U.S. position was later strengthened by a 6 April 1999 WTO ruling that upheld U.S. claims for damages against the EU for losses incurred because of the existing banana regime (*Caribbean Insight*, April 1994, 4). The final blow to the EU banana regime occurred on 12 April 1999, when the WTO issued its ruling on the illegality of the regime (see *Caribbean Insight*, 16 April 1999, 1; *The Guardian*, 8 April 1999, 23; *Financial Times*, 8 April 1999, 1).

Outside the WTO structure, a further blow to the Caribbean banana industry can be identified in the discussions over post–Lomé IV arrangements between the EU and its ACP partners. Those discussions signaled an early warning of the new EU approach that was taking shape and which would later became formalized in the European Economic Partnership Agreement (EPA) signed in 2008 between the EU and the Caribbean Forum of African, Caribbean and Pacific States (CARIFORUM). Increasingly battered in the WTO and elsewhere over its preferential trading arrangements with the ACP, the EU's expressed vision for a post–Lomé IV trading relation reflected the neoliberal concerns with free trade and the full integration of the third world into the global economy. This was clearly revealed in a 1996 EU "Green Paper" on the future of Lomé, which called for "an overhaul of trading arrangements in view of recent global changes." It emphasized notions of "differentiation, privatization, competitiveness, good governance, civil society and effectiveness" (*Caribbean Insight*, January 1997, 2). The post-Lomé scenarios proposed by the Green Paper also placed key emphasis on "helping ACP states to become more competitive" and to "go global." One such scenario called for the inclusion of "new areas of trade liberalization such as standards certification and intellectual property rights, as encouraged by the WTO" (ibid.). These new realities were emphasized by the British International Development secretary, Clare Short, before a House of Commons International Development Committee on the renegotiation of the fourth Lomé Convention. There, Short reiterated the notion that the "status quo is not an option" since "trade preferences are becoming less and less valuable because the barriers are eroding." Partly as a result of this conviction, Short expressed the view that "the ACP countries have not done particularly well under the Lomé regime." She was concerned that the thinking of the EC had been dominated by the embrace of "reciprocal free trade agreements" (House of Commons International Development Committee, 21 May 1998, 178–179).

This embrace of trade liberalization and global neoliberalism in EU-ACP relations between the mid-1990s and 2000 witnessed the fundamental overturning of the neatly packaged assumptions upon which John Compton had rationalized the notion of "limited sovereignty" as the most appropriate option for postcolonial St. Lucia. Central to this was the idea of continued "special protection" from Britain on the basis of historical colonial attachments. This assumption was to be swiftly eroded from January 1993, with the formation of the SEM and beyond, when new trade structures designed to facilitate the emergence of a liberalized global trading order were rapidly erected as part of the process of deepening globalization. These institutional structures eroded preexisting economic regulations that placed special consideration on the "development" of the formerly colonized world and marked a progressive attack on the St. Lucia banana industry. The St. Lucian state, along with Geest Industries, responded by restructuring the local banana industry, resulting in dramatic changes in the domestic political landscape.

Neoliberal Restructuring in the St. Lucia Banana Industry

In the early 1990s a number of significant transformations occurred in Geest's corporate structure. These transformations provide a useful starting point from which to explore the impact of global restructuring on the internal structure of the St. Lucia banana industry. The first significant shift was the company's transformation to a public liability company. This decision terminated the previous paternalistic relationship that had existed between the Geest family and the St. Lucia banana industry. Compton stressed the implications of these developments for the St. Lucia banana industry in a report to Parliament on 19 January 1993: "The Marketing company—Geest—is now a Public Liability Company, managed not by a family but by professionals, accountable to a vast number of shareholders concerned about the value of their shares quoted on the Stock Exchange and the dividends declared by a company in which they have invested these savings" (Compton, Budget Address 1993, 19). This concern was echoed by George Odlum, the former anti-Geest agitator, who argued that with these changes, "it is no longer the whims and fancies or the benevolence or otherwise of the Van Geest family which will determine the outcome of these contracts, but the profit-and-loss interest of the shareholders of the company" (Odlum n.d.b, 17).

Further, the company decided to terminate its involvement in Windward Islands bananas in 1995. Grossman (1998, 69–74) links this decision to the reduction in Geest's profits as a result of increased global competition. As seen earlier, the establishment of the NBR in 1993 had entitled the Windward Islands' governments to a percentage of dollar licenses, thus increasing the access of U.S. companies to the European market share. This had significantly empowered the Windward Islands' governments in relation to Geest, resulting in their success in winning in 1995 a contract that was far more equitable than earlier ones. This was a significant development given the fact that "the basis of Geest's profitability in the banana industry had always been the inequitable contracts that it had with the Windwards" (ibid., 75). Increased competition from Latin American bananas, lower Windward Islands production, and a reduction in prices as a result of the SEM overwhelmingly convinced Geest that a pullout was necessary.[4]

One response of the St. Lucian state to these developments was to secure, in conjunction with other Windward Islands governments, a greater role in the banana economy at the global level, beyond mere production. The earliest attempt by the Windward Islands governments to deepen their involvement in the banana industry occurred during the contract negotiations with Geest in the period following the SEM. A central objective was to gain greater returns from Geest's marketing operations in the United Kingdom (*Caribbean Insight*, February 1993, 2). This ambition was partly facilitated by the formation of the Windward Islands Banana Exporting Company (WIBDECO) in 1994. WIBDECO was intended to replace the noncommercial Windward Islands Banana Growers' Association (WINBAN) and to serve as a trading company for the banana industry (GOSL Strategy Paper 1999, 3). A further and more significant development in this process of domestic adjustment was the decision by WIBDECO to purchase Geest's banana interests. This was achieved in 1995, in association with a private multinational company, Fyffes, at a cost of £147.5 million. While this development was hailed as the fulfillment of "a long-held ambition within the Windward Islands to be involved in the shipping and distribution of our bananas" (*Caribbean Insight*, January 1996, 1), it also contained a number of negative features. First, the acquisition of Geest's banana interests occurred at a point of marked instability in the banana industry. Moreover, the price for these marketing and shipping operations was far higher than expected by market analysts (ibid.). These factors therefore militated against "empowerment" of the ordinary producer within the Windward Islands banana industry.

Another important response by the St. Lucian state was to readjust the role and place of the ordinary producer in the banana industry. These adjustment policies formed a key plank of the government's policies and dominated the politics of the St. Lucian state in the 1990s. Indeed, this policy of adjustment to heightened global liberalization was a logical continuation of the historical role played by the St. Lucian state under Compton, in which incorporation into the global economy (as distinct from national protection from it) had been the major objective.

Writing on the state's role in facilitating Geest Industries in the 1960s, Slocum (1996, 47–48) described the St. Lucian state as a "critical motivator" and "avid proponent" of "global integration," and this priority was markedly strengthened in the post-Geest period. Thus the increasing instability of the banana industry in the 1990s forced the Windward Islands governments to apply market and neoliberal perspectives to the running of the industry. Old structures, which had given a measure of economic protection and political empowerment to the ordinary producer, were eroded. While this process of commercialization was partly a consequence of the Windward Islands governments' increased financial stake within the banana industry, this empowering of the Windward states led to a corresponding disempowerment of individual producers at the domestic level.

In a sense, therefore, by embracing largely commercial values within the industry, the St. Lucian state was insulating itself from the political responsibility of the outcomes consequent upon deepening globalization.

As will be detailed more fully later, this process of adjustment was to reach its peak under the St. Lucia Labour Party (SLP), which was reelected in 1997 and which developed new commercialized structures within the banana industry consistent with an ethos of competitive capitalism. The first stage in this process occurred with the privatization of the St. Lucia Banana Growers' Association (SLBGA), which was first dissolved by an act of Parliament in 1998 and then re-formed as the St. Lucia Banana Corporation (SLBC), a privately owned concern comprising 3,000 growers each owning one share. Any other company wanting to purchase bananas to be exported to WIBDECO was legally entitled to do so. This led to the emergence of additional companies all competing for the loyalty of the local producers as the preferred sellers of produce to WIBDECO.

Privatization led to a period of continued instability in the St. Lucian banana industry. The various companies that sprang up following the formation of the SLBC all emerged to counter the political domination of key personalities within the industry. The main bête noire was Patrick Joseph, a former leader of the militant Banana Salvation Committee,[5] who emerged as the director of the SLBC with the dissolution of the SLBGA. Technically unqualified, his prominence in the St. Lucia banana industry was a direct consequence of his political activity. He consistently engaged in conflict with the government of St. Lucia and with WIBDECO, which he viewed as an expendable and expensive middleman between the St. Lucian banana producers and the U.K. market. In response to his control of the SLBC, Tropical Quality Fruit Company emerged as the second banana-purchasing company in St. Lucia. A third company, the Agricultural Commodities Trading Company (ACTCO), began operations in January 2000, evidencing a further series of political squabbles within the industry. Indeed, the raison d'être for the emergence of new banana companies in St. Lucia was far more political than economic, thus undermining one of the key neoliberal objectives of the privatization process.

The commercialization of the banana industry also reflected the ideological collapse of the historical association that had existed between the socioeconomic empowerment of the rural small landholders and the independence process itself. State subsidization of the SLBGA and the consistent pattern of political interventionism in the running of the industry had historically indicated the importance placed upon the empowerment of the small banana producer (see Banana Review Committee Report 1993, 11–13), particularly as an ideological safety valve indicating the advancement of the peasantry (the historical victims of colonialism) and as a basis of political support for Compton's United

Workers' Party (UWP). In contrast, the new emphasis on the application of strict commercial considerations to the relations between the government and the banana producers indicated the termination of an important feature of the independence state-society "social contract."

Quite significantly, this new emphasis on commercial criteria was advanced by international organizations such as the EC, the British Development Division, and the United Nations Development Programme, all of which were closely involved in devising strategies for the survival of the St. Lucia banana industry, and ironically was to reach its height under the newly elected SLP, which was returned to office in May 1997. The influence of these institutions in insisting on a process of depoliticization in the banana industry was clearly borne out in a St. Lucia government strategy paper for the recovery of the banana industry. According to the paper, these donor agencies agreed to "a plan for a core banana industry capable of competing in liberalized markets by the year 2002" in which "investments by the industry would be based on commercial, rather than by political, criteria." This was intended to allow "prices to growers to reflect quality differences, so as to encourage the emergence of a core group of efficient banana growers" (GOSL Strategy Paper 1999, 5). Central to this strategy was a diminished emphasis on ensuring the economic survival of the weaker producers.

The influence of global neoliberalism was reflected in several aspects of state policy in the banana industry. The emphasis on "commercial criteria," for example, was reflected through a device known as the Certified Farmers Programme. Under this program, only farmers who met the required quality standards could be registered as official exporters of bananas. Modeste Downes, a former board member of the SLBGA, was quite clear on the political and economic implications of this development:

> This initiative will have two major effects: (1) marginalization of the small grower, to the point of exclusion . . . and (2) the division of growers into elites and "lumper proletariats" [*sic*]. The elites even now are easily identifiable, and it will be a sad tale when some of these persons, Johnnies-come-lately, overtake the small grower who desperately needs to remain in business and cancel him out instead. . . . Finally, the present scenario actually sounds the death knell of the banana industry. We all would have wished otherwise, but when the market is in charge, I guess that's what it has come to. (*St. Lucia Mirror*, 12 September 1997, 2)

The influence of global neoliberalism in shaping the restructuring of the banana industry can also be identified in the pervasive language of neoliberalism among St. Lucian agricultural officials. The government strategy paper for economic recovery presented a number of neoliberal justifications for the commercialization of the industry. Included among these was the argument that commercialization would ensure "(1) . . . [an] effective system of corporate administration in the industry, (2) the banana companies operate in as cost-efficient a manner as possible, [3] there is a more accountable system of ownership and control with sanctions for nonperformance and rewards for performance." The report noted that "the privatization of the banana industry has also removed what has traditionally been identified as an unnecessary obstacle to efficiency—Government and political interference" (GOSL Strategy Paper 1999, 12).

The protection of the more vulnerable banana producers was also abandoned in the more technical aspects of the running of the industry (see Banana Review Committee Report 1993, 20), which placed greater emphasis on insulating the government from the economic losses of the industry. The St. Lucia government's decision to write off the entire debt of the SLBGA as a fresh start for privatization, for example, prompted concern on the part of local and regional neoliberal economists that the government had not undertaken greater efforts to insulate itself from future economic shocks.[6] These economists called for "conditionalities, based on compliance with selected financial and management performance criteria, to be attached to the write-off of the BGA debts" (see Williams and Darius 1998, 106). Neoliberal technocrats were unequivocal in their support for the elimination of the smaller and weaker producers from the industry. A report by Cargill Technical Services, a U.K. consultancy agency, for example, noted that "some 2,200 farmers are forecast to leave the banana export [*sic*] because of their lack of ability to meet quality requirements, their indebtedness or their lack of land and labour resources." Far from viewing this as a negative, the study called for new structures to "attract the better banana farmers and to dissuade the weaker producers." Among the structures proposed was a new pricing regime "based upon a revised revenue system that apportions costs and returns in a way that cuts down the existing high level of cross-subsidization from the more efficient farmer to the less efficient" (Cargill Report 1998, 62). Given that 14 percent of farmers were responsible for 45 percent of banana production (ibid., 19), this meant large-scale retrenchment.

Aspects of the government's pursuit of neoliberal adjustment suggested an "absence of choice" or even "powerlessness" in the face of global change. The government was aware that significant economic dislocation would occur in the banana-producing regions as a consequence of its commitment to neoliberal restructuring, but rationalized it on the basis of necessity. In a public address on the implications of the WTO ruling against the NBR, the prime minister of St. Lucia, Kenny Anthony, spoke of the pain of adjustment:

I can tell you that I am in the most unenviable position of forcing on our farmers very unpopular and painful measures aimed at getting them to adapt to the changing market environment. Our banana farmers are hurting, and quite understandably, . . . fear that the bitter medicine being administered to them, rather than helping, will end up destroying their livelihood. Be that as it may, we are determined to push ahead with those measures because we know that the preferential system will not remain in place forever. (Anthony n.d., 4)

In October 1999 Anthony presented a similar justification for his hands-off approach when a political dispute over the selection of a new board of managers of the newly privatized SLBC threatened to destabilize the banana industry:

We are aware that many persons expect Government to intervene to bring a hasty conclusion to the current situation. However, the expectation is conditioned by past experience that we do not wish to repeat. This is not the time for heavy-handed Government intervention. Nor will this Government, this Prime Minister, knowingly favour one candidate against the other. . . . We . . . believe that the current SLBC situation is an inevitable part of a natural transition within any recently restructured industry. While the situation is far from perfect, we can only imagine the magnified impact it would have on output if there were only one banana exporting company. As the competition between banana companies is healthy, so too is competition for more effective leadership within the SLBC. . . . Government's primary interest remains therefore an economic one. (Anthony 1999b, 1–2)

This general embrace of the tenets of neoliberalism in the face of obvious social dislocation suggests the further weakened and subservient nature of the state to global capital under heightened liberalization and globalization. Much of this incapacity was couched in a language that suggested a positive embrace of the necessity of adjustments. Yet it was widely recognized that the process of adjustment exacerbated the vulnerability of the weaker sections of the society that had previously been sheltered by the state. The magnitude of social dislocation occurring in the banana-producing regions was a central feature of the Cargill report:

For those banana-dependent families working in the most marginal areas or with the least labour resources, this study has confirmed . . . the profound social problems that are occurring. Farmers that have had respectable earnings for years are now the butt of other people's jokes. The loss of dignity and solvency manifests itself in such conditions as alcoholism, involvement with drugs, partner and child abuse, impotence, and occasional suicide. . . .

Responsibility for the welfare burden is now shifting, yet there is no well-defined agency or government program charged with meeting this burden either in terms of providing new areas of employment or meeting the emerging social needs. (Cargill Report 1998, 2)

In recognition of this high level of social dislocation, a significant feature of the government's strategy of adjustment involved the creation of social structures to absorb the economic "shock" of restructuring in the banana industry (GOSL Strategy Paper 1999).[7] The main issues emphasized were those of adult education and literacy, drug control, and support for rural women (Cargill Report 1998, 76–80). Another important response by the government was the establishment of special poverty reduction projects (see GOSL Strategy Paper 1999).[8]

This reality, however, far from challenging the dominant neoliberal discourse, can be seen as complementing its objectives. C. Y. Thomas has demonstrated persuasively the manner in which the emphasis on such "social recovery" projects fits into the neoliberal paradigm. Writing in the context of the wider Anglophone Caribbean, Thomas lamented that "earlier regional emphasis on development of the social sector" had been replaced by the introduction of "new modalities of social intervention," such as poverty programs and special social funds. According to Thomas, the "net effect of these has been to put social development somewhat on the back-burner, and to undermine the traditional roles of line ministries in the region" (Thomas 1996, 50). By relegating the issue of poverty reduction and the social advancement of the majority to the status of a "special project," the reality of the "incapacity" of the state in the face of global neoliberalism was reinforced rather than challenged.[9]

In sum, a process of economic adjustment at the global level resulted in a consequent embrace of neoliberalism within the St. Lucia banana industry. The most significant feature of these domestic adjustments was the reversal of the earlier emphasis on the economic and political empowerment of small banana producers. Given the close link between bananas and politics in St. Lucia, the process of adjustment had a profound impact on political developments in the country. One significant feature of the process of adjustment was its role in the fall of Compton's UWP between 1992 and 1997.

Adjustment, Political Instability, and Political Change

By 1992 the full impact of global restructuring was clearly reflected in the withdrawal of large numbers of farmers from banana production. The degree of social dislocation in the rural sector was captured by the Cargill report (1998, 17):

The . . . period has seen an overall deterioration in international market prices for bananas, while consumers, and correspondingly marketing agents, have tended to become more quality conscious. . . . A significant proportion of growers in St. Lucia have struggled to achieve the quality criteria demanded by overseas buyers, and have subsequently withdrawn from the industry. Some of the highest cost producers have also ceased production in response to falling prices and increasing input costs, and the consequent erosion of margins. It has been estimated that over the period 1992–97, 49% of St. Lucian banana farmers ceased production. In this sense the social fallout from the banana downturn has already happened on the island.

There were also significant shortfalls in banana revenue (see Table 5.1). Compton highlighted the impact of this development on the wider economy in the 1994 budget:

In 1993 . . . St. Lucia's banana exports fell by some 13,000 tons or 6,000 below quota, with a loss of income of $48 million. In 1992, St. Lucia exported 133,000 tons valued at $136.97 million. This decline, compounded by the depreciation of the value of the pound sterling, has been reflected in the shops, in the Banks and in Government revenues—this loss is felt all around. This loss must be recovered by greater productivity which is within our ability, because if this trend continue [*sic*] we will suffer a reduction in our quota which we will never recover. (Compton, Budget Address 1994, 7)

Economic decline was particularly acute in the post-1997 period. This followed the WTO ruling, and is clearly observable in Table 5.1, which shows a sharp drop in production and revenue between 1996 and 1997. The process of restructuring world trade had a clear impact on the broad economic progress of St. Lucia. This heightened economic instability undermined the relationship between the government and small producers that had sustained UWP political dominance, resulting in the defeat of the UWP after nearly three decades of political rule.

A series of political upheavals within the St. Lucia banana industry took place from 1992 onward, which coincided with the shifts in the global banana market. At the center of these upheavals was the attempt by the small banana producers to defend their right to participate in the decision-making structures of the industry. The political struggles of the small producers in the early 1990s constituted, arguably, an implicit "antineoliberal" project. These episodes revealed the "beleaguered" nature of the state in attempting to simultaneously facilitate the global neoliberal project and to safeguard domestic economic interests.

Table 5.1. Banana production, export, and revenue, 1990–1997				
Period	Banana Production (tons)	Banana Export (tons)	Banana Revenue (EC $ million)	Active Growers
1990	135,000	133,777	186.9	
1991	100,000	100,595	146.4	
1992	135,291	132,854	184.8	
1993	122,927	120,129	137.9	7,047
1994	90,909	90,119	115.7	6,252
1995	105,658	103,668	128.1	5,841
1996	105,547	104,805	128.5	5,698
1997	71,395	71,395	74.6	5,270
Source: Cargill Report 1999, 18.				

We have already seen in the preceding chapter that a conflict between the government and the banana producers had emerged in the late 1980s over the dissolution of the democratically elected SLBGA board and its replacement with government appointees. One internal consequence of this early government-SLBGA confrontation was the birth of the militant Banana Salvation Committee (BSC). Significantly, the role of the BSC extended beyond the issue of bananas to the wider internal politics of St. Lucia. The BSC was instrumental in the organization of "no-cut strikes" and in the mobilization of large groups of midsize and small producers against the government, Geest Industries, the global multilaterals, and the U.S.-owned multinational fruit companies. The agitation by the BSC was also a key factor in the erosion of the UWP–small producer alliance.

The most dramatic episode of BSC militancy occurred in October 1993 during three days of violent protest. Demonstrations and "no-cut strikes" were mounted in response to reductions in the purchase price of bananas, amid claims of corruption within the government-appointed SLBGA board. During these protests, a number of demonstrators were injured, and two farm laborers were shot and killed by the police. The strike was estimated to have cost the state about EC$2 million. Of this, EC$500,000 was owed to Geest Industries, whose "ships had left St. Lucia virtually empty during the strike" (*Caribbean Insight*, November 1993, 10). The strike was marked by the erection of roadblocks and the burning of banana sheds, and was intended to frustrate the economic activities of those banana producers who were not in sympathy with the "no-cut strike." The roadblocks seriously disrupted governmental and commercial activity, with a number of tourists having to be shuttled by air to the island's international airport, and with a number of school closures. On the second day of the strike Compton, himself a banana farmer, attempting to break the strike, narrowly escaped injury at the hands of striking farmers (*Caribbean Insight*, November 1999, 10; see also Slocum 1996, 135).

The 1993 farmers' strike marked a turning point in the internal political relations of St. Lucia. The conditions under which the strike was terminated validated the actions of the farmers and delegitimized the UWP. Not only did a government-appointed review committee recommend a price increase for banana producers (see *Caribbean Insight*, November 1999, 10; Banana Review Committee Report 1993, 104–105), but Compton dismissed the entire SLBGA board. He argued that the association was "completely bankrupt" with debts of EC$23 million compared with a surplus of EC$16 million in 1990 (*Caribbean Insight*, November 1993, 10). In light of this, it became increasingly difficult for the government to sustain its official stance of nonrecognition of the BSC. As an increasingly powerful, popular, and militantly antigovernmental group, the growing inability to delegitimize the BSC meant the existence of an alternative pole within the farming community to that of the UWP. The strikes in effect marked the end of the alliance between banana producers and politicians that had sustained the political hegemony of the UWP.

In addition, the period following the 1993 strike coincided with a series of antidemocratic responses on the part of the government, which led to a further erosion of its popular support within the wider community. Immediately following the strike, the government fired the general manager of the state-owned Radio St. Lucia, Alva Clarke, on the grounds that the station had opened its airwaves to "criminal elements" during the banana strike. This was a reference to the antigovernment tone of callers to the station's popular call-in programs during the strike.[10] The government was also unhappy with the nature of the reporting during the strike. The dismissal of the station's general manager was followed by a one-week strike by employees of Radio St. Lucia, who also complained of veiled threats from the chairman of the board of Radio St. Lucia (*Caribbean Insight*, December 1993).[11] A far more significant reflection of the antidemocratic tendencies following the 1993 riots was the passage on 14 March 1995 of the Criminal Code Amendment Act (see Francois 1996, 103–110). The main aim of the amendment had been to render illegal the "no-cut strike" tactic of the BSC, whose protest activities had remained a weekly fixture of St. Lucian political life.[12] Thus the "objects and reasons" clauses of the bill declared the intention to "create new offences and penalties with respect to the damaging or burning of banana trees, including the fruit thereof, and any building associated with the banana industry" (ibid.).

However, the language of the bill proved repugnant to a wide cross-section of the population, particularly since it hinted at the illegality of normal trade union activity. In the parliamentary debate on the bill, it was stated that the amendment was intended to "create new offences and penalties with respect to threats by words or gestures or by way of letters, etc., which cause a person to desist from performing or to discontinue any lawful activity on his property or on the property of another person" (Francois 1996, 104). Thus the Criminal Code Amendment led to a growing rift between the government and the "social partners" whose support had been crucial to the success of the neoliberal project in the 1980s. One of the first acts of the island's unions, acting under the auspices of the Industrial Solidarity Pact (ISP), was to withdraw their participation from the government's National Economic and Social Consultative Council (NESCC) (*Caribbean Insight*, April 1995, 10). Given the fact that the NESCC had been one of the main instruments through which national consensus around neoliberalism was proposed, the collapse of union support represented both a crisis for the UWP and, more important, a threat to the success of the neoliberal project.[13]

These developments indicate the extent to which external economic transformations were resulting in the erosion of the internal political relations upon which the "stability" of the postcolonial order had been based. Given the fact that the response of the BSC was rooted largely in its attempt to preserve the internal economic and political relations of the last three decades, the government's dilemma in facilitating a process of transition can be clearly understood. The situation was rendered more complex by the fact that the old status quo that the BSC was seeking to preserve had been sustained by a particular set of external economic relations that were being eroded and that were imposing the imperative of adjustment upon the state. This dilemma touches upon the reality of perpetual crisis of the postcolonial state under neoliberalism, given the need for constant adjustment as greater and greater levels of neoliberal facilitation are demanded. It is in this context that further challenges to the UWP, and its eventual collapse in May 1997, can be understood.

Several features of the circumstances leading up to the collapse of the UWP in the general election of May 1997 support the claim that this political development was rooted principally in the post-1992 transformations in the global political economy. In the first place, the global shifts of the 1990s worked against the economic and political approach that had defined the development thrust of the UWP. The UWP's project of national self-determination had been consciously formulated to accommodate itself to existing global realities. It had placed deliberate emphasis on the "economic" development of the state as a vehicle through which the circumstances of the previously marginalized domestic population could be transformed. Relatedly, this project had rejected the need for direct political intervention to resolve the colonial legacies of race and class inequalities. An important corollary to the legitimacy of the UWP, therefore, was the existence of a global economic environment that could sustain the specific approach preferred by Compton and the UWP.

However, the global shifts of the early to mid-1990s had rendered elements of that strategy untenable. Midgett (1998, 17) identifies the collapse of the global framework that had sustained the conservative project in the Anglophone Caribbean as a key explanation for the collapse of the UWP. He surmises that "it may be that regimes with this kind of orientation are ill-suited to small, independent societies where attention to social provision needs to be a feature of successful governance" (ibid.).[14] Intensified globalization of the 1990s therefore fundamentally challenged the ideological basis upon which the conservative philosophy of national sovereignty had been constructed.

The erosion of support for the UWP was clearly discernible among banana producers, who viewed the government's project of neoliberal adjustment as an attempt to create a situation in which "the grower will have no say in the SLBGA any more [*sic*]" (Patrick Joseph to Minister of Agriculture, 2 February 1994). A central demand of small producers throughout the 1990s was the need to retain an element of economic democracy within the banana industry. In a letter to the minister of agriculture dated 3 May 1994, the BSC demanded not only "an immediate conference of delegates to choose representatives of their choice" but also that the farmers' representatives "be included in the Geest contract negotiation." In order to facilitate this, the BSC demanded that "all information relating to the contract at this stage be made available to their representatives" (Patrick Joseph to Ira d'Auvernge, 3 May 1994). It was the government's inability to sustain the politics of inclusion within the industry, and its embrace of a less democratic approach, that led to the erosion of its most significant and reliable political base.

The government's response to the BSC led to the alienation of other significant sectors of civil society. The state-supported killing of rioting protestors was unprecedented in the postcolonial political annals of St. Lucia, and the deaths of the two farmers led to a further erosion of the government's popularity. The ill-fated attempt to amend the Criminal Code and the closure of Radio St. Lucia and an independent radio station, Radyo Koulibri, whose call-in programs provided an avenue for popular criticism of the government, served to further alienate the domestic population. This gradual embrace of antidemocratic tendencies was both a symptom and a cause of the crisis of the UWP under global neoliberalism.

The economic downturn encountered as a result of the crisis in the banana industry also contributed to the fall of the UWP. The clearest indication of a wider challenge to the UWP occurred with a public service demand for pay increases in mid-1995. This dispute between the government and the public service was particularly severe, lasting intermittently for up to about six weeks. The basis for the dispute was the claim for 30 percent increases by teachers and civil servants, which contrasted sharply with the 6 percent increase offered by the government for 1992 to 1995. One feature of the strike was the support given to it by the territory's customs personnel. Significant losses resulted in the business sector, which responded by laying off workers. The tourism sector also suffered significant losses as a result of the strike (see *Caribbean Insight*, July 1995, 2–3). Ordinary consumers were inconvenienced by shortages in essentials such as cooking gas, sugar, and rice.

Compton's response to the strike was a near exact repetition of his response to the events preceding the fall of his government in 1979. In a public broadcast, Compton described the strike as an "illegal action designed to hurt the country." He viewed strikers as pursuing the "clearly political" agenda of bringing the government down (*Caribbean Insight*, July 1995, 3). In terms that reaffirmed his 1979 stance, Compton claimed that "the position is not whether government is willing to pay, it is one that the country just cannot pay." He insisted that "agitation cannot change arithmetic" (Compton, Budget Address 1995, 7). In a move that further stiffened the resolve of strikers, Compton threatened to withhold payment from strikers for the days they spent away from work (*Caribbean Insight*, July 1995, 2–3).

Midgett (1998) has sought to contrast the political implications of the collapse of the UWP in 1997 with those that followed the election of 1979. While many parallels can be identified, the 1990s episode was of far greater significance insofar as the capacity of the state to engage in domestic policies that go against the interests of global capital is concerned. While the episode of the 1970s had been the result of the post–Bretton Woods financial dislocations, the 1990s economic upheavals marked the collapse of the political and economic relations upon which the postcolonial order had been constituted and the imposition of further demands for neoliberal adjustment. The 1990s economic crisis can be equated with the shift from sugar to bananas of the mid-1950s and can be viewed as marking the transition from one set of political-economic relations to another. Further, while the politics of the 1970s had witnessed a conflict between competing development strategies, the neoliberal global framework of the 1990s offered little space for the pursuit of alternative policies to those that had led to the crisis. The public servants' strike of the 1990s consequently represented a far deeper crisis for the state than that of the 1970s period. The political developments leading up to the defeat of the UWP, and the nature of that defeat itself, were results of that reality.

Two significant internal political developments indicate the manner in which the process of global change had weakened the political self-assurance of the

UWP. The first was a period of internal political crises within the UWP as a result of leadership changes and accusations of corruption against the government. The second was a related process of internal reorganization within the leadership of the SLP, resulting in the emergence of the previously marginalized Left-intelligentsia into the leadership positions within the party. Both of these developments can be partially attributed to the process of global adjustment of the 1990s.

Compton chose to retire as head of the government and head of the UWP in 1996. While his retirement was presented in terms of his age and the longevity with which he had served as head of the government,[15] the erosion of the political framework that had sustained his leadership was an important factor influencing his decision. Indeed, the fact that Compton's narrow escape at the hands of banana farmers had occurred in the Micoud-Dennery area, the region that had sustained his political career,[16] no doubt spurred him in the direction of retirement. On a more symbolic level, there were close parallels between Compton's own actions in the 1950s on behalf of the sugar workers and the action by the BSC against his regime. The symbolism of these developments in resulting in the final denouement of Compton has been captured in a rather exaggerated account by Francois (1996, 100): "By the time he went on national television on October 11th 1993, to denounce 'ungrateful' sugar-cane turned banana farmers 'who once called me daddy and now calling me murderer and thief,' his audience knew that the final fall of Compton was inevitable. John Compton had come full circle."

In addition, the nature of the 1990s global political economy had definitely revealed to Compton the bankrupt nature of the state as a mediator between global economic interests and St. Lucia's domestic population. By 1994 Compton explicitly acknowledged this in a response to the BSC uprising of October 1993, linking the political instability in the country with the increasing helplessness of the state: "We refuse to adjust to the changing tides of international affairs, and when we run into rough weather, instead of taking stock of ourselves we turn on the captain with all the venom we can muster. . . . The prices fall in the United Kingdom so we burn banana plants in St. Lucia as if this can cause the prices to rise" (Compton, Budget Address 1994, 2).

Compton's retirement coincided with a period of organizational uncertainty that contributed in no small measure to the UWP's defeat in 1997. The handpicked successor to Compton was Vaughan Lewis, the former head of the Institute of Social and Economic Research of the University of the West Indies and the former director of the OECS.[17] Local opposition groups that sought to capitalize on Compton's withdrawal from the political scene renewed their hostility when Lewis became prime minister (see Midgett 1998). Compounding Lewis's difficulties was the fact that he had inherited the leadership in the context of a growing rejection of the UWP's style of politics. Not only did Lewis inherit the government in the midst of an economic crisis surrounding the banana industry, but his leadership occurred against the backdrop of charges of corruption in which the UWP was implicated. The main issue in this regard was popularly entitled the "U.N. Fund Scandal."

At the center of the scandal was a retired U.N. ambassador, Stephen Flemming, who had fraudulently drawn funds from various U.N. funding bodies to establish a ghost organization known as the East Caribbean Research Centre. When brought before a government-sponsored Commission of Enquiry, Flemming charged that he had drawn the funds with the full knowledge of key members of the UWP hierarchy, to fund the 1992 election campaign. While the inquiry absolved the UWP leadership of responsibility, there was cause for much unease over the level of accountability within the government. For example, the inquiry revealed that a UWP parliamentary representative and former junior minister, Rufus Bousquet, had been drawing a U.N. salary prior to his election for a job for which he lacked the qualifications claimed in his curriculum vitae. His appointment was reported to have been facilitated by a deceased former chairman of the UWP and close confidant of Compton, Henry Giraudy (see Phillips Commission Report 1995, 63–69).

These revelations emerged following long-standing opposition charges of corruption and conflicts of interest in key ministries in the St. Lucia government, to which the prime minister had failed to respond (see *Combat*, 19 February 1994, 2). Though a central conclusion of the U.N. funds inquiry was that "Dr. Flemming alone solicited, procured, and disbursed" the funds, its wider conclusions implied a culture of corruption within the UWP. One of the commission's recommendations was that the "government of St. Lucia should in general exercise greater vigilance in [the] future and greater and more effective supervision of its operations at home and abroad." The report also recommended that the government "should consider the introduction of a Code of Conduct or Ethics" to guide the operations of its public officers (Phillips Commission Report 1995, 93).

Complementing this period of crisis within the UWP was a related process of reorganization within the SLP, leading to a more election-ready organization by 1997. A number of key developments characterized this process. The first was the replacement of the SLP's leader, businessman Julian R. Hunte, with Kenny Anthony. While Hunte had managed to hold the SLP together following its 1982 debacle, he had failed, in three general elections, to win the government. Hunte's failure to win the government had served to alienate a number of leading figures of the SLP, such as Calixte George and Lawson Calderon, both of whom had broken away from the SLP in 1995 and formed part of the leadership of the Citizens' Democratic Party (CDP) (*Caribbean Insight*, September 1995, 10). Anthony's selection as leader of the SLP, therefore, created a context where these weaknesses were reversed. One of the leader's first acts was to welcome the estranged CDP faction back into the fold of the SLP. Similarly, he ended the political rift between the SLP and the Odlum faction by inviting George Odlum and Jon Odlum back into the party.

The context within which George Odlum was welcomed back to the SLP further indicates the complexity of the process of political change that was taking place in St. Lucia in this period. Odlum's reemergence on the St. Lucian political scene had been motivated by his strong showing in a 1996 by-election through which Lewis had entered Parliament.[18] Odlum's hastily formed National Front Coalition, although defeated by Lewis, had outperformed the SLP candidate. This spurred the SLP hierarchy to replace Hunte as leader of the party. Thus, before the 1997 election, the Old Left had returned to the SLP fold. Its leader, Kenny Anthony, as has been seen, had been a leading figure of the Workers' Revolutionary Movement (WRM) in the 1970s. George Odlum, the key figure of the 1970s New Left period, had returned. Calixte George and Hilford Deterville, both of the 1960s Forum and who had been involved in the CDP, had also reentered the SLP. A younger generation of radicals who had been closely aligned with the People's Revolutionary Government (PRG) regime in Grenada and other popular organizations such as the National Youth Council were also reintegrated into the SLP under Kenny Anthony.

It is within this context that the UWP was defeated by the SLP in May 1997. The systemic crisis within the banana industry, coupled with the unresolved pay dispute with the public service, provided an economic climate of uncertainty against which the UWP contested the election. Charges of corruption and the resignation of key stalwarts and parliamentarians, including Compton himself, as well as the inexperience of the new leader, Vaughan Lewis, further served to undermine the ruling party. Faced with a unified opposition and the entry into the campaign of young technocrats and educated activists who mounted a modern and professional campaign, the UWP suffered near total defeat, retaining only one seat out of a possible seventeen. Three decades of political domination had come to an end. Midgett (1998, 13–14) provides a clear indication of the scale of the UWP defeat:

> In 1979 the swing from UWP to labour was 10.1 per cent; in 1997 it was 19.1 per cent. In 1979 the SLP lost just 32 polling divisions out of 86; in 1997 they lost only 11 out of 89. And of course, the SLP won 16 seats in 1997, whereas in 1979 they had won 12. But the differences are more profound than just the magnitude of defeat. . . . In 1979, although they lost badly, the UWP actually

increased their vote by more than 15% from 1974. . . . By contrast, in 1979 the swing resulted in the UWP losing over 7,000 votes, a 21.6 per cent decline from 1992. The party increased their 1992 vote totals in just 11 polling districts and only a single constituency. . . . Their defeat was comprehensive and island wide. Finally, the erosion of UWP areas of strength—the "safe seats"—that began in the 1979 election is now complete. The party can no longer be assured of *any* victories in a subsequent election.

Deepening Globalization and Independent Statehood: An Assessment

The impact of deepening globalization upon the process of political change in St. Lucia can be seen most clearly in the fact that the rise and fall of the UWP coincided very closely with the rise and fall of the banana industry. The UWP's project of state construction was premised on the existence of the Lomé framework, which had provided an external prop to internal sovereignty. This confidence in the existence of a benign external environment led to the articulation of an internal economic and political project wholly accommodating to these external relations. This was the basis for the dependent posture adopted toward Geest Industries throughout the 1970s and 1980s. The political hegemony of the UWP within the farming community had also been constructed on a similar basis. Deepening globalization, however, undermined the internal political relations of St. Lucia and fundamentally altered the framework that had sustained Compton and UWP dominance.

The state's pursuit of neoliberal policies in the banana industry was largely motivated by external forces. These policies were pursued, moreover, against the wishes of the domestic population. The state's embrace of neoliberalism was seen as leading to the marginalization of a class whose socioeconomic advancement had been a central promise of the independence project. Hence the violent response of the banana producers to the reduction of their power within the SLBGA was an indication of the degree to which the farmers had sensed their movement from the center to the periphery of the St. Lucian postcolonial project. Similarly, the emergence of antidemocratic practices was also the result of the narrowing of political choices, which had resulted from global neoliberalism, forcing the state to adopt an instinctively hostile stance to those sectors of the population perceived as disruptive to the process of adjustment. This tendency to increasing authoritarianism and counterdemocratic stances has been identified by several commentators as one of the main contradictions of the impact of neoliberalism on the postcolonial world. As Robinson (2008, 232) has noted:

"As globalization proceeds, internal social cohesion declines along with national economic integration. The neoliberal state retains its essential powers to facilitate globalization, but it loses the ability to harmonize conflicting social interests within a country, to realize the historic function of sustaining the internal unity of a nationally conceived social formation and to achieve legitimacy." By the mid-1990s all of these tendencies had become clearly evident in St. Lucia.

At the same time, several features of the politics of St. Lucia in the 1990s suggested the inefficacy of the tactics of domestic social movements seeking to resist globalization. The activities of the BSC provide a case in point. Of critical significance was the fact that the resistance of the farmers' movement was leveled almost exclusively at local structures of power. Thus the economic arrangements that had threatened the socioeconomic power of the small producers were largely unaffected by the protest. Indeed, Slocum (1996, 136) argues that a major weakness of the BSC was that while it used "the national context as its framework . . . economic issues gradually diminished as a central focus of the movement's public discourse." In this regard, Compton's plea to the farmers that "our battle is not in our banana fields or on the roads of St. Lucia but in the external market" (ibid.) contained a heavy dose of truth. The futility of national politics within globalization was therefore demonstrated both by the actions of the state and by the attempts of antisystemic forces seeking to influence the state.

Finally, there are several aspects of the UWP's defeat in the 1997 general election that reflect the impact of the process of globalization within the Caribbean sociopolitical space. These are specifically heightened when the 1997 experience is compared to electoral patterns in the other Anglophone Caribbean territories. The defeat of conservative regimes, which had dominated Caribbean politics in the 1980s, can be largely attributed to the process of globalization. These regimes were, in many of the elections in the mid-1990s to the early twenty-first century, replaced by left-of-center governments, which had fallen victim to heightened U.S. involvement in the region in the wake of the Grenada invasion (see Barrow-Giles and Joseph 2006). Midgett (1998, 14–18) has pointed to the defeats of Eugenia Charles's Dominica Freedom Party in 1995; the Peoples' Action Movement/Nevis Reformation Party coalition in St. Kitts and Nevis in 1993 and 1995; the Jamaica Labour Party (JLP) of Seaga in Jamaica in 1989, 1993, and 1997; and the UWP in St. Lucia in 1997 as indicators of that trend. The January 2000 electoral success of the previously marginalized Dominica Labour Party under the leadership of Rosie Douglas, and Ralph Gonsalves's Unity Labour Party in St. Vincent and the Grenadines in 2001, provides further evidence of this tendency (Barrow-Giles and Joseph 2006). Significantly, Midgett (1991) identifies the failure of the conservative regimes to pursue a project of postcolonial reconstruction as a major factor accounting for their failures in that period.

Table 5.2. Electoral landslides in the 1990s Caribbean		
Territory	**Year**	**Distribution of Seats**
Barbados	1999	BLP - 26 / DLP - 2
Grenada	1999	NNP - 15 / Others - 0
Jamaica	1993	PNP - 52 / JLP - 8
	1997	PNP - 50 / JLP - 10
St. Kitts and Nevis	2000	SKNLP - 8* / CCM - 2 / NRF - 1
St. Lucia	1997	SLP - 16 / UWP - 1
Source: Political database of the Americas, www.Georgetown.edu/pdbawww.skbee.com/election2000/liveResults.asp. *Note:* BLP = Barbados Labour Party; DLP = Democratic Labour Party; NNP = New National Party; PNP = Peoples' National Party; JLP = Jamaica Labour Party; SKNLP = St. Kitts Nevis Labour Party; CCM = Concerned Citizens Movement; NRF = Nevis Reformation Party; SLP = St. Lucia Labour Party; UWP = United Workers' Party. *The extent of the "landslide" in St. Kitts and Nevis can be better appreciated when it is noted that the eight seats won by the SKNLP were all based in St. Kitts, the dominant partner in the federation.		

He cites the withdrawal of the United States from involvement in Caribbean politics at the end of the Cold War as a critical factor eroding the conditions that had previously facilitated the success of these conservative parties, such as Compton's UWP.

The impact of globalization was also seen in the destruction of stable two-party systems, which had characterized many of these states since independence. On one level, this process was reflected in the disruption of the pattern of two-term electoral swings, which had characterized the electoral relationship of the dominant political entities, typified most clearly in the Jamaican case. According to Meeks (1996, 127), with the exception of the first election under universal suffrage in 1944 when independents outperformed the Peoples' Nationalist Party (PNP), "each party succeeded the other in a two-term, roughly ten-year cycle, with the loser never getting less than 40 per cent of the national vote." This pattern was first broken in the 1997 election, which saw the third consecutive defeat of the JLP. The JLP, one of the leading conservative parties, consistently trailed the PNP in electoral polls in the late 1990s. A second and related feature of recent electoral trends in the Caribbean has been the huge margins of victories within which electoral mandates have been secured in elections in the 1990s (see Table 5.2).

A number of writers have viewed these developments as indicating the direct impact of external economic events on the internal electoral process in the Caribbean. One of the earliest of such studies was Selwyn Ryan's work on the politics of structural adjustment in the fall of the Peoples' Nationalist Movement (PNM) in Trinidad and Tobago (Ryan 1989). Having won every election since 1956 under Eric Williams, the PNM was able to hold only three seats in the 1986 election under the leadership of George Chambers, following the death of Williams (see Emmanuel 1992, 54). Ryan observed that despite Chambers's bravado that "the IMF cannot dictate to me," his internally imposed policy of fiscal prudence was largely responsible for his downfall (Ryan 1989, 37). The impact of structural adjustment and global neoliberalism on electoral fortunes in the Anglophone Caribbean became more apparent in the 1990s and into the twenty-first century. One of the most spectacular of these was the fall of the Erskine Sandiford administration of Barbados in 1994 following a period of structural adjustment. Among the more problematic of Sandiford's measures was a reduction, by 8 percent, of all public service salaries (Sandiford 1992; see Joseph 1997). These developments indicated a process in which the internal political structures and relations of the postcolonial reality in the Caribbean were being fundamentally transformed, a process that, as will be seen, was to have an impact on the new governments into the first decade of the twenty-first century.

An important explanation of these developments is the fact of increasing disillusionment of Caribbean electorates with the "delivery capacity" of the state. Significantly, the most severe electoral defeats were felt by governments that had presided over processes of structural adjustment. This can be seen most clearly in the cases of the Sandiford administration in 1994 in Barbados and the Lewis-Compton regime in St. Lucia in 1997. Indeed, much of the politics of St. Lucia in the period following the return of the SLP can be understood as a continuation of a politics of adjustment out of agriculture into tourism and services, leading in turn to new challenges to the new government from its mass base reluctant to abandon the old ideology and unable to lower its expectations to the realities of the new constraints of globalization. Given its history as the party of the Left in St. Lucia, the experience of the SLP in government introduced new dimensions to the politics of adjustment to globalization that further elucidate the dilemma of small states under neoliberalism.

CHAPTER 6

Global Neoliberalism and the Left Agenda, 1997-2006

The Left Compromise to Globalization

The period leading up to and immediately following the 1997 electoral victory of the St. Lucia Labour Party (SLP) witnessed the philosophical repositioning of the party to embrace the objectives of global neoliberalism. This imperative of realignment required a number of responses from the SLP, largely fashioned and pursued by Kenny Anthony, appointed as party leader in January 1997. One of the clearest features of Anthony's early leadership was a deliberate attempt to transform his party in response to what he perceived to be the new global realities confronting the Caribbean Left and impacting small postcolonial states. Among the immediate tasks Anthony set for himself were the modernization and political reorganization of the party; the attraction of new, younger, more technocratic people to its ranks; the refashioning of its philosophical precepts away from the radical anticolonial nationalism and socialism of the 1970s toward a more pragmatic accommodation to hegemonic neoliberalism; and the careful crafting of a policy objective that was designed both to inspire confidence in the business, middle-class, and other sectors of the population historically hostile to the party.

At the same time, Anthony, having had his earliest political associations in the politics of the St. Lucian and Caribbean Left, was careful to position the party within the narrowing space available for social democratic thinking and practice in the late-twentieth-century post–Soviet Union era. Thus the new politics of the SLP represented a pragmatic blend of pursuing economic strategies at the macro level that were clearly commensurate with the standard neoliberal prescriptions, but which at the same time were marked by the sustained effort to offer protection and "social safety nets" to the poor and vulnerable. In addition, given Anthony's background in the St. Lucia labor movement, having served as president of the St. Lucia Teachers' Union, he also pursued policies aimed at creating an industrial relations environment in which the protection of the rights of workers and trade unions was a key priority.

One of the first responses of the newly elected SLP to what was perceived by its leadership as new global imperatives was to undertake a transformation in its frontline cadres and personnel. The political reorganization of the SLP was motivated by the notion that the process of globalization required a higher degree of technical competence than had hitherto existed in government, since the challenges of globalization had created a new order far more difficult than anything encountered in the previous years of pre- and postcolonial development. This was a consistent theme of the SLP's 1997 electoral campaign. The party's manifesto, for example, emphasized the notion that while the twenty-first century "holds far yet unfathomed challenges but limitless opportunities for the entire globe . . . St. Lucians find themselves without a coherent plan of action to address this new and complex world environment." The country was described as being "burdened by a government fatigued by nearly thirty years in office; a government that exhibits paralysis and intellectual bankruptcy as far as finding solutions to these problems is concerned" (SLP 1997).

The need for greater technocratic competence in government played a critical role in the party's rejection of its leader, Julian Hunte, in 1996. Hunte, though a hugely successful businessman, had ended his formal education at the secondary level and was widely seen as being unelectable due to his technical limitations. This need for a more "technically competent" leader assumed greater urgency following the selection by the United Workers' Party (UWP) of one of the Caribbean's leading intellectuals, Vaughan Lewis, as party leader. The replacement of Hunte by Kenny Anthony in 1996 was therefore a critical feature of the SLP's adjustment to the demands of global neoliberalism.[1] The academic and occupational backgrounds of the SLP candidates contesting the 1997 general election also reflect this emphasis on technocratic qualifications. Of the seventeen candidates, one—the leader—possessed a doctoral degree, five held master's degrees, and three held bachelor's degrees. This trend was also manifested in the leadership of the party structure itself, with academically qualified technocrats such as Calixte George, Hilford Deterville, Ernest Hilaire, James Fletcher, Didicus Jules, and Petrus Compton playing key roles in the election process and in the reorganization of the party. Significantly, these technocrats were to occupy key roles in the government, at both the ministerial and administrative levels, following the election.

This emphasis on the "technocratic competence" of leadership at the expense of its ideological orientation and class-based political aims and objectives is a critical aspect of the Left compromise to global neoliberalism. A key assumption behind this development was that managerialism, as distinct from leadership, had now become an important aspect of state's response to globalization. Implied in this assumption was that all major ideological questions and debates about alternative paths to development had been settled, leaving only the task of effectively managing the accepted reality to the existing global order (essentially a managerial function) (see Nettleford 1993). By embracing technocratic managerialism, the SLP appeared to be accepting the notion that the major political challenges of independence either had been resolved or the pursuit of alternatives had now been rendered futile, and that the party had entered a stage of practical accommodation to neoliberalism. This is borne out by the fact that after serving in opposition since 1982, two years after formal independence, the new SLP government raised no new issues critical to questions of sovereignty and national self-determination in the new environment, and settled into the mode of survival and development within the existing global order.

Once both major parties in St. Lucia had embraced the new technocratic ethos, a context was created in which political alternatives were delegitimized. This development stood in marked contrast to the earlier period of St. Lucian politics, from the period of universal suffrage to the immediate postindependence period (1950 and 1982, respectively), in which politics was marked by competing ideological notions about the role of the state in resolving and overcoming the internal relations implanted by the colonial past. While the early SLP governments of the 1950s–1960s had been widely recognized as administrations of limited academic competence, their ideological commitment to abolishing the internal relations of colonialism had remained central. Similarly, the embrace of socialism by the left wing of the SLP under George Odlum in the 1970s had been seen as an essential adjunct to the nationalist project.

In contrast, the years of political defeat experienced by the SLP (1982–1997), as well as the existential reality of neoliberal globalization, had effectively removed the concerns about race and class equity and the notions of domestic economic ownership and empowerment from the political agenda. This new emphasis on technocratic competence resulted in a corresponding marginalization of the more traditional "politician" types and, at the same time, widened the distance between the leadership and the party's rank and file.[2] Chosen because of their technocratic competence, candidates and party officials were politically unfettered insofar as their attachment to popular aspirations were concerned. It was symptomatic of these developments that George Odlum was excluded from office within the party structure.[3] In this sense, the political reorganization of the SLP resulted in a situation in which the decision-making process was further insulated from "popular" interference. Similarly, a decision to appoint a full-time "professional" general secretary to administer the party's affairs, as distinct from one elected at annual conventions, further established the managerial ethos within the party structure.

In keeping with the new dependency upon externally driven political and economic forces, the SLP's project of political restructuring was deliberately carved to mirror the "Third Way" project of the British Labour Party under Tony Blair. The SLP, under Kenny Anthony, was officially described as the "new" labor party (see SLP 1997), and a young, newly elected British female MP, Clare Ward, was invited as a special guest speaker at Kenny Anthony's formal launching as an electoral candidate.[4] Parallels were also drawn with regard to the youthfulness of the leaders of the two parties, both of whom were responsible for effecting a political reemergence of their parties after a roughly similar period of political marginalization. Several political commentators in St. Lucia saw the victory of the British Labour Party on 1 May 1997 as influencing the turn of events in St. Lucia on 23 May 1997 (Daher Broadcasting Television Panel Discussion, 23 May 1997).

The embrace of "new labor" established a considerable ideological distance in relation to the SLP of 1979, the last time it tasted electoral victory. In its 1997 campaign, the SLP stressed the need "not to go back to the past" but to "embrace the future and all its possibilities and probabilities" (see Anthony 2004, 4–15). While this was a response intended to blunt UWP campaign propaganda, which highlighted the "Communism" and "in-fighting" of previous SLP administrations, it reflected further the identification with the "Third Way" project in Britain. Given the deliberate and conscious emasculation of the Left engendered in Blair's "Third Way"—essentially an extension of Thatcherism into the British Labour Party—the SLP's adoption of Blair's rhetoric, tactics, and ideological assumptions portended a similar development in St. Lucia. In that moment of philosophical adjustment, the questions that had shaped the ideological orientation of the SLP's anticolonial project in the 1970s were consciously omitted from the new labor agenda.

The political reorganization of the SLP therefore necessarily involved a distancing from the project of radical internal economic reform, which had defined the earliest phases of the nationalist movement. It undermined the democratic fabric of the society by privileging "managerial competence" over the necessity of addressing the more overt political questions of social transformation. The process of reorganization also created a distance between the managerial goals of the party leadership and the economic aspirations of its mass base. As will be seen later, this was to result in a near perpetual tension between various ideological wings of the Labour Party divided roughly along lines of "new labor" versus "old labor," although these categories were never subject to a critically thorough analytical dissection that was required. Nevertheless, the later collapse of the SLP in 2006 was partly a result of the unresolved tensions springing from the ideological differences within the party over the adjustment to neoliberalism and globalization.

These organizational transformations by the SLP, though critical in effecting the party's electoral victory over the UWP, also signaled the end of sharply defined ideological and policy differences between the two parties. Indeed, given the UWP's own embrace of managerialism, seen in its selection of Vaughan Lewis as party leader, the election results can be read as indicating the public's acceptance of the SLP as having completed its managerial transformations more fully than did the UWP. In other words, the SLP was seen as being more ready for the technical adjustments required by globalization. The anxieties over the future of bananas, the withdrawal by the militant leadership of the banana producers of their support for the UWP, public servants' discomfiture with the growing cases of corruption in the UWP, and the resignation from active politics by inaugural prime minister and founder of the UWP, John Compton, were all factors that resulted in handing the SLP the biggest electoral victory ever achieved by a party in postindependence St. Lucia.

In keeping with these shifts were new policy approaches and assumptions. Of first importance was an ideological commitment to the state's withdrawal from the economic sphere. This was complemented by a political agenda of "good governance," which emphasized notions of accountability, constitutional reform, anticorruption, and other "noneconomic" issues as the basis for the party's electoral challenge to the UWP. The party also defended the process of neoliberal adjustment as a process of economic and political empowerment. While the SLP recognized that a retreat of the state was liable to be attacked as an abrogation of state responsibilities, it was presented as allowing for "real" ownership and control by the population. A distinction was made between state ownership and popular ownership. This ideological shuffle was an attempt to respond to the contradictory demands emanating simultaneously from the global and domestic environments and was an essential part of the SLP's compromise to globalization.

This development also required subtle shifts in the internal assumptions and strategies that had influenced the independence movement in its earliest incarnation. The SLP therefore assumed that the challenges of colonialism had been largely resolved, and it emphasized the existence of a new postcolonial reality. In a speech at an annual conference of the Unity Labour Party in neighboring St. Vincent and the Grenadines, Kenny Anthony declared that while "the years after adult suffrage focused on social and economic transformation, then in the twilight of this century the focus needs to be on political innovations" (Anthony 1996). This assumption that the economic and social challenges of independence had been solved was expressed even more clearly to a Barbadian audience in October 1999. There, Anthony expressed the notion that "there had been societal evolution beyond the involuntary amalgam of opposing classes that we inherited at independence." This was viewed as indicating a shift in "societal needs" (Anthony 2004, 147–155). Underlying these assumptions was the idea that a process of local political and economic empowerment had occurred. This was echoed by George Odlum, foreign minister in the new labor government, in a speech to the St. Lucian Chamber of Commerce, symbolically addressing an audience before which he would previously have been persona non grata. In his speech, Odlum made much of the fact that he was addressing a chamber "which in the past has been elitist," but which "has metamorphosed into a more egalitarian body" (*The Crusader*, 29 November 1997, 2). Clearly implied in these interventions by leading members of the SLP was an attempt to downplay the need for critical opposition to the internal economic relations of the existing order and to signal that the era of radical opposition was no longer possible or desirable. In its place was a concentration on the transformation of the "governance" framework as distinct form the socioeconomic order.

An important feature of the SLP's new philosophical orientation was the attempt to present its neoliberalism as being internally driven as opposed to externally imposed. For example, the government claimed that the formulation of its announced policy of public-sector reform had been guided by a perspective "that accords unto us the responsibility for designing our economic, social and political spaces" (Anthony 2004, 124). According to Anthony, "while the global environment certainly influences *how* we procure our needs, as communities we remain wholly responsible for determining what those needs may be" (ibid., 125). In his view, while external forces had made necessary the need for efficiency reforms, this was a "matter of timing not ideology." He argued that "we need efficiency for our own purposes and must see it as a pre-requisite for welfare maximization. . . . We do not need global competition to acquire this truth" (ibid., 129).

This determination to demonstrate the sovereign basis of neoliberal adjustment marks an important distinction between the approaches of the two dominant political parties in St. Lucia. The SLP, given its history in the radical anticolonial movement, felt a greater intellectual urgency to explain and justify its new approach. The UWP, in contrast, had been largely unapologetic about its adherence to a narrow concept of sovereignty. Thus the SLP in the late 1990s spent a great deal of time explaining and defending its response to globalization out of its concern to demonstrate its "social-democratic" and "leftist" pedigree. This ideological tension was clearly evident in a speech by Kenny Anthony at the annual conference of the SLP in November 1997:

> We must be strong and remain focussed in our historic mission. We are new labour, new in organization, new in spirit, new in vision and new in direction. But we are still labour and that new spirit has been erected on our cherished values and anchored in our historical roots. This party came from the poor and its workers. We were born in the struggle for a better life for the disadvantaged. . . . There is no doubt that we must correct some historical wrongs because it is the only way the society can be restored to decency and fairness. (Anthony 1997)

Similarly reflective of ideological tensions within the government's philosophy was the concern to highlight the dangers of neoliberal structural reforms. A central concern of the party was that neoliberalism had led to the "abandonment of principles of social equity." As a result, the party's project of internal reform was described as an attempt to "capture a middle ground; an economic and political ideology that is neither pure laissez-faire nor leftist; a moral ideology that is just but pragmatic; that produces economic growth with a social consciousness" (Anthony 2004, 126).

This definition of an ideological "middle ground" was also motivated by the awareness of the Caribbean electorate's resistance to global neoliberalism, given that several governments had tasted electoral defeat as a result of their unquestioning implementation of neoliberal policies driven by the International Monetary Fund (IMF). An example foremost in the mind of Anthony was the Barbadian structural adjustment experience under Erskine Sandiford, which had resulted in the early exit of the Democratic Labour Party (DLP) from office. Thus, in expounding on the "middle ground," Anthony observed that "recent history is full of free-market heroes—all of them in developing countries—who saved the economy and lost the election. So reform with civil unrest is not an option" (Anthony 2004, 130).

Given the fact that the economic role of the state had been de-emphasized, the question of "good governance" became a central focus of the new philosophy of the party, further reflecting the closing of the ideological gap between the economic philosophies of the SLP and UWP. The SLP therefore exploited the UWP's political failures as the main plank upon which it justified its bid for election. This was evident in a speech by Anthony delivered to the conference of the SLP on 2 November 1997 (Anthony 1997):

During this election there is much talk about the growth index of the economy. We say to the UWP, we will also look at the misery index of the lives of our people. Their hunger index; the neglect and victimization index; the dishonesty index in government; the un-kept and broken promises index; their bluff index. . . . Let us substitute capable ministers for inept ones. Let us substitute compassion for contempt and most of all let us substitute a democratic and benevolent way of life for a dictatorial and uncaring one.

The emphasis on "good governance" was effective in allowing the SLP simultaneously to join the UWP in its economic outlook and to assert its distance on the issue of governance. Economic questions were largely removed from the arena of electoral contestation, and in their place was a far greater emphasis on governance as the main issue on which the electorate was invited to vote.

However, this shift to "good governance" as the main basis for electoral contestation signaled the emergence of critical tensions between the party's commitment to global neoliberalism and the project of domestic empowerment. The essence of these contradictions lay in the fact that while the party envisaged a more direct intervention of civil society in the administration of the state and on the question of governance, its economic commitment to neoliberalism created a context for greater conflict between the state and society. In other words, the effort at insulating the economy from public censure was undermined by the deeper attention paid to issues of governance, central to which were greater levels of public participation in decision making and in the scrutiny of government's decisions. As will be seen later, the SLP's democratic orientation became a critical factor testing the party's commitment to global restructuring. These tensions between concessions to popular aspirations, on the one hand, and the adjustment to the imperatives of globalization, on the other, become even more marked when the SLP's record in government is examined.

Globalization and the SLP in Government

The economic policy of the SLP in government between 1997 and 2006 reveals a shaky balance between the nationalist concern with establishing domestic control over economic and social policy and the adjustment to the imperatives of globalization. This tension had been clearly anticipated in the party's manifesto, which stressed the need to "provide a more conducive environment to enable St. Lucians with drive and initiative to make a more comfortable living at home," despite its broader recognition of global constraints on the independent actions of the state. In an attack on the UWP's foreign investment policy, the manifesto stressed that the party was "against preferential access being given to foreigners while locals have to fight so hard to make it happen for them" (SLP 1997, 5). Among the measures promised to facilitate domestic entrepreneurial capacity was the pledge to "reserve certain sectors . . . for St. Lucian and OECS [Organization of Eastern Caribbean States] citizens" (ibid., 7). Moreover, these expressions of economic nationalism were secondary relative to the commitment to neoliberalism. The manifesto stressed that "these are global times and we need foreign investment to energize our economy" (ibid., 5). Much of the new direction was advocated on the basis of the "negative" impact of globalization. Neoliberal restructuring was thus seen as an unavoidable necessity (ibid.).

The tension between the need to demonstrate a commitment to the empowerment of the local majority and the pursuit of neoliberalism was evident in other aspects of the SLP's internal policies. The first party convention following the election was used to outline a number of initiatives that were intended to demonstrate the party's commitment to a labor agenda. Typical of these were the abolition of medical fees at health centers, the free provision of textbooks, and the abolition of school fees for a large number of underprivileged children (Anthony 1997, 13). Another important "socialist" policy of the government was the Short Term Employment Project (STEP). Under this project, the government, with the help of the private sector, engaged in Keynesian-style strategies designed to alleviate the unemployment problem among the youth and other segments of society who had never had the opportunity or capacity to sustain gainful employment (ibid., 15; George, interview).

In addition to these measures at the domestic level, an important feature of the "Left" content of the new SLP government was its foreign policy. One of the earliest and most dramatic episodes in the life of the new government was the breaking of diplomatic relations with Taiwan and the consequent deepening of relations with mainland China (see *St. Lucia Mirror*, 12 September 1997, 9).[5] While the establishment of relations with China in the late 1990s was no longer essentially radical given the embrace of the market within China itself (Odlum, interview), this move was important to the SLP's promotion of itself as a party of the Left.[6] These relations were strengthened with the promise of financial and technical assistance with capital projects from the Chinese. The establishment of ties with China was also justified on the basis of China's emergence as a leading global economic power. As such, the SLP was able to identify itself as a party aware of shifting global realities but politically astute enough to maintain ties with a socialist ally that was a leading player on the world stage. In this regard, therefore, the example of newly emergent China as a socialist state that had made the necessary adaptations to the market—and was not only successful but thriving—was specifically attractive to the SLP, given its attempts to demonstrate its relevance as a party of social democracy able to navigate the challenging waters of modern, competitive trade liberalization and globalization. By turning to China, the SLP was able to maintain its socialist pedigree and at the same time assure itself of a relationship that could deliver concrete material and developmental assistance, in a period when the traditional partners of the Caribbean had reduced their involvement in regional development.

An early attempt was made to increase commercial ties between China and St. Lucia through a weeklong visit by a St. Lucian trade delegation to China in early 1999 (*St. Lucia Mirror*, 5 February 1999, 1–2). By the end of the SLP's first term in office, China had emerged as one of the principal development partners in St. Lucia, with agreements having been won for the construction of sports stadia, a duty-free storage and clearance complex, a cultural theater complex, and a new general hospital and a modern psychiatric hospital.[7] China, for its part, was able to advance its foothold in the Western Hemisphere and Latin America and deepen its trading links in a vastly expanding global network that was growing commensurate with its productive capacity and overall economic expansion. China's ties to St. Lucia provided a further outlet for its vast labor pool, expanded its trading opportunities, and, as a member of the Caribbean Development Bank, allowed it access to participate in the development projects on offer in the island. Significant, too, was the fact that St. Lucia became the newest member of China's growing list of diplomatic friends able to lend support for its claims to Taiwan as a renegade province, and for its "One China" policy. In this sense, therefore, St. Lucia's link to China was a mutually beneficial undertaking, and it was an important cog in the foreign policy of the SLP in the era following the collapse of Soviet Marxism and in the period of the rise of neoliberal globalization.

In addition to its adoption of diplomatic relations with China, another important element of this shift to the left in St. Lucia's foreign policy was the renewed declaration of solidarity by the SLP with Cuba (*The Voice*, 9 October 1997, 1). In January 1999 Kenny Anthony paid a state visit to Cuba, where he received Cuba's highest honor, the Jose Marti award (*The Voice*, 30 January 1999, 5).[8] This renewed closeness with Cuba was marked by a heightening of public statements in condemnation of the U.S. economic embargo (*St. Lucia Mirror*, 29 January 1999, 3). The most direct benefit to St. Lucia from these ties was an increase in the number of scholarships to Cuban universities for St. Lucian students; the free access of St. Lucian citizens to specialized medical care in Cuba, as under the miracle eye care program, for example; and the increase in technical support from Cuba in the areas of sports, education, and health care. Cuba's miracle eye care program was funded by Venezuela, which had emerged as a leading player in the region, and which, following the consolidation of power by

Hugo Chavez, had pursued a socialist project designed to shift the region away from dependency on North America and to explore alternative development paths that had been stifled in the period since the 1980s.

Thus, with the fashioning of this more aggressive involvement in the Caribbean by Hugo Chavez of Venezuela, a further opportunity was opened up to the SLP for the deepening of ties with the global social democratic movement. This became particularly heightened in the closing years of the SLP's final term in office when the government of Venezuela fashioned a special facility for the provision of oil and petroleum products below existing market rates for countries of Latin America and the Caribbean. The Petro-Caribe initiative, as it was called, was essentially a system that offered participating countries the opportunity to pay for Venezuelan oil in part with agricultural products, thus effecting a system of barter, and with significant grace periods before the commencement of actual payment. The Petro-Caribe initiative was part of a wider Venezuelan thrust into the Caribbean, dubbed the Bolivarian Alternative for Latin America (ALBA), which Chavez touted as a genuine alternative to the U.S.-led Free Trade Area of the Americas (FTA). One of ALBA's critical features was the formation of an ALBA Development Bank, which was intended to provide members with soft loans for developmental purposes. Although the SLP government was never fully a signatory to the ALBA plan or the Petro-Caribe initiative, the options offered by the presence of a Venezuela with a renewed interest in assisting the Caribbean region with its development efforts provided psychological and structural support, justifying the social democracy of the SLP.

In addition, the existing global context, the specific challenges that the country faced with the onset of trade liberalization, and the movement away from protectionism that it had historically enjoyed also provided the SLP with the space to shape a critique of the existing order. The new foreign policy orientation of the SLP government was marked by strong stances against the external forces of global neoliberalism. Locked as it was in a struggle to preserve its banana economy, St. Lucia condemned the multilateral institutions for not being sufficiently open, transparent, and responsive to the needs of small developing societies (*The Voice*, 23 September 1997; 7, 9 October 1997, 7). Similarly, given the role of the United States as the principal supporter for Latin American banana producers, much of the SLP's critique of global neoliberalism was leveled at the United States over the issue of the World Trade Organization (WTO) ruling against the European Union (EU) banana regime.

The specific thrust of the SLP's foreign policy orientation proved troubling for the more conservative sections of the population, who had continued to associate the SLP of 1997 with that of 1979. In particular, the SLP's renewed alliances with China and Cuba were denounced in the local press as indicating "a return to the left" (*St. Lucia Mirror*, 10 October 1997, 2). In response, the St. Lucian foreign ministry defended the SLP's new foreign policy stances as being necessary in the age of globalization. In the clearest statement on foreign policy since the SLP's return to power, the St. Lucian foreign minister, George Odlum, provided a number of reasons for St. Lucia's new foreign policy orientation. Paramount among these was the argument that "with political ideologies fading into the sunset of Cold War international relations," St. Lucia could "no longer rely on those whom we had considered traditional friends." This situation was seen as one demanding that St. Lucia "find creative ways of sustaining our economy in the face of this onslaught" (see *St. Lucia Hansard*, Budget Debates 2000; see also Anthony in *The Voice*, 23 September 1997, 7). It was clear that central to the SLP's approach was the assumption that with heightened globalization had come the erosion of support from the United States and Britain. As a consequence, the SLP believed that it was necessary to lessen its historical dependence on these "traditional partners" not only as an ideological response but equally important as a technical response to what was required by the existing global order.

However, despite these elements of an "Old Left" agenda in the government's policy, particularly in the sphere of international relations, many of the SLP's policies in the domestic sphere belied a tendency to pursue neoliberal objectives. This is because while the arena of international relations is relatively removed from domestic political contestation, except in cases where sharp ideological divisions exist and where sharp reversals from previous political practices can be discerned, the arena of domestic economic policy allowed little room for the pursuit of policies that conflicted with the dictates of hegemonic neoliberalism. As such, a Left "compromise" to globalization is most clearly discernible in the SLP's conduct in the domestic economic sphere.

One of the central planks of the SLP's economic policy was a withdrawal by the state from the economy in order to allow market imperatives to determine state-society relations. Policies of divestment and corporatization were central to this process. Where government ownership was retained, an attempt was made to administer these enterprises along strict commercial lines. This commitment to a withdrawal from direct participation in the economy was clearly articulated in the party's manifesto, where the SLP proposed to "divest some interest in the National Commercial Bank (NCB), St. Lucia Development Bank (SLDB) and St. Lucia Electricity Services (LUCELEC) to a broad cross-section of the public." The SLP promised that "the proceeds of privatization and divestment will be used to create a National Development Fund which could spawn new and viable productive sector activity, possibly in joint ventures with competent private sector interests" (SLP 1997, 6). Privatization and commercialization were extended to essential services such as water and public information.

In many of these cases, the government's divestment was motivated not by the economic failure of these enterprises but in pursuit of the government's ideological objective of reducing "nonmarket distortions" in the economy. While recognizing the "healthy dividends to . . . the government from these enterprises," the government rationalized divestment on the basis of resolving the "tangled loyalties of the government" (Anthony 2004, 127). In the case of LUCELEC, this "tangled loyalty" lay in government's role of "profit maximization shareholder" and "its paternal role as regulator." In the case of the NCB, the nonmarket distortion lay in the "government's ability to significantly influence liquidity in the private banking system." This was due to the government's ability to shift national insurance deposits in a context where the government-owned NCB "just happened to hold the lion's share of social security deposits and just happened to be where government went to borrow for projects" (ibid.).

However, the government's commitment to a "social-democratic" path necessitated that its embrace of neoliberalism was defined as part of a strategy of economic empowerment. On one level, the government argued that the process of divestment would lead to "welfare maximization" by freeing up capital to be allocated to the social sector. Welfare maximization was also to be furthered by the government's intention to terminate its role in noneconomic enterprises such as the Water and Sewerage Authority (WASA), which had proved to be a severe drain on the government's resources. On another level, it was argued that divestment encouraged direct "public ownership" as distinct from "government ownership." It was therefore seen as furthering a process of "economic democratization." These claims to economic democratization were clearly articulated by the government in its policy of divestment in the NCB:

Should privatization be designed to ensure that the national bank remains essentially, the peoples' bank? Government had to ask itself what un-quantifiable, priceless intangibles of our community psyche would we be discarding if we turned exclusively to market forces. Our reform compromise was to so package and price shares as to be accessible to all St. Lucians. Moreover, we were careful to inform and educate the general public that we considered our primary market. While institutions were also targeted to ensure a successful public offering, there was a definitive pecking order that reserved share allotments for individuals and nationals. Needless to say, we were overwhelmed. The offer was oversubscribed by some EC $11,000,000 and the allotment to nationals fully taken up. (Anthony 2004, 128)

Despite its definition of its efforts as a project of "empowerment," the government's policy of divestment, commercialization, and state retreat can nevertheless be seen as resulting in an abandonment of the weaker sections of society whose empowerment had been at the center of the national self- determination project. One of the clearest instances of the abandonment of an ideological position of direct commitment to the poor and vulnerable was the result of the corporatization of the water company, WASA.[9] One of the most significant implications of the corporatization of the water company, as proposed, was a 100 percent increase in water rates. This huge increase in the cost of this essential service was clearly facilitated by the application of "private-sector norms" to the administration of the company and was intended to widen the process of commercialization of the industry. While observing that "only 35% of households in St. Lucia were connected to the water supply," the prime minister proposed that monies gained "would be used to fund a six-month free connection policy to enable WASCO to widen its customer base" (*St. Lucia Mirror*, 24 December 1999, 20). Corporatization was also intended to break the population's dependence on the state. While greater financial efficiency of the water company was to be achieved, the government's willingness to apply commercial principles in the provision of a commodity as essential as water provides a clear indication of the commitment to neoliberalism.[10] Indeed, the government came under sharp criticism from the opposition for its failure to take into account the impact of its policy on the poorer sectors of the population (ibid., 13).

It was clear that the government's stance was the result of continued pressure from the external capitalist environment for a further application of neoliberal principles to the business of the state. Following its decision, the government was confronted with the persistent claim by a North American company, Posedon Resources, that its alternative proposals for water investment in St. Lucia would have been far more cost efficient. Most significant, the U.S. firm insisted that it was willing to invest "$EC 67 million or more over a long period of time" to guarantee potable water to every resident. The company also claimed that the 100 percent increase in water rates would have been avoided under its proposals. This episode reveals the manner in which the government's reliance on a neoliberal ideological justification for the corporatization of WASA opened it to further demands, and it also reveals the extent to which the state was caught between the external demand for further privatization and its need to serve as a shield against the external economic sphere. In this regard, the basis upon which the government rejected the firm's offer was that the company was "only interested in what we call green fields projects, which involve minimum risks." The new managing director of WASCO, Martin Satney, insisted that "government . . . must be careful about entering into agreements with private overseas-based

Table 6.1. The distribution of power in the privatized National Commercial Bank		
Shareholders	% of Shares	No. of Potential Directors
Government of St. Lucia	38	3
Caribbean Assoc. of Indigenous Banks	20	2
Barbados National Bank	10	1
2,750 St. Lucian Shareholders	12	1
Source: St. Lucia Mirror Online, 22 October 1999.		

organizations claiming to have access to lots of money and giving the impression that they want to be kind to St. Lucia" (see *St. Lucia Mirror*, 4 February 2000, 1–2). The language of nationalism was used both to advance and to resist neoliberalism.

Similar contradictions were identifiable in the privatization of the government-owned NCB. In this case, the challenge to the government lay in its claims that the privatization process had led to the possibility of direct ownership of the company by St. Lucians. Much of this ideological claim was based on the notion that the divestment of government ownership had resulted in a consequent transfer of ownership and control to the local populace. Indeed, given the historical domination of the St. Lucian economy by a narrowly based propertied class, an egalitarian process of domestic ownership was an unfounded, overly optimistic assumption. The nonegalitarian nature of share ownership of the NCB was pointed out by a disgruntled Lawson Calderon, a former SLP executive member who wanted to see the role of the government on the board of the NCB weakened.[11] According to Calderon, the "three largest shareholders own 68% of the company, the 67 largest own 87% and the smallest 2,750 own just about 12%." Calderon also charged that the share ownership structure of the NCB had made it difficult for the majority of small shareholders to control the board and to reduce government domination of the institution. Under the company's constitution, the board was to be composed of eleven directors. Anyone with 10 percent of the share ownership was entitled to appoint one board member. Calderon's complaint was that the nature of share-director distribution made it difficult for the majority of small shareholders to break government control of the board (*St. Lucia Mirror*, 22 October 1999, 2–3). An examination of the share-director vote of the privatized NCB indicates the limit to which an empowerment of ordinary shareholders had occurred and the continued control of governmental and quasi-governmental bodies over the NCB (see Table 6.1).

In addition to the mere share-director distribution, Calderon complained that the process of director selection had essentially destroyed the possibility of small shareholder control. Calderon identified the close identification of regional institutions such as the Barbados National Bank (BNB) and the Caribbean Association of Indigenous Banks (CAIB) with the government of St. Lucia. Further, the government used its additional 8 percent of shares to influence the selection process of the remaining directors. Moreover, the eleventh director of the board, the manager of the NCB, was a government appointee. Calderon was also disappointed that the small shareholders could "not muster enough share-power to influence the election of even one director to the board." Accusing the small shareholders of "battered woman syndrome," Calderon lamented the absence of a consciousness of economic democratization (*St. Lucia Mirror*, 22 October 1999, 2–3). Essentially, therefore, Calderon's challenge to the government was a demand for the government's ideological commitment to neoliberalism to be translated into a further limitation on the role of the government in the economic sector. As such, it represented a continuation of the increasing pressure for a further neoliberal retreat on the part of the government. Similar tensions in the government's embrace of neoliberalism were evident in the other major pillar of government policy, the banana industry, much of which has been discussed earlier.

As in the case of the NCB, the SLP government pursued a process of commercialization of the banana industry and presented this development as a process of empowering the ordinary St. Lucian. The SLP manifesto had argued that "mere power to control decision making in the SLBGA [St. Lucia Banana Growers' Association] is not the same as 'ownership of the industry'" (SLP 1997, 13). In contrast, the SLP had promised that full control and ownership were to be effected through the abolition of the SLBGA and the formation of a company "owned and managed by farmers." Under these arrangements, it was proposed that "government will be cast in the role of a minority share holder with the responsibility for managing the external affairs of the industry" (ibid.). These justifications were further expressed during the actual process of commercialization of the industry. In a speech announcing the structural changes in the industry, the prime minister suggested that such a "rationalization of this institutional structure will . . . enable growers to move closer to the marketplace, which is a key objective . . . , allowing growers to become involved in pricing arrangements which can be more transparent" (Anthony 1998).

It is clear from the prime minister's unabashed use of the ideological terminology of neoliberalism that such a policy was motivated less by the need for domestic empowerment and more by the pressures of global competition and the ideological hegemony of neoliberalism. Indeed, the manifesto had stated explicitly that the "SLBGA must be transformed into a commercial entity to enable it to make decisions on a more commercial basis and to cope with external competition" (SLP 1997, 13). Moreover, the actual implementation of the process of commercialization by the government revealed a far greater incidence of governmental withdrawal than was presented in the manifesto itself. The manifesto had spoken of the government's retention of a minor shareholder role to facilitate the external relations of the industry, but in practice a wholesale withdrawal was undertaken. Not only did the government relinquish all domestic participation in the local banana companies, but it also expressed a willingness to terminate its involvement in the Windward Islands Banana Exporting Company (WIBDECO), the external arm of the industry (Anthony 2004, 143).

The government's policy of restructuring in the banana industry was undertaken amid calls for greater government regulation by the very constituency in whose name the privatization process was undertaken. A joint call by otherwise politically divided banana companies for greater governmental regulation was not supported by the prime minister. Instead, the demand was met with the response that "each step by government would reduce and weaken your independence as a private company" (see *St. Lucia Online News*, 29 April 2000). This position was later modified by the government following sustained calls for regulation. In a significant volte-face, the minister of agriculture, Cass Elias, declared that the calls for government intervention "give some legitimacy to the idea that to some extent the banana trading business should be regulated" (see *St. Lucia Online News*, 13 May 2000). Despite this concession however, the ideological commitment to governmental withdrawal remained dominant. The minister of agriculture reiterated the position that the government was "opposed to a monopolistic situation, and . . . to interfering with the fundamental rights and freedoms of persons who may wish to trade" (ibid.).

Given this general commitment to a reduced economic role for the state, a project of political reform was an essential pillar of the policy program of the government. The intention to widen the democratic space of the society had been clearly enunciated in the party's manifesto, and, in addition to measures proposed for increasing government accountability and reducing the incidence of corruption, the manifesto proposed a number of initiatives to give effect to notions of "participatory democracy." Among these were proposals to "allow greater participation by the public in the legislative process," to be achieved by the "opening of discussions on Bills coming before parliament, and the introduction of more white papers for public comment to influence the shaping of laws and policies." Similarly, the party proposed to "decentralize decision making by putting in place a system of local government more relevant to the needs of today's communities." The party also announced its intention to "recognize representative social, economic and cultural organizations as legitimate voices expressing citizen's [*sic*] concerns on vital societal issues" (SLP 1997, 3–4). The initial step in the realization of such a "people-oriented" approach was facilitated within the party system itself through the mechanism of "primaries" and "run-offs" between prospective candidates as a basis for their selection.

This attempt to deepen the democratic political culture was vigorously pursued following the party's assumption of office. These objectives were clearly enunciated by the prime minister in a public address in November 1997:

> To implement our new vision, our people must be able to say that government now belongs to us. Government must not become a remote and . . . self-serving entity. Government cannot continue to be seen as the enemy of the people. This structure which always seems to be doing things to people must now be re-fashioned to be an instrument working for people. The institutions of government must be transformed from command centers to become service centers for our development. We must encourage public servants to serve the people. The traditional approach of privatising information, maintaining absolute secrecy, must be abandoned and be replaced by openness and transparency. (Anthony 1997)

In order to achieve these democratization objectives, a number of concrete procedures were implemented. These included the strengthening of the Integrity in Public Office Act, which included mechanisms for the declaration of assets to an independent Public Accounts Committee by all parliamentarians and governmental officials at the upper grades of the public service. The new democratization mechanisms also saw the emergence of a procedure for the submission of periodic reviews by cabinet members to Parliament on the achievements of their various ministries. Cabinet members tabled a similar report at the party's annual conference. These measures were intended to achieve greater ministerial accountability. Efforts at ensuring people-centered government were also pursued by allowing for the presentations on preferred priorities to the government from relevant community interests prior to the formulation of annual budgets (Anthony, Budget Address 1998, 6).

This process of democratization, however, created a context in which the "beleaguered" nature of the state as a facilitator of neoliberal reform, on the one hand, and the defender of social and economic interests, on the other, was further exacerbated. Thus, while the government sought to widen internal democratic practice, this proved problematic given the inherently antipopulist nature of neoliberal logic. In other words, while democratization implied the opening up of spaces for popular influence over governmental decision making, the nature of neoliberalism implied an expectation that issues such as efficiency, profit, and market determinism would shape public policy and priorities. This, it can be argued, was one of the main factors accounting for the eventual defeat of the SLP in the December 2006 general election.

One of the clearest instances of these contradictory demands on and expectations of the SLP government was in the response by the business class to the SLP's attempt to modernize the labor laws of the country, in keeping with the party's commitment to social democracy. The arguments and rationale by the SLP for insisting on the Labour Code, the hostility of the employer class to the passage and implementation of the code, the place of the debate in the 2006 general election, and its contribution to the defeat of the SLP, as well as the broader implications for the lessons for social democracy in the era of globalization, require deeper examination for further understanding of the problematization of social democratic nationalism within the context of hegemonic neoliberalism.

The Labour Code and the SLP Defeat: Contradictions in Social Democracy in the Era of Globalization

One of the clearest instances around which the SLP sought to carve a space for social democracy within the context of global neoliberalism was by proposing to "encourage the modernization" of labor and industrial relations "so that our industrial relations practice is brought in line with internationally accepted standards and provisions" (SLP 1997, 17–18). In fulfillment of this aspiration, the SLP promised to "replace the existing patchwork of labour legislation with a labour code." Among the arguments raised by the SLP in justifying the need for the Labour Code was the need for the establishment of wages tribunals to cover "certain categories of workers such as shop assistants, agricultural workers, and domestic workers," who "have not been amenable to unionization because of the peculiar nature of the employment relationship" (ibid., 18). The manifesto also promised that "occupational health and safety laws [would] be revised and the labour department [would] be given adequate inspection staff to carry out its responsibilities." In addition, the manifesto proposed to establish provisions for unfair dismissal," which would "strengthen the job security of workers and provide, among other things, for the re-instatement of a worker who is unfairly dismissed." Significantly, too, the manifesto promised to "review the system for the payment of severance to workers who have been employed with one employer for a minimum number of years." Finally, the manifesto promised that the labor government would "ratify all of the international conventions on labour and industrial relations of major United Nations bodies such as the International Labour Organization [ILO]" (ibid., 19).

Once elected to office, and in fulfillment of its manifesto pledge, the SLP sought to implement the process of establishing the Labour Code by first engaging the services of the ILO. One commentator, the ILO's legal consultant engaged in the process, Rose-Marie Antoine, noted that in keeping with the government's promise for democratic participation on key issues, consultation with the social partners was the main basis upon which the work on the Labour Code was conducted. In her words,

> Consultation and dialogue was at the centre stage of the process from the onset, which was initiated way back in 1998. . . . Once the then government approached the ILO for assistance to construct the Code and it was agreed, the ILO took sole responsibility for the project up till the time of delivery of the document in 2001. What this means is that the ILO funded the *entire* project.[12] . . . The ILO also laid down the terms of its process which, as is characteristic, is tripartite, i.e. unions, employers and state dialoguing together. . . . Tripartism and meaningful dialogue was also an important component for the Government when it made its request to the ILO. The ILO also supervised the Labour Code process with myself as consultant and the ILO's Caribbean administrative officer (Michele Jankanish) as a member of the Task Force. (Antoine 2007)

Similarly, reflections on the draft code also captured the close synergy between the promise of the SLP in its manifesto and its actual intent and practice once in government. According to another commentator, Mario Michel, a former government minister in the Anthony administration, the main objective of the Labour Code, as contained in the long title, was to "reform legislation applicable to labour and industrial relations in Saint Lucia taking into account existing local standards and international labour law standards." He argued that "although the proportion of the Labour Code that is reform is small as compared to the proportion that is consolidation, there are still some significant reforms contained in the Code which render its passage and implementation desirable" (Michel 2007). Among the proposals that Michel singled out as indicative of genuine reformist intent were "the introduction . . . of the concept of unfair dismissal and the establishment of the Labour Tribunal." In these developments, the movement from manifesto promise to policy and legislative actualization was clearly discernible.

The seriousness of purpose with which the SLP pursued its plans to modernize the labor and industrial relations climate led to an equally determined stance on the part of private capital to frustrate the government's objectives. Throughout the SLP's two terms in office, the efforts at passing the Labour

Code were continuously obstructed by the employer group, who mounted stiff and resolute resistance at every stage in the process. The first opportunity for such obstruction came following the submission of the draft code, which the social partners were invited to review. From the outset, the stance adopted by the employers was not one that was designed to improve the draft, but to bury the entire process. Their first response was to hire the services of a regional attorney whose job was to "find fault" with the several provisions of the draft. The employers' second response was to insist on withholding their assent to the Labour Code until all of their demands had been met. These obstructionist tactics have been effectively captured by Rose Marie Antoine:

> I must tell you that although I welcomed much of this consultation, not all of it drove the process forward. Indeed, very often, I found myself going over and over the very same ground, to'ing and fro'ing, even within the same group, for example, with one group of employers often contradicting what a previous employers' group had proposed, changing their minds constantly. I plodded along even though we were constantly going over so called "concerns" which had been fully debated, consensus arrived at in the Task Force and at previous meetings with groups of employers and unions. An instructive example is that of sick leave. The Task Force held extensive discussions on how to implement a sick leave provision which made it possible for workers who were genuinely ill not to be prejudiced, while at the same time, enhancing productivity by ensuring that workers did not abuse sick leave. It was decided that a twelve-day yearly sick leave without certification would work with a proviso which I added that even within this period, an employee could be penalized if proven to have taken sick leave when not sick. ... The employers then objected to this provision on the ground that it would encourage workers to take sick leave as an entitlement, akin to holiday (something we had considered, of course). The Code was then amended and the twelve days omitted. Lo and behold, in the final Retreat Consultation, the very employers came to the table proposing (as if new) that a twelve-day sick leave provision be included as without a set number of days there would be abuse! So we were right back to the very same provision that had been in the original Draft. (Antoine 2007)

Given the wide level of consultation that had gone into the code, Antoine was led to conclude that the actions of the employer group were intended to defeat the objectives of the government. Thus she argued that "those who are calling for [more consultation] ... are misguided or worse. It is, in my view a sure invitation to not only further misinformation and confusion, but a way to hijack the Code and frustrate its objectives" (Antoine 2007).

Concrete and real evidence of the employers' hostility to the Labour Code was to be seen in clear and direct terms in the last days of the SLP in government. In his bid to fulfill his manifesto pledge, Anthony ensured that the very last sitting of the House, prior to its dissolution before the 2006 general election, was devoted to the debate on and passing of the Labour Code.

In the days prior to the sitting, however, the Sandals Hotel chain, owned by Jamaican magnate Butch Stewart, announced the laying off of nearly 200 workers, an action that was interpreted by many to signal his hostility to the code and particularly its provisions for the legal right to trade unionization among all sectors of workers. If the intention of the proprietor of the island's largest hotel chain was to secure worker and voter hostility to the ruling government, then the strategy was an unequivocal success.

Thus in the days leading to the debate, and on the day of the debate itself, a number of Sandals workers, joined by opposition politicians and activists, seized the opportunity to mount demonstrations around the Parliament buildings and in the streets of the capital. The leading trade unions in the country, though widely supportive of the government's stance on the Labour Code, failed to respond with a show of support for the government's objectives. In addition, there was very little public education on the part of the unions on the benefits of the Labour Code for workers themselves. Therefore, with no support from their representative organizations, and with little expressions of public sympathy for what the SLP was seeking to do, the view of the individual worker toward the Labour Code was largely negative. Confronted with clear and incontrovertible evidence of the "consequences" of the Labour Code in the dismissal of the Sandals workers, the rank-and-file worker began to see the SLP's passage of the Labour Code as a threat to job security. On the eve of a general election, and with the opposition groups painting themselves ironically as simultaneously defending the interests of workers and employers alike, a common hostility to the SLP was effected.

However, beyond the narrow issue of employer hostility to the modernization of the industrial relations environment is the larger question of the contradictory nature of the SLP's pursuit of social democracy in the era of neoliberal ideological dominance. At the heart of the employers' hostility to the Labour Code was their assumption that any move to formalize the regulatory environment of employer-employee relations was an erosion of their hegemony as controllers of capital. In the view of employers, the actions of the SLP government appeared to go against the prevailing neoliberal norms of the global environment, and they thought that the government was too bullish in facilitating the empowerment of labor. Further, much of the employers' resistance was rationalized on the basis of the implications of the Labour Code for St. Lucia's international competitiveness. In the view of employers, any increase in the cost of labor, and any tightening of regulations in the industrial environment, would redound to the country's competitors in the region and elsewhere. Finally, the deep-seated "feudal" nature of employer-employee relations in St. Lucia (see Chapter 2) cannot be ruled out as an explanation for the hardened opposition of the employers to the code. Accustomed as they had become to relative freedom in the determination of their treatment of employees, several employers believed that that government's pursuit of the code was an unwelcome intrusion. Their resistance was therefore set in the context of both historical and contemporary opposition to what was perceived as the SLP's ideological commitment to social democracy.

What is significant, however, is the fact that the Labour Code played a critical role in consolidating the neoliberal environment to which the employers were committed. Thus, while the labor unions had remained silent in support for the Labour Code, the SLP itself vacillated in the face of public demonstrations against the passage of the code, particularly given the precariousness of the impending election. Such vacillation was due to the party's desire to be seen as "friendly to business," particularly in light of its socialist history and particularly against the SLP's own intention to reclaim the middle ground, appealing to all groups and persuasions. It is important, too, that the SLP had been critical in effecting the shift from an economy based on agriculture to one based on tourism and services, a shift that had led to the class consolidation of the very forces opposing the Labour Code. Ironically, Butch Stewart had enjoyed his greatest level of tourism expansion under the SLP, acquiring the Sandals Grande, the largest and most upscale of his three hotels, after the property formerly owned by the Hyatt group had fallen into receivership. The scale and extent of his investment in St. Lucia suggested confidence in the business environment created by the Anthony administration.

These realities might explain the unwillingness of the prime minister to condemn as political the motivations behind the Sandals firings, and to expose the move as an overt attempt to arouse voter anger against the SLP in the days leading up to the election. Indeed, the only member of the SLP administration to openly condemn the Sandals action was Victor La Corbiniere (who was serving as a senator and attorney general, and was not a candidate in the upcoming election). La Corbiniere, in a television interview, argued that he was "convinced that the firing of the workers on the eve of the general elections was not accidental but was an attempt on the part of the company to destabilize the country." However, his remarks earned a quick public disclaimer from Anthony, who distanced the leadership of the party from La Corbiniere's anti-Stewart comments (see *The Gleaner* online, 23 November 2006). Clearly evident in this episode was Anthony's own "beleaguered" position as both an advocate of neoliberalism and as a promoter of worker interests. Indeed, the beleaguered and overwhelmed nature of the postcolonial state in the era of globalization in attempting to fulfill contradictory demands from its various publics have been thoughtfully analyzed and presented by Bgoya and Hyden (1987), and the SLP in late 2006 appeared to conform to many of the features they described. Indeed, given the revolt against Anthony by both capital and labor, it can be safely concluded that the marriage between neoliberalism and social democracy that he had attempted had proven a failure. So complete was the failure that when the elections were held on 11 December 2006, the SLP, which had been swept into office in 1997 with a 16-1 mandate, was routed at the polls by the UWP (under the leadership of eighty-two-year-old John Compton, who had come out of retirement for the sole purpose of defeating the SLP), winning only six seats to the UWP's eleven.

Assessing the Efficacy of the Left Compromise to Neoliberalism

Much of the success of the SLP's neoliberal project had been premised upon the assumption of the willingness of the populace to accept immediate short-falls in their economic well-being as a necessary price of adjustment. In short, it depended to a large extent upon the government's success in achieving domestic ideological consensus for neoliberalism. The huge popular mandate of the SLP government and the virtual decimation of the opposition UWP in the 1997 election provided a wide degree of "political space" for the pursuit of neoliberal reforms. This reality partly accounted for the pace and manner in which these reforms were implemented. Nonetheless, the government's consciousness of the unpopularity of these policies was reflected in its constant appeal to its support-ers for the need for loyalty "in an increasingly insensitive and harshly competi-tive world," which "involves hard choices and difficult decisions" (Anthony 1997, 17).[13] The earliest cracks in the SLP's neoliberal agenda can be identified, there-fore, in the popular resistance to the government's abandonment of its welfarist role.

Given the huge popular mandate enjoyed by the SLP following the 1997 elec-tion, the earliest and most significant challenges to the government's neoliberal-ism had come from the party's mass base itself. One of the earliest of such chal-lenges occurred during the party's 1997 annual convention, mere months after the general election. A resolution from a member on the floor called for a policy of "affirmative action" to address the needs of SLP supporters neglected dur-ing the thirty-year rule of the UWP. It was motivated by a growing impatience with the government's extension of an "olive branch" to the local beneficiaries of UWP rule, who continued to enjoy prominence on the boards of the various statutory corporations (*St. Lucia Mirror*, 5 November 1997, 1–2). While this was a demand for a crude form of patronage and "clientelism," it indicated a growing dissatisfaction by the party's mass base with the delivery capacity of the state and represented an early challenge to the new philosophy, which downplayed the need for direct government intervention to assist vulnerable groups. By challenging the SLP's new "politics of inclusion," the resolution also expressed impatience with the emphasis on political reform at the expense of economic change.

This episode provides an example of the widely noted phenomenon in Caribbean politics of the impact of globalization undermining the "clientelist" basis of party-mass relations (Stone 1980; Edie 1991, 1994; Ryan 1994). While presenting a criticism of clientelism against the standards of modern liberal democracy, these studies have argued that much of the legitimacy of the Caribbean political system depends upon the ability of the various parties to deliver goods and services to their constituencies. According to these writers, the clientelist system, despite its defects, has kept the political system functioning in a stable manner and has made it "work" in the eyes of the ordinary citizen (Ryan 1994, 245). According to Ryan (ibid., 236), through clientelism, "the political system became an arena in which rival political and trade union elites promised the 'moon' and sought to outbid each other to dispense patronage to their followers." Such writers also point to the availability of global aid and preferential trade in sustaining the clientelist system. These writers argue that by eroding the conditions supportive of these clientelist relations, the new global environment has created a context that challenges the legitimacy of the political process. Given these developments, Ryan (ibid., 249) expresses the concern that the "critical problem is whether the Caribbean masses weaned as they have been on state-dispensed patronage, will accept choices which have been made as beneficial to their long-term interests, or whether they would opt for radical alternatives which continue to promise them the 'moon.'" The early conflict between the SLP's hierarchy and its mass base over the question of "affirmative action" therefore appeared to suggest a growing challenge to the political order as a result of unfulfilled local expectations.[14]

In addition to this early challenge, a number of subsequent developments during the SLP's first three years in government raised other questions about the ability of the party to balance the conflicting demands emanating simultaneously from the external and domestic environments for a further lessening of the economic interventionist role of the government and for its enlargement, respectively. While the marginalized sections of society had desired a greater degree of intervention, those sections of the domestic population more committed to neoliberalism demanded a further weakening in the government's role. At the same time, various groups that had been expected to benefit from the process of privatization, as was seen in the case of the banana companies, made unending calls for a degree of governmental intervention to provide protection for the existing companies. These conflicting and contradictory tendencies reinforced the "beleaguered" condition of the state.

Thus the earlier examination of the privatization process in the NCB and WASA provided evidence of a process in which a further retreat by the government was demanded. In the case of WASA, the demand had come from a foreign company frustrated in its economic ambitions by the government's continued role in the provision of water services. The foreign firm had appealed directly to popular sentiment by suggesting that cheaper water rates could be attained through further deregulation by the government. In the case of Lawson Calderon's demand for a reduction in governmental control of the NCB, the motivation was more political than economic. It expressed a desire for the majority of shareholders to seize the opportunity provided by privatization to limit government domination of the NCB board. These developments suggested a demand for a process of state withdrawal beyond that envisaged by the government. A public declaration by the government of the need for "managed change" might well have been directed at the government's hyper-neoliberal detractors. The declaration spoke of the need to "strategically manage the political side of the process" and highlighted the need to safeguard against "cracks of doubts and indifference in the party rank and file," which would leave the "architects of reform weakened and isolated." Such a development was viewed as being "suicidal" in the "pragmatic world of politics." According to the declaration, "change has to be negotiated. It requires leverage and compromise, and these are best invoked from a position of strength" (Anthony 2004, 130–131).

The clearest contradictions in the SLP's project of neoliberal reform, however, had been manifested in the banana industry. As we have seen, the privatization of the banana industry was rationalized on the basis that the removal of political interference in the industry was essential to its economic recovery. It was also done on the basis that privatization would have resulted in the political empowerment of small banana producers and the economic democratization of the industry. However, the heightening of political infighting following the privatization of the industry fundamentally challenged these assumptions. Much of this political infighting was due to the continued application by the newly enfranchised owners of the industry of the political tactics that had been employed in an earlier context of marginalization. Thus the director of the SLBC, Patrick Joseph, failed to apply a "management" or "business" approach in his attempts to resolve various economic disagreements with the other players in the industry, such as WIBDECO. The most poignant illustration of this reality was his call to local farmers to engage in protest action to "shake WIBDECO off their backs." The response by WIBDECO was to perceive this as a threat "from a security point of view, which may be directed at our property and staff" (see *St. Lucia Mirror Online*, 5 November, 24 December 1999; 8 January 2000). The continued politicization of the St. Lucia banana industry in the early years of the SLP government, however, can be viewed as a consequence of the sustained economic and political marginalization of local producers and the global instability of the industry at the time. Thus the calls by local players for a reintroduction of governmental intervention can be viewed as a demand that was intended to arrest this process of marginalization or as a call for greater governmental resistance to global and extralocal sources of their economic marginalization.[15]

Finally, in assessing the contradictions of neoliberalism as they impacted the SLP in government, mention must be made of the continued discomfort of elements of the Old Left represented by George Odlum, and the SLP's shift to neoliberalism. Odlum used the 2000 budget debate to launch a stinging attack against the continued disillusionment of the party's supporters and society as a whole with the government's performance. An important basis of Odlum's criticism was that a general decline in the popularity of the government was evident despite an economic growth rate of 3.1 percent from the previous year (*St. Lucia Hansard*, Budget Debate 2000). Relatedly, Odlum noted the "serious . . . dichotomy between the Government's claim that it is working and performing more than any previous government had done and the mass disillusionment with the government for its nonperformance." Odlum observed that "it took the UWP thirty years to follow this graph of decline and it is almost inexplicable that this Government should race headlong down this road in three measly years after the brilliant record of performance we have heard from every speaker." Odlum noted that while the 2000 budget could be described as "clever," it "failed to address the central dilemma of the Government." At the heart of this dilemma was the question of "why should such a show of brilliant government result in the alienation of all the important sections of the community" (ibid.).

While there was a heavy dose of political opportunism in Odlum's attack on the leadership of Anthony and the performance of the SLP as a whole, the phenomenon of grassroots alienation despite macroeconomic growth resides at the heart of the failure of the neoliberal model, particularly when pursued by social democratic political forces. Indeed, one of the consequences of neoliberalism throughout the Caribbean has been its tendency to separate the objective of economic growth from the question of the economic and social advancement of the majority. Thus, while the SLP had achieved a growth rate of 3.5 percent between 1999 and 2000, this occurred alongside a process of economic marginalization of the small farmers in the banana-producing areas. Odlum's query about the contrast between the three-year rise and fall in popularity of the SLP with that of the thirty-year trajectory of the UWP touched upon the impact of global economic change upon domestic politics. Indeed, the thirty-year rise and fall in the popularity of the UWP had coincided with the period of the rise and fall of the banana industry. In contrast, the SLP had inherited the government in a context where the global framework that had sustained the banana economy had been eroded by the entrenchment of global neoliberalism. As a consequence, the issue points to the increasing limits in the ability of the small peripheral state to influence internal economic processes. By eroding the external economic environment in which the political system had been sustained, the process of global neoliberalism had rendered it difficult for the democratically elected SLP government to satisfy the aspirations of its electorate. It is in this context that the midterm fall in the popularity of the SLP, as well as its eventual defeat in the 2006 election, can be understood.

There were a number of related reactions to the budget that point to public dissatisfaction with the SLP. The Chamber of Commerce expressed dissatisfaction with the state of the economy despite a 3.5 percent growth. It conceded that there was "little to criticize about the budget itself" but noted that the "constant whispering among the business community" was that "the economy is at best, stagnant." Central to the Chamber's critique was that the business community and wider populace "may not be benefiting significantly from the growth in the economy." While the Chamber's stance might have reflected the business sector's historical hostility to the SLP, there was much validity in the Chamber's argument that the poor performance of the banana industry "may be the prime reason why the wider community and business sector have not shared much in the growth of the economy" (see *St. Lucia Mirror Online*, 7 April 2000, 1). The leader of the opposition, and the only UWP member of the lower house at the time, pointed to growing unemployment in the country following a series of closures by foreign-owned manufacturing enterprises in the months preceding the budget presentation (see ibid., 9). This gap between the government's perception of the "correctness" of its policies and the observations of growing dissatisfaction was a consequence of the privileging of the demands of global capitalism over the immediate needs of the national population. While the SLP government was sophisticated enough to present its neoliberalism as part of a project of popular empowerment, the wider population, confronting the reality of economic marginalization, held a diametrically opposite view of its actual circumstances.

The demands for affirmative action by the party's mass base further suggested dissatisfaction with the government. Central to the SLP's project of economic and political reform was the need to restructure the state-society relationship. This largely involved the imposing of an ideological shift upon the populace to reduce its dependency on the state. This was intended to create a context in which the state was unfettered by local expectations in its response to the pressures from the global environment. As such, the state's "besieged" and "beleaguered" condition (Bgoya and Hyden 1987) would have been partly overcome through a reduction in the demands on the state, effected through a process of state withdrawal. However, the continued demand by the party rank and file and the society as a whole for state intervention provides a clear indication that the ideological shift aimed for had not materialized, and popular expectations continued to reflect the assumptions of a strong, interventionist sovereign state. Thus, while the political leadership had identified openness to global economic dictates as a priority, the population continued to demand and expect protection from the global economic environment.

The politics of the new SLP therefore suggested a number of ways in which globalization lowered the expectations of the Left in the independent state as a tool for radical change. The SLP's recognition of the need for political reform was a tacit acknowledgment that the existing global environment was hostile to the institutions, strategies, and ideas that had earlier shaped the expectations of independence. Not only did the economic structures of global neoliberalism, such as the WTO, represent a challenge to the postcolonial economic development strategies, but the absence of global political alternatives further militated against the pursuit of the project as earlier defined. The main response of the Left was to abandon these objectives. Instead, greater emphasis was placed on the need to "consolidate" independent statehood as opposed to advancing it. This was to be achieved through a project of "political reform" that would allow the state more freedom to disengage from its nationalist objectives. One consequence of this was that it weakened the capacity of the domestic political sphere to influence internal economic relations. In this sense, the notion of the independent state as a buffer between the global and the local was no longer central to the SLP's approach.

In contrast, the SLP's goal of economic empowerment of the ordinary St. Lucian was pursued within a framework that highlighted the opportunities for all citizens in a context where the state reduced its involvement in economic activity. This marked a sharp reversal in the assumptions of the role of the state in the task of ensuring the economic and social development of the marginalized majority. The marginalization of the Left in the 1980s and the related increase in the power of global capital led to a fundamental rethinking of the assumptions of both the independence project itself and the role of the state in the fulfillment of that project. On this basis, the SLP developed the ideological notion that the challenges of the earlier independence project had been resolved. Such an ideological orientation was necessary in order to remove the necessity for state intervention from the political agenda. As such, it was an ideological construct consistent with the dictates of global neoliberalism.

While the SLP's approach might have worked for St. Lucia in the broad macroeconomic sense, the continued frustration by the SLP to win wide popular acclaim for its policies seemed to have realized Kenny Anthony's fear of being a "free market hero" who saved the economy but lost the election (see Anthony 2004, 144). Indeed, toward the end of the party's second term in December 2006, and despite the rapid transformation and modernization of St. Lucia from a banana-dependent economy to a largely services-based economy, the electorate was not sufficiently moved to allow the SLP a third term in office. One of the interesting features of the 2006 election was the return of John Compton, at age eighty-two, as leader of the UWP. The fact of his return, the public disaffection over the performance of the SLP, the hostility of the media, the ongoing call for change in response to the SLP's bid for a third consecutive term in office, and the tensions and insecurities surrounding the passage of the Labour Code all led to the SLP's defeat and the return of the UWP to the seat of office.

However, the election of the UWP did little to resolve the contradictions of the postcolonial state in the era of globalization. Indeed, the developments following the election suggested further erosion in the sovereign space and that the room for sovereign maneuvering was narrowing considerably. This was reflected most critically in a period of considerable confusion and uncertainty in the foreign policy of St. Lucia, where the new government controversially broke relations with China for the reestablishment of ties with Taiwan. What is significant in this development was not the breaking of ties in itself, but the narrow materialistic basis upon which the decision was taken, as well as the increasing influence of Taiwan in the domestic politics of St. Lucia once formal diplomatic relations had been established. In addition, the politics of the break involved intrigue and political machinations by a rebel gang within the cabinet led by the minister of foreign affairs, who was later fired by the prime minister for the act. The subsequent illness (and eventual death) of Compton following closely upon the cabinet revolt opened the way for the full surrender of the principle of sovereignty on the altar of material economic considerations.

CHAPTER 7

"Sovereignty for Sale"

Domestic Politics and International Relations in the Early Twenty-first Century, 2006–2010

The 2006 Election and Political Turmoil in St. Lucia

When St. Lucians voted the United Workers' Party (UWP) into office on 11 December 2006, they did so against a background of having witnessed a largely upheaval-free transition from an economy dependent primarily upon banana production to one based on tourism and services. Given this reality, the St. Lucia Labour Party (SLP) had contested the 2006 election on the basis of the SLP's managerial competence, its success in taking St. Lucia through the early pressures of trade liberalization and the onset of a globalized neoliberal economy, and its general success in achieving economic growth and political stability in one of the most difficult periods of economic change in St. Lucia.

Cognizant of the social fallout from the decline of the banana industry, the SLP government had placed a heavy emphasis on providing social safety nets and alternative employment for once-prosperous banana producers now facing the prospect of economic marginalization. The Poverty Reduction Fund (PRF), the Short Term Employment Program (STEP), and the Basic Needs Trust Fund (BNTF) to finance small work projects were intended to provide a degree of financial assistance to persons to cushion the impact of the production shortfalls in the banana industry. St. Lucia's involvement in the 2007 Cricket World Cup had ensured a construction boom as a number of incentives were offered for the expansion and building of new homes and residential properties, and this significantly cushioned the impact of the postbanana economic fallout. Further, a significant public-sector investment program assisted not only with providing a necessary Keynesian-type stimulus to the economy but also advanced the promised social modernization. A number of police and fire stations were either built or repaired, a new correctional facility was constructed to replace the old Royal Gaol inherited from the colonial period, several new fisheries complexes were constructed with the aid of the Japanese to modernize the fisheries sector, major highways were expanded and rehabilitated, and several secondary and primary schools were built, repaired, refurbished, and expanded as part of the World Bank Education Sector Enhancement Programme.

Further, as part of the program of social modernization, the SLP also ensured the realization of a program of universal secondary education, securing for the first time in the country's history an adequate number of secondary school places to absorb all students from the primary school system. Another major social program of universal health coverage through utilization of resources from the country's National Insurance (Social Security) system was being put through its pilot phase at the time of the 2006 general election.

In addition to its efforts at strengthening the social sector, the SLP was confident that it had democratized the political landscape of St. Lucia. During the SLP's term of office, despite the dislocations that had taken place in the banana industry, at no point were there any of the strikes, work stoppages, and other instances of civil unrest that had punctuated the political life of St. Lucia from the early 1970s to as late as the banana strikes of 1993. Under the Anthony administration, a culture of open discussion and public dialogue had taken root, with a number of independent radio stations airing popular call-in programs minus the official harassment that had characterized the UWP's response to the press immediately preceding and following independence under the Compton regime. Typical of this new democratic ethos was the fact that the official radio station, Radio St. Lucia, was put under professional management, and its news department was given a wide degree of editorial independence. In his own party as well, Anthony had introduced a series of "run-offs" or primaries through which party members could participate in choosing the candidates to contest elections on behalf of the party. In addition, Anthony had also introduced the practice of holding public consultations on major legislation and public reforms, as was seen in the case of the Labour Code and prior to the presentation of the annual budget.

Further, as part of his reading of the technical requirements for the challenges of the early twenty-first century, Anthony presented a slate of highly qualified and experienced individuals, many of whom had served in his cabinet in the previous two terms. One of the more notable of these candidates was the experienced regional technocrat Vaughan Lewis, who had served as prime minister of a UWP government following the first retirement of John Compton in 1996. The entry of Lewis into the SLP had emerged out of his increasing disillusionment with the quality of leadership within the UWP, but his formal exit from the party was hastened by the reemergence of Compton as leader of that party. Similarly, Julian R. Hunte, who had served as the leader of the SLP and leader of the opposition from the mid-1980s to the early 1990s, was also a candidate for the SLP following his period of service as president of the General Assembly of the United Nations. In Anthony's thinking, therefore, he was presenting to the voters a potential government and a unified party, in keeping with his commitment to the democratic advancement and economic development of St. Lucia.

Despite these developments, however, the 2006 general election resulted in the defeat of the SLP. While the previously examined contradictions in Anthony's adjustments to neoliberalism help to explain the UWP's victory, other compelling explanations can be found in the normal cycle of electoral renewal following two consecutive terms of SLP rule, the attrition in SLP support given charges of aloofness and arrogance of its leadership, the weight of unsubstantiated allegations of corruption and administrative lapses, and an upsurge in crime—in particular, homicides. The most significant, factor accounting for the UWP's success, however, was the return of John Compton as the party's leader. At the time of his reemergence Compton was eighty-one years old,[1] and a number of questions were raised about his physical and mental capacity to shoulder the burdens of leading a country and managing an economy in the postbanana era.[2] Nonetheless, the voters, in keeping with the Caribbean's historical attachment to messianic and charismatic leadership (see Allahar 2001), demonstrated a nostalgic affinity to Compton's aura as the "father of independence," the leader associated with St. Lucia's economic and infrastructural development in the postcolonial period, the "strongman" who had successfully retained political power for over three decades, and, most important, the individual most closely associated with the so-called banana revolution and therefore most likely to effect a return to its "golden age." While the SLP campaigned on the issues of Compton's history of authoritarianism and political high-handedness, his inability to meet and understand the challenges of a new technological era, and the uncertainties associated with his age and physical health, the voters confirmed their strong attachment to Compton's historical legacy and elected the UWP to office with eleven seats in the St. Lucia Parliament to the SLP's six.[3]

The general election in St. Lucia would set in motion a pattern of defeats of incumbents in several Caribbean Community (CARICOM) countries between 2006 and 2010 (see Barrow-Giles and Joseph 2008). Following the SLP's defeat in December 2006, the region witnessed the defeat of Perry Christie's Progressive Labour Party (PLP) in the Bahamas in May 2007, Portia Simpson's Peoples' Nationalist Party (PNP) in Jamaica in September 2007, Owen Arthur's Barbados Labour Party (BLP) in January 2008, Said Musa's People's United

Party (PUP) in Belize in February 2008, and Keith Mitchell's New National Party (NNP) in Grenada in July 2008.

The exceptions to this pattern within CARICOM occurred in Trinidad and Tobago, where the plural nature of the society along ethnic lines ensured the reelection of the Afro-dominated Peoples' Nationalist Movement (PNM) in 2007. However, the PNM was to fall from office in an ill-advised snap election in 2010, with a coalition (Peoples Partnership [PP]) government led by Kamla Persaud-Bissessar winning the government, confirming the pattern of incumbent defeat. In Antigua and Barbuda, Baldwin Spencer's United Progressive Party (UPP) held off a stiff challenge from Lester Bird's Antigua Labour Party (ALP) to retain office with a significantly reduced majority (see Table 7.1). Antigua's deviation from the wider pattern can be explained by the fact that the UPP had served only one term in office and therefore had escaped the attrition faced by other parties in the region that had enjoyed two, three, or even four terms in office.[4] However, the closeness of the UPP's victory provides evidence that the factors that had taken root in St. Lucia and the other Caribbean countries were also at play in Antigua and Barbuda. The other exceptions to the pattern occurred with the repeat victories of the St. Kitts Labour Party of Denzil Douglas, the Dominica Labour Party led by Roosevelt Skerrit, and the Unity Labour Party led by Ralph Gonsalves in St. Vincent. In these cases, the victories by the incumbents can be attributed to the weakness of the opposition parties and the high levels of state-led "pork barrel" strategies in the periods leading up to the elections in a context of high levels of clientelist politics.

Given the fact that the St. Lucian electorate, like voters in the rest of the Caribbean, appeared to have reduced their emphasis on the traditional issues of economic growth, infrastructural development, and increased employment opportunities, and had instead focused on the need for democratic renewal around the all-inclusive mantra of "time for change," this development appeared to suggest a degree of democratic maturation on the part of the electorate. However, while the shift to new democratic considerations can be seen as indicating advancement in the political development of the region, the unidimensional nature of the demand for change for its own sake suggests room for further democratic development in the region. One danger in this emphasis on change for the sake of change is the tendency to magnify the weaknesses of incumbents while the potential weaknesses of the government-in-waiting are significantly diminished or underplayed.

Indeed, this tendency appeared critical in determining the outcome of the 2006 election and, as will be seen later, played a critical role in the events that led to the reestablishment of diplomatic relations with Taiwan. Prior to the general election, one UWP candidate, Keith Mondesir, an optometrist, had pleaded

Table 7.1. General elections in the English-speaking Caribbean, 2006–2010

Country	Election Date	Winning Party	Previous Ruling Party
St. Lucia	11 December 2006	UWP	SLP
The Bahamas	2 May 2007	FNM	PLP
Jamaica	3 September 2007	JLP	PNP
Trinidad and Tobago	**5 November 2007**	**PNM**	**PNM**
Barbados	15 January 2008	DLP	BLP
Belize	7 February 2008	UDP	PUP
Grenada	8 July 2008	NDC	NNP
Antigua and Barbuda	**12 March 2009**	**UPP**	**UPP**
Dominica	**18 December 2009**	**DLP**	**DLP**
St. Kitts and Nevis	**25 January 2010**	**SKLP**	**SKLP**
Trinidad and Tobago	24 May 2010	PP	PNM
St. Vincent and the Grenadines	**13 December 2010**	**ULP**	**ULP**

Taken and adapted from Barrow-Giles and Joseph 2008. The **bold** print indicates the deviations to the pattern of incumbent defeat.

Note: UWP = United Workers' Party; SLP = St. Lucia Labour Party; FNM = Free National Movement; PLP = Progressive Labor Party; JLP = Jamaica Labour Party; PNP = Peoples' National Party; PNM = Peoples' National Movement; DLP = Democratic Labour Party; BLP = Barbados Labour Party; UDP = United Democratic Party; PUP = Peoples' United Party; NDC National Democratic Congress; NNP = New National Party; UPP = United Progressive Party; DLP = Dominica Labour Party; SKLP = St. Kitts Labour Party; PP = Peoples' Partnership; ULP = Unity Labour Party.

guilty before the Provincial Court of Manitoba, Canada, of violating the Private Health Information Act by disclosing his patients' personal health information to a third party (see Ombudsman of Manitoba 2002, 19–20). Another candidate, Guy Joseph, a bus driver by profession and president of the association of private bus operators, had admitted to paying himself a stipend from the association's funds as compensation for his loss of earnings in instances where he was called to attend meetings on behalf of the association. While this action was not illegal in itself, it did suggest a deviation from the traditional practice of volunteerism associated with the performance of such civic duties. Both of these candidates were elected to office in the 2006 election, and both were nominated to the cabinet as full ministers of government in the new administration. In addition, within the first six months of the new administration, two UWP parliamentarians, Edmund Estaphane and Marcus Nicholas, were arrested, on separate occasions, for traffic violations, and a third, Richard Frederick, the minister of housing, was arrested on an allegation of customs fraud (see *The Voice Online*, 22 January 2008).[5]

The most glaring instance of the process of political degeneration, however, was the appointment of Rufus Bousquet as the minister of foreign affairs in the new cabinet. Bousquet had been at the center of the events that had led to the fall of the UWP government in 1997, given his role in what became known as the "U.N. Fund Scandal" (see Phillips Commission Report 1995; see also Chapter 5). Bousquet's involvement in the scandal arose out of his receipt of a "U.N. salary" under false pretences, after claiming to be in possession of a university degree (Phillips Commission Report 1995, 77). He was subsequently fired from the cabinet for violating a "gag order" that Compton had placed on his ministers, barring public discussion of the matter. Given this specific history, Compton's appointment of Bousquet to the important and sensitive post of minister of foreign affairs ran counter to the expectations of good governance and democracy that the UWP had promised. While Compton's choice of Bousquet may be explained by the paucity of technical talent at his disposal, his decision was a further extension of his tendency to underestimate the importance of a sophisticated handling of international relations to the country's development. It also betrayed his historically weak sensitivity to the concept of sovereignty itself, in particular as it relates to the importance of presenting a face of self-respect and national seriousness to the rest of the world. He appeared to be unaware of the manner in which, by presenting a credibility-compromised Bousquet as St. Lucia's first contact with the rest of the world, he was weakening the effectiveness of St. Lucian sovereignty in elevating its standing within the global family of nations. The weakness of that decision would become even more glaring when Compton would subsequently fire Bousquet from the cabinet in his last official act as prime minister (see *Guyana Chronicle Online*, 9 June 2006), and when Bousquet would admit publicly, following a newspaper probe, that he had served time as a federal prisoner in the United States in the mid-1980s for passport fraud and grand theft auto while living in that country under the assumed name of Bruce Duane Tucker (see *HTS News Online*, 15 August 2007).

It is in this context of political confusion following the 2006 general election that the decision was made to switch diplomatic relations from China to Taiwan, an event that itself was to unleash further confusion and uncertainty in the political life of St. Lucia.

The Unfolding of the Taiwan-China Affair

When the UWP cabinet was sworn in on December 2006, one of the most pressing questions was the future relationship between St. Lucia and China. The early response of the UWP to this persistent question was to insist that the relationship with China would continue along the lines established by the deposed SLP. Indeed, at the swearing in of the cabinet the leading ministers clearly affirmed their commitment to a continued relation with China. The high point of this identification with China was reached when the minister of foreign affairs, Rufus Bousquet, agreed to accept an invitation to visit China. Following that visit, a memorandum of understanding was signed between China and Bousquet committing the two countries to continued relations and declaring St. Lucia's support for the "One China" principle (see *The Voice*, 5 May 2007, 4).

Despite these assurances, however, there were early and persistent signs of confusion in UWP policy toward China. While a number of ongoing projects in the country were being financed by China, several UWP parliamentarians criticized aspects of China's engagement with St. Lucia during the first post-election budget debate on 19 April 2007. One of the main targets for criticism was the practice of Chinese companies to employ large numbers of Chinese labor on local projects, a tendency that was seen as disadvantageous to St. Lucian workers. UWP parliamentarians also criticized China as being interested in large "show projects" as distinct from small community projects, which they claimed were more responsive to the needs of people at the grassroots level. While these claims are of little analytical value in themselves, they are important as an indication of a growing ideological hostility toward China by members of the UWP cabinet despite the official continuation of relations with China. Significantly, one of the leading anti-China voices in that budget debate was Bousquet, fresh from his visit to China.

In the period surrounding the 2007 budget, therefore, there was an increasing number of signs that the promises of continued relations were being reneged upon. Early reports of Taiwanese officials making quiet inquires into available properties for the setting up of an embassy proved discomforting to the Chinese and provided a clear indication that the UWP, or as later evidence would show, important factions thereof, had been favoring Taiwan at the expense of China.

While it is normal for cabinets to be split on issues both critical and minor, it would later shock the country, and indeed the wider Caribbean region itself, when information surfaced that the formal decision to establish relations with Taiwan had been taken without cabinet approval, and against the expressed wishes of the octogenarian prime minister, John Compton.

As it happened, Compton himself had been deeply divided about the decision on China. For historical-sentimental reasons he had felt indebted to Taiwan, since Taiwan had been one of the first countries to establish ties with St. Lucia immediately following its independence in 1979, and had had close relations with the UWP throughout that party's life in office. Indeed, in the middle of the election campaign reports surfaced that Compton had secretly met, in St. Vincent, with the Taiwanese president, who was visiting that country, despite the fact that the government of St. Lucia had no official relations with Taiwan.

While Compton had denied these meetings, the prime minister of St. Vincent, Ralph Gonsalves, had declared publicly that such a meeting had in fact taken place. Following Compton's meeting, the political leader of the SLP issued a statement alleging that Compton had received election funds from Taiwan and condemned the actions of Taiwan as interference in the domestic politics of St. Lucia. In a significant twist, following his visit to St. Lucia in January 2008 the president of Taiwan, Chen Shui-Ban, openly acknowledged that he had met with Compton in 2005 in St. Vincent and had discussed the question of resuming diplomatic relations in the event that the government changed (see *HTS News Online*, 17 January 2008).[6]

In addition, Compton's Cold War–era anti-Communism had meant that the Chinese were not his natural allies. Further, the establishment of ties with Taiwan was seen as an important act of distancing the policies of the UWP from that of the SLP, in a context where the UWP, after ten years away from the government, was eager to establish a new course for itself, independent of the trajectory set by the SLP. All of these factors made it difficult for Compton to ignore the pressure that he was no doubt under, from Taiwan and within his own cabinet, to reestablish St. Lucia's historical association with a province considered a renegade by China.

Nonetheless, there were some important factors that made it difficult for Compton to reject China. First and foremost was the inescapable political and economic reality of China's emergence as a leading player in the global economy. Compton, who had based much of his understanding of St. Lucia's sovereignty as residing in the country's potential and ability to extract developmental assistance from the leading economies, understood far more fully than his cabinet colleagues the importance of retaining the formal diplomatic relations that the SLP had established with China. A second consideration prevailing upon Compton was the scale and depth to which China had already committed itself to St. Lucia, with several projects in actual progress at the time of the election and with others anticipated in the future. Of critical importance was China's construction of a new psychiatric hospital, which was at an advanced stage of completion, and a promised cultural theatrical complex expected to commence immediately upon the hospital's completion. Compton was also aware of the implications for the image of St. Lucia were its diplomatic relations to be switched with every change of government. Given these realities, Compton could not be cavalier or overtly sentimental in arriving at his decision on the continued relationship between St. Lucia and China. Indeed, a leading public commentator and Compton confidant, Rick Wayne, would later declare that during this period of reflection, Compton had been advised by several leading regional prime ministers and technocrats on the importance of retaining diplomatic ties with China.

Whatever the explanation, Rufus Bousquet would later use Compton's vacillation on the issue as an excuse to explain his eventual decision to sign a memorandum of understanding on 30 April 2007 with his Taiwanese counterpart, effectively reestablishing diplomatic relations with that country (see *The Voice*, 3 May 2007, 1). At the signing were Bousquet and seven other elected cabinet colleagues, whose presence demonstrated their support for and complicity with the action. More notable, however, were those absent from the signing. The absentees included the leading and most senior of the elected members of the cabinet: the prime minister, John Compton; the deputy prime minister, Lennard Montoute; and Stephenson King, the only member of the cabinet to have served with Compton in earlier administrations and who would eventually emerge as prime minister following Compton's death. None of the nominated members in the cabinet had attended the signing, beholden as they were to Compton for their positions in the Senate and in the cabinet.

This development led to a rebuke of the government of St. Lucia from the Chinese ambassador, Gu Huaming. In a strongly worded statement, he accused the government of St. Lucia of interfering in the internal affairs of China:

> We are shocked by Saint Lucia Government's decision to resume the so-called "diplomatic relations' with Taiwan and by signing of relevant communiqué. It is known to all that there is but one China in the world, that the Government of the PRC [Peoples' Republic of China] is the sole legal government representing the whole of China and that Taiwan is an inalienable part of China's territory. The Taiwanese issue is China's internal affair. It concerns China's core interests, namely, its sovereignty, territorial integrity and reunification. China strongly opposes the development of any official relations with Taiwan by a country that has diplomatic relations with China. This is a clear and firm position of the Chinese Government, which is recognized and supported by the vast majority of countries. (*The Voice*, 3 May 2007)

Added to the rebuke of the Chinese ambassador was the voice of the leading international relations expert in the SLP, Vaughan Lewis, who identified several concerns with the switching of diplomatic relations to Taiwan. Arguing that while Taiwan was free to help St. Lucia in many ways and that "St. Lucia was free to accept" such help, it was "not acceptable, and can never be acceptable, that any assistance to St. Lucia from Taiwan, must only come at the price of diplomatic recognition of Taiwan as the true or legitimate China." Lewis also noted that while "none of us will deny that any sovereign country, including our small country of St. Lucia, can change its mind on any issue of international importance . . . a small country like ours will surely lose its self-respect if it appears to the international community to change its mind on this most important matter every weekend." Lewis also referred to the initial letter sent from the foreign minister to the ambassador of China, in which Bousquet had reconfirmed St. Lucia's recognition that "there is but One China." Lewis therefore urged the government to "reiterate its earlier statement" and to put a stop to the present situation in which St. Lucia was "being laughed at all over the Caribbean and . . . beyond." A significant argument raised by Lewis in his call for the return to the Chinese status quo was the fact that China was "a full member of the Caribbean Development Bank and the World Bank, and will soon be a member of the Inter-American Development Bank." Lewis warned that they would "sit in judgement on any loans that we seek from those institutions," and that "they will not be able to help us in our hour of need" (*The Weekend Voice*, 5 May 2007, 4).

Later events would show that Bousquet's group, "the super-eight" as they would later be described in popular parlance, had defied Compton's wish to place a halt on the process of formalization of diplomatic relations with Taiwan to allow for more reflection and discussion within the cabinet. Indeed, there appeared to be a degree of undue haste with which the communiqué was signed and the Taiwanese embassy formally opened.[7] According to Bousquet's version of events, however, his assurance in proceeding with the matter had been based on the decision reached by the cabinet on 26 April with the full agreement of Compton, three days before the formal signing of the memorandum of understanding with Taiwan. In contrast, there were clear indications that while such a decision had been taken, Compton, following further reflection, had specifically called for a pause pending deeper consideration of all issues by the cabinet. Despite Bousquet's protestations, it was clear that he and his seven colleagues had undertaken a palace revolt on the important question of the establishment of diplomatic relations with China.

Compton never recovered from their actions. On the very day that the decision was taken, he left for the United States for his annual medical checkup and suffered a severe stroke. What he left in St. Lucia was a severely torn and divided country and party, split over these political developments and angered by the events that had befallen Compton and the country. St. Lucia was immediately plunged into a period of uncertainty given that no discernible leader was identifiable within the ranks of the UWP cabinet, and given the centrality of Compton not only to the UWP's electoral success but also to the future prospects of the new administration. Later revelations by Rick Wayne would reveal deep divisions within the party and further add to the confusion in the county. Reading from a document purported to be written by Compton himself, and originally intended as an address to the nation, which was never delivered, Wayne asserted that Compton, prior to his illness, had intended to retain diplomatic relations with China and to explain his reasons for doing so (see *The Voice*, 5 May 2007, 1).

Compton's budget address would be his last public utterance to the people of St. Lucia. Upon his return to St. Lucia, a severely weak and frail Compton made his final public appearance at his office in the prime minister's official residence and summarily dismissed Bousquet from the cabinet. Any doubts over whether Bousquet had acted with the consent and concert of Compton had been publicly and comprehensively answered by his firing. Compton would eventually die on 7 September 2007, surviving no more than nine months into his final term as prime minister, leaving behind him a severely weakened and divided administration.

Sovereignty and Political Confusion After Compton

With the death of Compton, the stage was set for the full embrace of Taiwan. Following a series of hostile missives directed at the government of St. Lucia, the Peoples' Republic of China broke formal relations with St. Lucia and recalled its ambassador and key personnel, making St. Lucia only the twenty-fourth country claiming diplomatic recognition of Taiwan. In a farewell letter to the people of St. Lucia, Ambassador Gu Huaming reminded his readers that the "Chinese side had repeatedly expressed good wishes for the developing and deepening relationship between China and Saint Lucia ever since the UWP came to power." He stated that the UWP, "disregarding the solemn representations and opposition from the Chinese side," had "allowed Taiwanese personnel to stay in Saint Lucia and engage in activities jeopardizing relations between China and Saint Lucia." He noted with regret that St. Lucia had gone a step further to make an erroneous decision to resume "diplomatic relations" with Taiwan. He concluded his message with the hope that "the Saint Lucian people, sooner or later, will overrule the wrong decision of the government," and ended with the affirmation that in the long term, "the friendship between China and Saint Lucia is irresistible" (*The Weekend Voice*, 12 May 2007, 4).

Considering the broader Caribbean pattern where the few countries that had retained ties with Taiwan had progressively severed such links in exchange for ties with China, the developments in St. Lucia raised interesting questions about the motives, thinking, and priorities of the new government. While in 1969 Taiwan had full relations with sixty-seven countries, including the world powers of Western Europe and the United States, the general pattern was to switch relations to China, particularly in light of the rise of that country as one of the world's leading economies. By 2008, of the twenty-four countries that had ties with Taiwan, twelve were in Latin America and the Caribbean. Thus in the late 1990s into the early twentieth century, both Dominica and Grenada, which had maintained what had appeared to be beneficial ties with Taiwan, terminated those relations in exchange for the perceived greater benefits to be derived from association with China.[8] Prior to the UWP victory in 2006, only St. Kitts and Nevis, St. Vincent and the Grenadines, and Belize had remained as countries in CARICOM that retained ties with Taiwan. In each case where ties were established with China, the countries witnessed massive injections of capital-intensive infrastructural investments, developments that proved beneficial both to China and the host governments.

In St. Lucia, however, Taiwan would become involved in the domestic political life on a largely unprecedented scale. Almost immediately following the election, allegations surfaced that Taiwan had engaged in "dollar diplomacy" to facilitate its entry into St. Lucia. These allegations were not assuaged when Taiwan adopted an approach of giving financial support to "parliamentarians" for community projects, while by-passing the central government's consolidated fund. Instead, the practice of the Taiwanese was to invite parliamentarians to submit projects for consideration, and the monies were handed over directly to these elected members for implementation. This approach not only angered the opposition, who on several occasions demanded an end to the practice, but it also led to a scathing rebuke from the then minister of economic development, Ausburt d'Auvergne.

In a letter to the minister of finance and acting prime minister and the director of audit, Kenny Anthony, the leader of the SLP, expressed his concern that, according to his information, "funds allocated to each UWP member of Parliament amounted to US $1,000,000 with an amount of at least US $200,000 to be made available to at least three members of parliament and that these funds are for the purpose of undertaking political activities and small projects in each of the constituencies which the said parliamentarians represent." Anthony expressed concern that "such funds are being personally given to UWP members of parliament and that they are making what amounts to personal arrangements with specific individuals namely UWP supporters, for undertaking what are described as 'contracts' in the respective constituencies. Individuals are being paid directly by the Parliamentary Representatives." He noted also that he had "no indication that the Ministry of Finance or the Treasury are involved in the transmission of such funds, nor is there any indication that any institution of the Government of Saint Lucia is responsible for ensuring proper use of, and accountability for such monies as are being distributed." Anthony reminded the government that the "personal authorization of the UWP parliamentarian to specific individuals, and outside of due process, of the use of funds for works pertaining to government property (or property to be acquired by Government) without appropriate budgetary authority of a specific Ministry of government represents a breach of the use of public property, and is therefore an illegal act" (*The Weekend Voice*, 22 December 2007, 1–4).

While the Taiwanese ambassador, Tom Chou, would later refute the claims that he gave funds to UWP parliamentarians for use by each member "according their personal direction" (*The Weekend Voice*, 22 December 2007, 1), a later demand by the minister of economic development, Ausburt d'Auvergne, himself a member of the Senate and a Compton loyalist, that Taiwanese development assistance be paid not to individual parliamentarians but to the consolidated fund appeared to suggest the existence of tensions between the central government and the individual parliamentarians over the manner in which Taiwanese funds were being allocated, disbursed, and spent. What was clearly evident, however, is the fact that Taiwan's modus operandi in St. Lucia was contributing to the erosion of the authority of the central government, in a context where the cabinet was split over the foreign policy decision, and was contributing to the erosion of democratic accountability and transparency.

This approach by the Taiwanese in their diplomatic relations was apparently not unique to St. Lucia. A critical feature of Taiwan's global modus operandi involved the fostering of close personal ties between the Taiwanese leadership and other world leaders, particularly those in the third world, whose diplomatic support was being courted. This personalization of the diplomatic relations was reflected in the relationship that was being fostered between the Taiwanese president and, first, John Compton and, following his death, Rufus Bousquet and later Stephenson King. Within the first three years of the UWP's term of office, the Taiwanese president had visited St. Lucia one time, and, in turn, King had visited Taiwan on two occasions. This pursuit of a personalized approach to the forming of diplomatic relations had also been clearly seen in the case of Costa Rica, where in 2004 the country's former president and former secretary-general of the Organization of American States (OAS), Manuel Ángel Rodriguez, was arrested and, among other charges, was accused of receiving monies illegally from the government of Taiwan (see *Global Integrity Commons*, 5 May 2009).[9]

Despite these and other events suggesting a pattern of corruption in Taiwan's approach to international relations, its development of personal ties with selected members of the ruling establishment in St. Lucia was imperative in light of the delicate political situation in St. Lucia and in light of its global race with China for diplomatic recognition. Taiwan's approach in St. Lucia therefore ensured that it could continue to reward the ruling government's parliamentarians who had supported the breaking of diplomatic relations with China. Foremost among such parliamentarians was, of course, Rufus Bousquet, who, having been expelled from the cabinet, would have limited say in the allocation of Taiwanese funds had such funds been diverted to the consolidated fund. Bousquet would later embark on a campaign to drive the unelected d'Auvergne out of the cabinet and to have himself reinstated by threatening to withhold his support for King as prime minister. Acceding to his demands, King would relieve d'Auvergne of a cabinet position and reinstate Bousquet, effectively removing any residual internal opposition to Taiwanese domination of St. Lucia's political life.[10]

Under the leadership of Tom Chou, and with little resistance from within the UWP itself, the Taiwanese embassy would engage in a series of actions further diminishing the preexisting limited understanding of St. Lucian sovereignty. One of the tendencies of Ambassador Chou was to identify closely with the political aspirations of the UWP parliamentarians, immersing himself in the politics at the constituency level. One of the more glaring of such episodes was his decision to appear at a community football tournament, accompanied by the parliamentary representative for the area, personally handing over the winning prize money in cash and wearing the political colors of the ruling party. When invited by the media to respond to opposition allegations about the incident's implications for the level of Taiwanese involvement in St. Lucian politics, the ambassador's response was to blame his ignorance of St. Lucian culture, dismissing the negative public reactions to his role in the incident as unwarranted (see *Radio St. Lucia Online News*).[11] Similar incidents were to become a regular feature of Chou's tour of duty in St. Lucia, a reflection of the further deterioration of the protective hedge sustaining the sanctity of sovereignty in St. Lucia.

Nearly one year following the "football incident," the SLP would again demand that Ambassador Chou be recalled from St. Lucia for interfering in the country's internal political affairs. On this occasion the calls would come following the decision by the ambassador to attend a handing-over ceremony of a network of computers, intended as a "community learning center," but housed in the political office of a UWP senator and government minister. While the minister claimed that his office was open to the public, it was clear that the ambassador, emboldened by the tacit support for his activities from the leadership of the UWP itself, was operating in an environment that facilitated these basic sovereign violations (see *The Voice Online*, 26 March 2009).[12] For his part, the ambassador, following a denunciation of the action from his own foreign ministry, declared himself innocent of any wrongdoing on the grounds that he had merely been invited to the ceremony but was not responsible for determining the venue. He also denied any responsibility for the location of the computer center. Nonetheless, it was clear that Ambassador Chou was operating in an environment that was permissive cf his diplomatic tactlessness. The historical diminution of the importance of sovereignty as a tool of national defense against external interference, coupled with the deepening economic dependency of the UWP administration in the face of a morally and politically weakened political leadership and compounded by a deteriorating global financial situation, which will be discussed later, was being reflected in the actions of the Taiwanese ambassador.

In addition, Taiwan's approach to international relations was particularly suited to the situation in St. Lucia. Locked as Taiwan was in its need for recognition as an independent country, the small cash-strapped countries in Latin America and the Caribbean proved excellent allies to advance Taiwan's claims to statehood. Indeed, in the months after the election in St. Lucia, Taiwan itself would be facing a parliamentary and presidential election of its own in which one of the central issues was the allegation of corruption involving the government's bribery of foreign governments in exchange for diplomatic recognition. At the center of the allegations was the Taiwanese president, Chen Shui-Ban, who during his 2008 visit to St. Lucia created a minor scandal for handing out gifts of cash in red envelopes to leading public officials,[13] the most prominent of whom was the commissioner of police, who later returned the money to the Taiwanese embassy (see *HTS News Online*, 12 November 2008).[14] Further evidence of the reality of these tendencies as a central aspect of the foreign policy of the Taiwanese government under the administration of the pro-independence Democratic Peoples' Party was seen in the eventual arrest of Chen Shui-Ban on charges of corruption, bribery, forgery, money laundering, and illegal possession of state assets following the defeat of his party in the March 2008 presidential election and his eventual replacement by the nationalist president Ma Ying-jeou of the Kuomintang (KMT) (*The Guardian Online*, 12 November 2008; *Time Online*, 12 November 2008).[15] All of these developments suggest the centrality of the use of money in Taiwanese diplomatic politics and point to the very strong possibility of a similar approach being used in St. Lucia.

The historically diminished significance attached to sovereignty in the period leading to St. Lucia's independence had manifested itself in the lack of restraint shown by Taiwan in the manner in which it defined and conducted its relations with St. Lucia. By the middle of the UWP's term of office, an environment of dependency and subservience had been created between the government of St. Lucia and the government of Taiwan. It was a relationship in which the St. Lucia government demonstrated very little capacity or willingness to restrain the conduct of Taiwanese officials in the country, despite the implications of their actions for the sanctity of St. Lucia's independence.

St. Lucian Sovereignty and Independence in the Period of Global Neoliberal Crisis

It is clear from the earlier examination of the evolution and understanding of sovereignty and independence in St. Lucia that the specific issues surrounding the foreign policy undertakings of the UWP government were the logical culmination of this historical trajectory. Given the definition of St. Lucian sovereignty in the narrow terms of a vehicle for economic development, at the expense of other issues such as self-determination, freedom from external domination, and the advancement of domestic culture and national personality, the events in the early twenty-first century reflected the impact of the weakened application of independence and national sovereignty that Compton had championed. Ironically, however, as is often the case where the founder of a movement or ideology dies, a process of ideological degeneration was unleashed, and Compton's "limited sovereignty" was crudely adopted and applied by the generation that succeeded him. Compton's hesitation over Taiwan prior to his death, when compared to the crude and unbridled diplomatic carte blanche that his successors gave to the Taiwanese officials, is evidence of this process of ideological degeneration. Indeed, the sight of St. Lucia's prime minister, Stephenson King, using his allotted time at the forum of the sixty-second session of the U.N. General Assembly to make calls for the body's recognition of Taiwan (see *St. Lucia GIS Online*),[16] at the expense of more pressing domestic issues, was a symbolic, yet poignant, reflection of King's dependency on Taiwan and his opportunistic use of the instrumentality of sovereignty.

These developments cannot be fully understood, however, without understanding the domestic and global political-economic contexts in which they were unfolding. At the domestic level, these events were taking place in a context where a new government had been elected to office after ten years in opposition. Moreover, the one person who was effectively the glue that held the group together, and upon whose shoulders had been placed the responsibility of navigating the country through the early stages of government, had become incapacitated nearly four months into the new administration. In addition, the quality of the personnel in the government, their lack of experience, and their unpreparedness for the challenges of public life meant that the expected technocratic expertise and ideological and intellectual leadership to meet the challenges of managing a modern economy in the postbanana political economy was glaringly absent. The narrowness of the UWP election victory and the continuing strength of the opposition further contributed to the perception of the government as being beleaguered by its responsibilities and overwhelmed by circumstance. It can be argued that the entire period following the election of the new government was a period of continuous uncertainty, with the ruling administration demonstrating little ability to restore national confidence and to respond effectively to the basic challenges of governance and national development.

In this context the sanctity of national sovereignty was the earliest casualty. Taiwan, aware of the gaps in the technocratic ability of the government and facilitated by St. Lucia's dependency, pursued its relations with St. Lucia in a manner that resulted in further limiting the understanding of national independence as a bulwark against external control and interference, particularly in domestic political affairs. At the same time, the government, encountering significant difficulties in fulfilling its 2006 manifesto pledges and aware of the growing public disillusionment with its performance, leaned heavily on Taiwanese support, with little consideration given to the impact that such unbridled dependency was having on the public sovereign consciousness. The sovereignty of the country had in a very real sense been "sold" on the altar of economic dependency, political expediency, and moral degeneracy and infantilism at the highest levels of government. The insistence that sovereignty should only be used in the narrow sense of securing economic development, coupled with the absence of genuine technocratic expertise among the upper echelons of the government, in addition to the high doses of political opportunism on the part of the new ministers, meant that there was no alternative philosophy within the government to facilitate a more politically sophisticated use of the country's independence in a period of difficulty.

Events at the global level also contributed to the erosion of sovereignty in St. Lucia. The most significant of these events was the onset of the global economic crisis, which began to manifest itself around the middle of 2008, further compounding the governmental difficulties of the UWP. One of the first challenges for the UWP was managing the transition out of bananas that the SLP had set in motion. Part of the difficulty was of the UWP's own making given that throughout the 2006 election campaign, it had promoted itself as the "banana-friendly" party and had painted the SLP as the party that had destroyed the "green gold" that had sustained St. Lucia in the previous decades. Much ado had also been made of Compton's role as the historical champion of the banana industry. The UWP had campaigned on the promise of restoring the banana industry to its former glory, effectively lifting public expectations in this regard. However, the structural adjustments away from dependency on bananas that had been set in motion in the mid-1990s had been essentially a response to the process of liberalization occurring at a global level. There was little that Compton and the UWP could do to reverse these tendencies. The result was one of frustrated public expectations, which further diminished public confidence in the ability of the new administration.

While the banana industry had been decimated by global trade liberalization, the global economic crisis of mid-2008 and beyond was to have its greatest impact on the tourism industry, which had been developed and pursued as the alternative to bananas. The new government, amid the instability and political turmoil associated with its early transition to office, was confronted with managing the effects of a global economic recession, largely touted as the most severe to have hit the global economy since the Great Depression of the 1930s.

The origins of the global recession have been associated with a subprime mortgage crisis in the United States, which later translated to a broader crisis in the financial sector, manifested in the drying up of credit and the collapse of some of the leading banks in the global economy. Given the difficulties in obtaining credit, the crisis moved into the manufacturing and other productive sectors in the main centers of global capitalism. Mass layoffs soon followed, resulting in sharp drops in consumer credit and a further worsening of the problems in the credit and financial sectors. In a direct sense, these developments represent, to many, the beginning of the end of the global hegemony of neoliberal ideology and practice and the possible return of a global neo-Keynesian perspective (see Robinson 2004, 163).

For St. Lucia, these economic developments manifested themselves most directly in sharp drops in visitor arrivals, landing a telling blow to the mainstay of the economy. By early to mid-2009 the government was bombarded with pleas for support from the hotel sector. Led by the tourism minister, Allan Chastanet, who was from a hotel-owning family, the government's main concern was with mechanisms to "bail out" the tourism sector in the face of these economic difficulties. During this same period, a number of hotels announced layoffs in order to reduce expenditures in light of the sharp shortfalls in arrivals. Among the earliest was the Sandals chain, which, it should be recalled, had been vehemently opposed to the SLP's enactment of the Labour Code and had fired a number of workers in protest. By early 2009 it is clear that Butch Stewart's opposition to the Labour Code had not been sufficient to stave off the impact of the global neoliberal economic crisis. In December 2008 the hotel chain announced that 210 workers were to be laid off due to the impact of the global crisis on tourism arrivals (see *CANA News Online*, 12 December 2008).[17] A further round of public discontent was being set in motion.

At the macroeconomic level, these economic challenges severely hampered the ability of the state to act. In an ironic twist of historical fate, the UWP, like other governments in the Caribbean, found itself constrained in the use of Keynesian-type countercyclical interventionist measures at the very point when such measures were gaining ideological currency at the global level. The existing high levels of debt, coupled with the reductions in the availability of credit, meant that the government's option of "priming the pump" could not be readily pursued. It was only after the world's leading economies met in April 2009 in London at a summit of the G-20 countries that a decision was made to create mechanisms to make financing more readily available to third world countries in order to quicken the global economic recovery. An important element of this mechanism was the decision to "quadruple the financial capacity of the IMF [International Monetary Fund] to US $1 trillion to invigorate its involvement in helping to ease the crises afflicting developing nations with emphasis initially on the most vulnerable" (*Sunday Sun*, 26 July 2009).

Thus by mid-2009 St. Lucia and several other Caribbean countries, including Jamaica, St. Vincent and the Grenadines, and Dominica, had all announced their intentions to seek "emergency financial aid under the IMF's concessional funding arrangements, such as its Exogenous Shocks Facility" as a way out of their economic difficulties (*Sunday Sun*, 26 July 2009). This decision, however, did not come without a heavy dose of ideological conditioning to soften the public for this about-turn in the governments' stance toward the IMF. Regional governments, aware of Caribbean resistance to the "recolonization" tendencies of the IMF, attempted to paint this new embrace of the IMF in a positive light. The general argument was that there were no "conditions" attached to this new borrowing, and that the IMF no longer operated in the same manner as it had in the 1970s. Despite these claims, these developments represented a material shift in the economic independence of the governments in the region. Following the first blast of the 2008–2009 global economic crisis, by mid-2009 St. Lucia was set to continue its participation in the global economy in a condition of deepened dependency and with its sovereignty further compromised.

This environment of global economic instability compounded and deepened domestic challenges confronting the UWP government. Thus, despite a change of government and president in Taiwan, there was no immediate material change in the relationship between the two countries. While the new leadership of the victorious KMT had espoused a policy of positive engagement with China, no discernible shift in relations between Taiwan and St. Lucia was detected. Nearly four decades of the consistent pursuit of notions of inadequacy, smallness, and helplessness in the face of global realities had conspired to create a notion of St. Lucian sovereignty as a largely ineffectual tool. At the very least, St. Lucian sovereignty was understood strictly in the narrow economic terms of an instrument to be used to "buy" favors from friendly governments. It was a notion that had evolved from the period of the country's earliest battles against colonialism, when feelings of the country's smallness and lack of resources overwhelmed the alternative readings of sovereignty, which emphasized the right to self-determination and freedom from domination. With the return of the UWP under

Compton in 2006, there was very little shift in that party's understanding of sovereignty and its possibilities. Indeed, ten years in opposition at the height of globalization had meant that the UWP had very little understanding of the manner in which global adjustment had impacted upon its traditional understanding of the requirements for St. Lucia's development. For instance, the party genuinely believed that it could restore the banana industry to its former glory. Compton, in the early weeks prior to his illness, was firm in his conviction that his goodwill and links to Tesco, Sainsbury's, ASDA, and other British supermarket chains could secure the market for St. Lucian banana producers. In a similar way, Cold War notions of combating Communism factored very heavily in his party's vacillation on the Taiwan-China issue. Having promoted and defended a narrow and limited understanding of sovereignty throughout his political career, Compton left his party with no basis for pursuing an alternative framework at a time when new thinking was required. Perhaps the most tragic episode of Compton's political career is the fact that at the very point when global political events forced upon him the possibility of a new direction, he found himself deserted and betrayed by his own party. It was a challenge that came at a point when he was too weak, frail, and outmaneuvered to save his country and himself. Future developments and intellectual reflection in the decades to come will no doubt determine whether this error will prove minor, tragic, or fatal for the later development of St. Lucia.

Conclusion

The exploration of the independence experience of St. Lucia reveals that much of the politics revolved around tensions between the local demand for sustaining the economic and political objectives that had given rise to nationalism, on the one hand, and the imperative of adjustment to the largely external demands for adjustment of neoliberal capitalist hegemony, on the other. Central to the earliest impulse for national self-determination had been the issue of economic development and viability and the questions of internal political democracy beyond the historical experience of colonialism. These aspirations were largely seen in the politics of working-class nationalism in the 1950s and in the later expression of a reformist independence project in the 1960s. However, the prenationalist historical experience, coupled with the limitations of economic size, led to the articulation of a view of tentative anticolonialism and limited sovereignty as the dominant expression of nationalist aspirations in St. Lucia. This was reflected in the anxieties involved in transcending the constitutional status of Associated Statehood. It was also reflected in John Compton's internal economic policy, which was hostile to the interventionist state and which was geared toward facilitating the activities of external capital as a basis for economic development. It was also seen in Compton's narrow understanding of foreign policy, which essentially was reduced to retaining the friendship of the former colonial power and the dominant Western capitalist powers.

This narrowly defined understanding of postcolonial existentialism was rendered unworkable by the emergence of a global neoliberal order, which demanded further adjustments of the postcolonial state and a further narrowing of postcolonial possibilities. In this work, the origins of the emergence of the neoliberal order have been located in a period commensurate with the collapse of the Bretton Woods order in the mid-1970s. This fundamentally challenged the global structures, ideologies, and political-economic relations that had shaped the assumptions of the independence project and produced sharp tensions between the juridical and real powers of the state, and between internal economic and political objectives and external economic relations. An ideological perspective that was hostile to a radical framework of national sovereignty was therefore dominant. This reality, to a large extent, explains the political economy of St. Lucia in the 1970s and 1980s. The nationalist politics in St. Lucia in this period, in contrast to those of Jamaica, Guyana, and Grenada, was marked by the absence of a project of radical internal reform, and even of the mild anticolonial reformism evident in states such as Barbados and Trinidad and Tobago. This pattern was consolidated by the retreat of the St. Lucian Left in the period following the U.S. invasion of Grenada in 1983.

The defeat of the Left defined the independence project in St. Lucia in the 1980s, and the politics of the period was one in which the ideology of global neoliberalism became further entrenched. In practical terms, this was reflected in the reality of U.S. political, economic, military, and ideological hegemony in the region. In this context, Compton's notion of independent statehood enjoyed hegemonic status. This was also facilitated by St. Lucia's economic success due to a favorable international economic environment within which the banana economy was able to flourish. However, by the late 1980s the first challenges to Compton's deliberately carved notion of limited sovereignty began to manifest themselves, due largely to the political shifts in the global environment associated with the collapse of the Soviet Union and the end of the Cold War. The developments surrounding this reality were largely viewed within the Caribbean region as resulting in a process of marginalization. Within this context, the economic assumptions upon which the legitimacy of the "narrow" independence framework was based were rendered unsustainable.

The response among the Organization of Eastern Caribbean States (OECS) countries to these developments was to pursue a project of political unification, and an attempt was made to broaden the concept of St. Lucian sovereignty to include a subregional focus. In short, a stronger basis for the viability of St. Lucian sovereign statehood was being sought as a response to the process of marginalization. In the main, however, the narrow framework of sovereignty continued to shape both the external and internal relations of St. Lucia in this period. This partly accounts for the failure of the United Workers' Party (UWP) government to seek the necessary legislative instruments that would have made OECS political union a reality.

The process of "deepening globalization" of the 1990s fundamentally challenged postcolonial development assumptions. Most pertinent to the St. Lucian experience were the challenges to the external economic relations that had sustained the banana industry. Among the features of this process was the emergence of the World Trade Organization (WTO) with a powerful mandate to pursue the objectives of free trade. Given the importance of the banana industry in St. Lucia's economic development and as a determinant of internal political relations, deepening globalization posed a fundamental threat to the strategies that had defined St. Lucian independence. The threats to the banana industry undermined the link between the interests of the weaker sections of rural society and the broader goal of the economic development of the state. The disruption of this link explains the conflict between the state and small banana producers in the early 1990s. This development also led to the defeat of the UWP in the general election of 1997.

These challenges continued to persist despite the huge popular mandate enjoyed by the St. Lucia Labour Party (SLP). The main weakness of the SLP during its two terms in office (1997–2006) was its failure to devise a strategy that could effectively reestablish the link between the sovereign ambitions of the state and the economic advancement of the domestic population. Throughout the period of the SLP in government, the impact of globally hegemonic neoliberalism significantly militated against the realization of such an objective. Indeed, the SLP's neoliberalism effectively increased the capacity of global capitalist economic relations to influence the internal economic relations of the society. Central to the SLP's project was a retreat by the state from activities that had previously occupied a central place in governmental activity. Typical of such a retreat was the party's policy in the banana industry. One of the positive features of the industry prior to the neoliberal challenge was its inclusion of a large number of small farmers in the economic and political decision-making structure, through the St. Lucia Banana Growers' Association (SLBGA). In contrast, the SLP's project of commercialization witnessed the economic and political disenfranchisement of the majority of the producers in the industry. A related policy of economic neoliberalism in other sectors of the economy resulted in a gradual but perceptible challenge to the party's neoliberalism within the wider society. Thus, despite the attempt by the SLP to create wider spaces for democratic expression and participation in the society, its concessions to global neoliberalism resulted in huge gaps between popular expectations and the party's perception of its activities as progressive. The persistence of this contradiction between governmental administrative success and popular disillusionment was a critical factor in accounting for the defeat of the SLP in December 2006.

These contradictions, however, deepened and widened in the twenty-first century under the UWP government, led first by John Compton and, since September 2007, by Stephenson King. A critical factor in widening these contradictions is the reality of a global economic recession, which in scale, intensity, and duration has drawn comparisons to the Great Depression of the 1930s to 1945. Compounding these difficulties was the reality of political instability in the wake of the death of Compton, who had led St. Lucia from 1964 and through nearly all of its years as an independent state up to 1996, and also during 2006 and 2007. Coupled with the evidence of political inexperience and the absence of technical training and know-how by its key leaders, a framework for continued political error and degeneration was established in St. Lucia in the middle of the global recession. Between 2006 and 2010, St. Lucia experienced a measure of political turmoil that it had not seen in the previous twenty years. It had witnessed the death of a prime minister, the arrest of three ministers of government, revelations of a criminal history of one senior minister, the instability of a cabinet revolt against a sitting prime minister, a long and disruptive strike in the public sector, and an unprecedented upsurge in crime, particularly drug-related homicides. By the end of 2010 the new government had not resolved any of the structural factors that had resulted in these developments, signaling the strong likelihood of continued instability.

It is in this context that the political noises surrounding the establishment of diplomatic relations with Taiwan were isolated for examination in this work. The central argument raised in examining the China-Taiwan affair was that the episode represented the culmination of the narrowly defined understanding of sovereignty and independence that had been consciously advanced by the sections of the political class that had led the independence movement and had responsibility for determining the direction of the postcolonial state.

The fundamental assumption of this tentative anticolonialism was to emphasize the "weakness" and "vulnerability" of the St. Lucian state, and, on the basis of this interpretation of "helplessness," to pursue a policy of dependency and mendicancy as the key feature of its international relations. A critical weakness of this approach, however, is that alternative possible formulations of the state as an instrument of development, resistance, and democratic and economic empowerment of the national citizenry is avoided. In addition, the interpretation of "helplessness" becomes a permanent feature of the country's international existence. Thus Compton pursued his notion of limited sovereignty sans modification throughout every stage of his leadership—from the period of nationalist ferment, to the period of independence, and into the period of heightened neoliberalism in the 1990s. The embrace of Taiwan as the "savior" of St. Lucia in the early twenty-first century was thus a logical consequence of this narrow interpretation of the possibilities of independence.

The most important factor militating against the unmitigated application of notions of limited state interventionism and participation in domestic economic and social life has been the continued resistance of the people and their insistent demand for an alternative approach. The presence of mass resistance to dependency was seen at every stage of the independence experience examined in this work. It is widely accepted that the period of the 1930s to the 1950s, with its heightened level of political agitation, gave birth to the modern Caribbean as it exists today in terms of its political culture, institutions, and internal and external political relations. This period of political agitation had come about as a popular response to the economic conditions of the Great Depression. With the approach of the second decade of the twenty-first century, as economic indicators approximating those of the Great Depression begin to emerge, it is not far-fetched to assume that another round of postcolonial political agitation is on the horizon. It is therefore expected that the timid and limited understanding of the independent state as an instrument of economic and political empowerment of the mass of the population will come under scrutiny, as the economic and social conditions give rise to political agitation and deeper reflection in St. Lucia.

A Normative Word:
The Anglophone Caribbean State in the New Global Economy

It is in this context that possible responses by Caribbean states to neoliberal globalization and economic crises can be considered. One of the first and obvious issues that will and should occupy intellectual attention is the need to ensure the economic viability of the Anglophone Caribbean sociopolitical space in a period of global economic and political dislocation. A second is the need to ensure that the internal politics of the state reflect the privileging of domestic economic and political aspirations over the demands of global capitalism. In short, any normative reflection on the future of the postcolonial Anglophone Caribbean state must seek to connect the present role of the state with the aspirations that had shaped the nationalist project in its earliest incarnation. In this regard, three possible options continue to impose themselves as logical responses to the current impasse. The first possibility is the pursuit of a strategy of regional integration among territories of the Anglophone Caribbean. The second involves a deepening of the democratic system within Caribbean societies. A third and more general prescription recognizes the need for Caribbean political activists to connect with the new social protest movements that have taken root at the core of the global capitalist system as the crisis of capitalism continues to awaken the consciousness of new generations of humankind. These considerations assume even greater urgency in the context where the previous champions of neoliberalism have been resorting to Keynesian responses in light of the failure of the global failures of neoliberalism.

These prescriptions are, of course, guided by a normative orientation that is sympathetic to the independence of the Caribbean postcolonial states and the national self-determination of its peoples. It is an orientation that identifies the strengthening and perpetuation of the nationalist project as an important basis upon which the impact of global economic relations on the internal realities of

Caribbean societies can be mediated. In this regard, the prescriptions reject the assumptions of global neoliberalism, which are generally hostile to the barriers placed by state-level processes upon the activities of global capital. These prescriptions, while ideologically delegitimized in the period of neoliberal hegemony in the years between 1980 and 2007, are now being positively reexamined in the wake of the global economic crisis of 2008. For example, many of the strategies that had earlier defined the Caribbean independence project, such as the nationalization of the "commanding heights" of the economy, which had been rejected since the mid-1980s, are now being reexamined in light of the threats to jobs, livelihoods, and the national economy as a whole, as the global economic crisis continues to deepen. However, the Caribbean states' political responses to the twenty-first-century crisis of neoliberal capitalism must be undertaken, not on a fixed ideological basis, but from a perspective of Realpolitik. In other words, the responses must issue from a sober recognition of the existing capacity of hostile global (and domestic) forces eager, able, and willing to defeat these nationalist objectives. As opposed to making a "fetish" of any specific strategy, it is therefore far more instructive to focus on why these strategies emerged in the first place. This offers far greater insight than is provided by a focus on what these strategies should be. It is in this spirit that a response by Caribbean states to globalization, in the period where neoliberalism has "lost the vitality of its youth," can be constructed.

Notes

CHAPTER 1. CONCEPTUAL ISSUES

1. The tendency to oscillate between a positive and a negative evaluation of nationalism is clearly evident within Marxism (see Davis 1978). Blaut (1987, 40–41) observes that after the First World War had destroyed the "internationalist" orientation of Marxism, two competing tendencies emerged. One was Lenin's, in which nationalism was seen "as a central feature of imperialism," and the other was Luxemburg's, in which nationalism was denounced as inevitably "reactionary" and overwhelmed by global imperialism (Davis ed. 1976, 289). Thus, according to Blaut (1987, 41), "Marxists were debating the issue of the decline of national states and national struggle nearly seventy years ago. And they are doing so still."

2. In *Latin America and Global Capitalism*, Robinson moves from the task of a general description of global capitalism to a specific account of the Latin American experience. In this work, I present a specific account of the St. Lucian experience. As neoliberal globalization unfolds, similar efforts will be necessary to capture the various domestic experiences of the Caribbean states.

CHAPTER 2. TENTATIVE ANTICOLONIALISM

1. For an account of the 1930s labor revolts in the Caribbean, see Bolland (1995), Hart (1989), Post (1978), and Lewis (1977). Most of the accounts suggest that their expression was relatively mild in St. Lucia (see Bolland 1995, 78–81; Lewis 1977, 21–23).

2. As late as 1963 St. Lucia surpassed only Montserrat among the territories of the Anglophone Caribbean in terms of GDP per capita (O'Neal 1964, 941).

3. The coal industry was established in St. Lucia in 1863. Given the island's strategic location and natural harbor, Port Castries became an important refueling station. Romalis (1968, 39) reports that between the 1880s and 1920, the coal industry brought in over half of the island's income, with as many as 1,000 ships per year calling at Castries.

4. This was due to the reduced reliance in St. Lucia upon foreign exchange to cover food imports as a result of the high level of domestic food production and consumption in the territory.

5. Allusions to the "feudal" aspects of plantation society were found in a number of colonial reports. One report described the owner of the Dennery sugar estates, Denis Barnard, as "living in a world which vanished many years ago, and . . . [he] retains the outlook and behaves in a manner which is feudal in the extreme, and which cannot possibly continue to exist in the West Indies as they are today without causing disaster" (PRO 1031/2809, 1 May 1957).

6. This was widely recognized by the political class in St. Lucia. A Colonial Office security report records George Charles during a strike in 1957 claiming that St. Lucia "was now going through the same experience of the other West Indian islands in 1937" [*sic*] (PRO-CO 1031/2808, 4 April 1957).

7. The mass following of this movement sprang largely from sugar plantation workers and small rural landholders. In a sense, therefore, the social context in which the movement emerged does not fit classical descriptions of the "working class." However, I use this designation largely because of the trade union origins of the movement. It was also the description utilized by the leaders of the movement (see Charles 1994).

8. The *Workers' Clarion* was the organ of the SLCWU and the SLP.

9. Reference here is being made to the West Indian Federation, which existed between 1958 and 1962.

10. The SLP emerged as the political party of the working-class nationalists in 1949 (Kunsman 1963, 609), on the eve of universal adult suffrage in 1950. Typical of the wider Caribbean experience, its popular base came from the SLCWU. Members of the professional middle class, such as Allen Lewis, played prominent roles in the party during this period.

11. Brown was expelled from the Legislative Council for being an undisclosed bankrupt in his native Bermuda. He was subsequently deported from St. Lucia, despite having lived there for nearly twenty years. There is evidence to suggest that the British authorities were uncertain about the legality of their actions with respect to Brown's deportation (see PRO CO 1031/1528, 29 January 1954).

12. The results of the federal elections proved a shock to the West Indies Federal Labour Party (WIFLP), which won twenty-two out of a possible forty-five seats. The more conservative Democratic Labour Party won twenty, while independents gained three seats (see Mordecai 1968, 86).

13. This tendency is clearly revealed in a letter written to Eric Williams by the representatives of the local propertied class, which berates the premier of Trinidad and Tobago for not sending troops during the 1957 sugar strike. They contended that "if the conclusions to be drawn from this are that, under the federation, the smaller islands are to be deprived of protection in cases of emergency, the outlook is indeed ominous" (Chase et al. to Eric Williams, 17 May 1957).

14. This linkage between federation and sovereignty was the central theme of the various conferences, dispatches, and technical papers devoted to the question of West Indian federation in the 1940s and 1950s (Cmnd. 7120 [1947]; Cmnd. 7291 [1948]; Col. 218 [1948]; Col. 255 [1950]; Cmnd. 8895 [1953]; Cmnd. 8837 [1953]; Cmnd. 9618 [1955]; Cmnd. 9733 [1956]; Cmnd. 804 [1959]).

15. This had been raised in the British House of Commons as early as 1922 as an argument against the recommendations of E. F. L. Wood (later Lord Halifax), who had chaired the Wood Commission: "the Honourable Gentleman considers Dominica is suited for self-government, but that Antigua, Montserrat and St. Kitts are not.... He points out that in St. Kitts there are big plantations ... with labourers. The planters object.... The Colonial Office is not there in order to protect vested interests and to get cheap labour for employers" (British HC Sessional Papers, 4 July 1922, 239).

16. Of the three presidents of the SLCWU who served before 1945, R. G. H. Clarke, Henry Belizaire, and Charles Augustin, only Augustin can be considered, by virtue of his occupation as an agricultural laborer, to be of the working class.

17. The bill was opposed on the grounds that "there had been no labour riots in St. Lucia" (SL Leg. Coun., 14 June 1938, 2).

18. Following the 1957 strike, the trade union leaders in the Executive Council were forced to make declarations of loyalty to the government and to distance themselves from the violence of the strike. In a clear act of intimidation, the administrator warned the ministers of the need to resign from office "if they were not openly and unequivocally on his side ... if a state of emergency

were declared" (PRO-CO1031/2809, 22 April 1957). Union leaders were required to resign from their trade union posts once they had been selected to the Executive Council.

19. The NLM was short-lived. It later merged with the PPP to form the UWP.

20. Compton denies a class orientation to the party and sees its raison d'être as lying in the greater focus on nationalism. In his view, "the trade unionists lagged behind the nationalist movements" in that their main objective was "getting an extra penny a day for the workers" (Compton, interview).

21. Compton's UWP rose to power following the resignation of two members of the SLP cabinet, J. M. D. Bousquet and Allan Bousquet, in 1964. On 29 March 1964 Compton's NLM, along with the Bousquet brothers, joined the PPP to form the UWP. Largely supported by small banana producers, the UWP emerged as the dominant political force in St. Lucia in the 1960s and 1970s.

22. As will be seen later, Geest had kept his plans to convert St. Lucia to total banana production hidden from the government. He had promised the government that sugar production would continue alongside bananas.

23. The "Little Eight" was an organization comprising the smaller territories of the Eastern Caribbean, which, unlike the larger states of Jamaica, Trinidad, and Guyana, were widely perceived as unlikely to sustain sovereignty unilaterally. It was an attempt to salvage a federal framework following the collapse of the larger federation. With the eventual independence of Barbados in 1966, the "Little Eight" project came to an end. Arthur Lewis places a significant share of the blame for the failure of the federation on Compton, whose freshness, according to Lewis, meant a reduced commitment to the decisions that had been painstakingly arrived at before his emergence (see Lewis 1973). This sentiment is also shared by Hunter Francois and Earl Huntley (interviews).

CHAPTER 3. THE POLITICS OF ST. LUCIAN DECOLONIZATION

1. As late as 1972 Compton had envisaged independence via a federal framework. Referring largely to Grenadian independence in 1974, Compton argued that his shift toward unilateral independence was the result of frustration, "like a jilted bridegroom at the altar," at the advances toward independence by prospective federal partners (*The Voice*, 22 April 1976, 1; SLP 1978, 8–9; Compton, interview). The abandonment of the federal objective was strongly opposed by a section of the political class, most vocally represented by Hunter Francois, who resigned from the UWP in the mid-1970s (see *The Crusader*, 20 April 1974, 1; *The Voice*, 13 May 1976, 2). Francois continues to insist that "our failure to go into independence jointly . . . struck a blow from which I don't see us recovering at all" (Francois, interview).

2. Following the failure of the West Indies Federation, Caribbean leaders shifted the focus to economic union. From 1968 features of CARIFTA were established and later formalized under a treaty of 1973 into CARICOM, a loose common market agreement among twelve Anglophone Caribbean territories (see Eckstein 1978, 8–9).

3. Under the European Association Policy, the Associated States as U.K. dependencies were associated under Part IV (Article 136) of the EEC treaty (Thomas 1987, 157).

4. Sixty percent of St. Lucia's import trade was outside the U.K. area and payable in U.S. dollars (SL Budget 1975, 3).

5. In 1974 the manufacturing sector comprised fifty enterprises employing 1,000 workers. This low level of industrial development forced the government to rely on foreign capital in the establishment of export-oriented, labor-intensive enterprises (GOSL National Development Strategy 1977, 29–30).

6. The Lewis model of development emerged out of an influential body of work produced in the 1950s by St. Lucian Nobel Laureate W. A. Lewis. His prescriptions for industrialization of underdeveloped countries heavily influenced political practice in the Caribbean. The basic premise of the Lewis model held that since the formerly colonial world lacked domestic savings, managerial expertise, and technical knowledge, the early phase of their industrialization development could be effected through special incentives to attract foreign capital. Lewis's "industrialization by invitation" model played a key role in Compton's development strategy in St. Lucia.

7. The president of the SLTU at the time and the main spokesperson on these issues was Kenny Anthony, who would lead the SLP to electoral victory in 1997.

8. Compton's foreign policy received wide support from the propertied class. *The Voice* described it "as an emphatic rebuff to those who have been advocating a brand of socialism for St. Lucia, similar to that of Communist Cuba," and argued that Compton's foreign policy was "on the level" with the St. Lucia Chamber of Commerce, whose president, Ornan Monplaisir, had described capitalism as "the only system that attracts our attention" (*The Voice* [Independence Supplement], 19 February 1979, 21).

9. Hunter Francois, who had served as a deputy premier to Compton, had sought to distance himself from UWP hostility to the Forum. He argues that he "had spoken in favor of what they were doing" and believed that "they had made a serious contribution to political thinking in St. Lucia" (Francois, interview).

10. In 1973 an able-bodied man on the Geest estates received 40 cents per hour, or EC$3.20 per day (Stoby Commission Report 1973, 5).

11. This organization had been largely inactive prior to its takeover by Odlum and his satellites. Following the failure to gain recognition for NOW, the Farmers and Farm Workers' Union provided a convenient vehicle through which Odlum continued his struggle against the Compton regime.

12. Peter Josie had risen in the executive of the Seamen and Waterfront Workers' Union, while Calixte George led the Civil Service Association (CSA).

13. The claim that the SLP radicals opposed independence is, and was at the time, strongly denied. However, as subsequent discussion will show, this charge is largely vindicated.

14. The full extent of Odlum's militaristic intentions later emerged in 1983 when "two Western intelligence sources" alerted Compton to the fact that a number of Odlum supporters were to receive military training in Libya (see *Caribbean Insight*, September 1983).

15. Equally sinister was the use of electoral manipulation by the UWP regime during the 1974 general election to retain political office. This charge has been the subject of much political speculation (see Wayne 1977), but was confirmed in a reliable study (Midgett n.d., 1983, 143–146). One indication of electoral manipulation was the huge disparity in enumeration levels between the 1974 and 1979 elections. The more accurate enumeration procedure in the 1979 election was due largely to British involvement in the process. Under pressure from the SLP for allowing independence under Compton, the British government closely monitored the electoral process. There was also an instance of a deviation in one particular ballot box from the voting pattern in a particular constituency after a second count (see Midgett n.d., 16).

16. Odlum served as minister of trade, industry, and foreign affairs in the SLP administration.

17. At the time, the St. Croix refinery was the largest oil refinery in the world, producing 700,000 barrels of oil a day and employing 1,300 people and contracting 1,700 U.S. workers (*Multinational Monitor*, April 1981, 1).

18. In an ironic twist of fate, the Amerada-Hess license became up for renewal in 2007. The country was denied an opportunity to see how an SLP administration would have handled the

negotiations since the SLP had lost the general election in December 2006, mere months before the old agreement was due to expire. The new UWP administration, led by an ailing eighty-two-year-old John Compton, signed a new agreement, which made no new demands upon Amerada-Hess for its continuation.

19. At the time of the declaration, the CECS was a loose confederation of the former and existing Associated States that shared a number of key institutions. These included "a common currency, the East Caribbean [EC] dollar; a common currency board, the East Caribbean Currency Authority, later upgraded to a central bank; and economic cooperation arrangements in the East Caribbean Common Market (ECCM)," as well as limited joint diplomatic representation abroad (Lewis-Meeks 1991, 44). These arrangements were formalized via the OECS treaty of 1981 (see OECS 1981). The original parties to the treaty were Antigua, Dominica, Grenada, Montserrat, St. Kitts and Nevis, St. Lucia, and St. Vincent and the Grenadines.

20. The formation of a regional defense force was a reaction to the Grenada revolution and to the leftward swing in the Caribbean as a whole.

21. Reeve (1999), in a related study, has suggested that Halliday's third period of structural realignment was when the microstates like St. Lucia that had been left behind by the first wave of universal decolonization were able to move into independent statehood.

22. This project was formalized in 1985 with the formation of the Caribbean Democratic Union (CDU). Launched by Edward Seaga, with the backing of the United States and strongly supported by Eugenia Charles of Dominica, the CDU was aimed at fomenting anti-Communist sentiment in the Caribbean (*Caribbean Insight*, January 1986, 1).

23. According to the commission, Geest Industries was one of the five largest growers on the island (Thomson 1987, 71).

CHAPTER 4. ST. LUCIA UNDER GLOBAL NEOLIBERAL HEGEMONY

1. Among the more beneficial features of Lomé I were "free access, without reciprocity, to the European market for goods exported from the ACP [Africa, Caribbean, and Pacific states]; a stabilization scheme (STABEX) to compensate ACP states for a reduction in export receipts for their principal primary products; and financial aid for the ACP" (Long 1980, ix).

2. The term "more developed country" (MDC) continues to be a misnomer in the context of Anglophone Caribbean political economy. It was used in the early 1960s and 1970s to distinguish the larger states of Guyana, Jamaica, Trinidad, and Barbados (because of economic size) from the smaller, semicolonial territories of the Eastern Caribbean, the less developed countries (LDCs). However, the strong economic performance of the Eastern Caribbean states, coupled with the economic decline of the MDCs, has rendered these historical distinctions nebulous.

3. Eight Caribbean states share a common currency, the EC dollar, administered under the unified central banking authority of the East Caribbean Central Bank (ECCB), based in St. Kitts (rate of exchange U.S.$1 = EC$2.70). These are Anguilla, Antigua and Barbuda, Dominica, Grenada, St. Kitts and Nevis, St. Lucia, St. Vincent and the Grenadines, and Montserrat.

4. One of the most prominent of these institutions was the Caribbean Association of Industry and Commerce (CAIC). Its revitalization was celebrated as a "counteroffensive" measure designed to overcome the defensive posture into which the regional private sector had been placed as a result of the activity of the "pseudo-radical intellectuals of the various university campuses" (see Blackman 1984, 29).

5. One local trade unionist pointed to a letter written in *The Voice* of St. Lucia by Edward Rock, a member of the executive of the UWP, as an indication of the manner in which the

pressures of the CBI shaped the thinking of the government. The letter claimed that government should seek to regulate wages since potential investors would need to know in advance the size of their profit margins before committing themselves to St. Lucia (Poyotte, interview).

6. They included Vere Bird of Antigua, Tom Adams of Barbados, John Compton of St. Lucia, Eugenia Charles of Dominica, Edward Seaga of Jamaica, and James Mitchell of St. Vincent and the Grenadines.

7. The GFS was an arm of the Ministry of Communications and Works concerned with repairing government vehicles and involved in minor road repair.

8. The average pay of a female worker in St. Lucia's EPZs was EC$60.00 per week (EC$1.00 = U.S.$0.37) (Kelly 1986).

9. "Roro" is a St. Lucian term that refers to quarreling, disturbances, or any noisy disagreement.

10. While the meetings were dubbed "constituent assemblies," their task was not to write a constitution but rather to serve in a "consultative" capacity (OECS n.d., 3).

11. Martinus Francois, an attorney, held the dissolution of the SLBGA board ultra vires. He believed there was little "evidence to support any fault or default on the part of the board or its chairman" to justify his sacking. He argued that in 1988, "a new banana production and earning record was set under the chairmanship of Mr. Gajadhar" (Francois 1996, 96). Francois maintained that Compton's involvement in the dissolution of the SLBGA board had violated the "fundamental legal principle that in the exercise of a statutory discretion a Minister must bring his independent judgement to bear" (ibid., 96–97).

12. SCOPE was a regional grouping of opposition parties formed to coordinate the response to the unification initiative. It was originally an acronym for Standing Committee of Opposition Parties of East Caribbean States. It was later changed to Standing Conference of Democratic Parties of the East Caribbean States (see P. Lewis 1999, 52).

13. Regional opponents of the initiative described it as the "Organization of Eugenia, Compton and Son" (see *Caribbean Insight*, July 1987, 7).

14. Two general elections were held in April 1987, the first on 6 April and the second on 30 April. Dissatisfied with a one-seat majority of the first election, Compton dissolved the house on its first sitting and called for fresh elections in the hope of attaining a more positive mandate.

15. Compton's one-seat majority was shortly increased. This was facilitated by the crossing of the floor of a former leader of the opposition, Neville Cenac.

16. It was also the case that a two-thirds parliamentary majority was required before any substantial amendments could be made to the St. Lucian constitution (Lewis 1988b, 17).

17. Among the factors accounting for the rapid reversal of SLP fortunes were the reorganization of the SLP under the leadership of Julian Hunte and the failure of the PLP to sustain the momentum of its 1982 electoral showing. With the electoral marginalization of George Odlum, the SLP had stabilized to a more centrist position of the political spectrum.

CHAPTER 5. DEEPENING GLOBALIZATION AND THE UNMAKING OF THE POSTCOLONIAL ORDER

1. These special arrangements were not a result of mere altruism. Grossman (1994) has noted a number of reasons why a pattern of protectionism emerged as a feature of British-Windwards relations. Included among these were concerns about the cost of aid. Also, these special marketing arrangements rebounded to the benefit of Geest Industries, which was itself a British company.

2. These were Colombia, Costa Rica, Guatemala, Nicaragua, and Venezuela.

3. This decision was reversed in September 1996 following a protest to the WTO dispute panel

by the Caribbean ambassador to the EU, Edwin Laurent (*Caribbean Insight*, October 1996, 2). This insensitivity to the concerns of small, weak states was one factor that led to the now famous Seattle disturbances in December 1999 (see *The Economist*, 27 November–3 December, 11–17 December 1999).

4. Geest had, in 1991, purchased 9,600 acres of land in Costa Rica, as part of a strategy of "multisourcing." This venture proved a wholesale failure due to an outbreak of "black sigatoka" banana disease as well as significant industrial unrest on these plantations. In 1993 Geest recorded a pretax loss of 3.8 million pounds (Grossman 1998, 73).

5. The BSC emerged in the early 1990s. Its raison d'être was to resist the process of political and economic disempowerment of small producers in the banana industry. Very militant in its tactics, it was responsible for acts of arson and property damage in the banana-producing areas. Its activities will be further explored later in this chapter.

6. The full cost to the government was EC$43 million (see Cargill Report 1998, 19). This process of restructuring fell upon the shoulders of a left-of-center SLP, which was victorious in general elections in 1997. The party had made the privatization of the SLBGA an important feature of its election campaign. The full implications of this political change will be explored in Chapter 6.

7. This was reflected by the permanent secretary in the Ministry of Agriculture, who, though aware that "the external situation for bananas is still unresolved," was convinced that "whatever the new regime we end up with, it will not be as good as what we were accustomed to before. Which again will precipitate a departure from the industry" (Fletcher, interview).

8. A poverty reduction unit was established in St. Lucia in January 2000.

9. A poverty survey conducted in St. Lucia in that period concluded that "18.7% of the households of St. Lucia can be considered poor on the basis of their expenditure on food and nonfood items." A further 5.3 percent were considered indigent in that their level of expenditure fell below that required to fulfill their nutritional requirements. When assessed in terms of the spatial distribution of poverty, the high incidence of poverty of the rural areas was clearly highlighted, with the self-assessed poor in one rural enclave reaching as high as 73.4 percent (Anthony, Budget Address 1997, 26). The report noted that "proper roads, adequate potable water supply, toilet facilities, transport facilities, proper housing and sanitation are lacking in almost every community, both urban and rural" (ibid.).

10. According to Francois (1996, 103), one such caller had "expressed the view that the angry lynch mob of farmers . . . should have come out with [Compton's] testicles on a platter."

11. Further industrial disturbances were to occur in September 1994, when the entire staff of Radio St. Lucia was dismissed following a sit-in strike over pay and working conditions (*Caribbean Insight*, October 1994, 10).

12. *Caribbean Insight* reported that a BSC strike led to a fall of about 3.5 percent in the bananas exported from St. Lucia in the first week of 1995. Acts of roadblocks, farm damage, and arson were reported during the strike. The strike was called in response to the government's failure to convene an extraordinary meeting of the SLBGA to discuss the new Geest contracts and the formation of WIBDECO (*Caribbean Insight*, January 1995, 10).

13. The government's amendment to the Criminal Code was quietly withdrawn by Compton in October 1995 (see *Caribbean Insight*, October 1995, 10).

14. Midgett presents a largely geopolitical, security-centered analysis of the fall of conservative regimes in the Caribbean. He attributes the crisis of conservative movements to the abandonment of such regimes by their erstwhile benefactor, the United States, in the post–Cold War context (Midgett 1998, 14–18). My analysis, in contrast, focuses on the broad economic shifts associated with globalization. Barrow-Giles (n.d.), in her study of the 1997 election, focuses on the strengths and weaknesses of the two parties as an explanation for the SLP victory.

15. Compton was seventy years old in 1996. He had been a member of Parliament since 1954, leader of the UWP since 1964, and head of the government from 1964 to 1979 and 1982 to 1996.

16. When Compton began his political career, the Micoud-Dennery region formed one constituency. The constituency was later split into four electoral districts. Compton contested the Micoud South seat but remained popular throughout the banana-producing eastern sections.

17. I have argued elsewhere (Joseph 1997) that the selection of Vaughan Lewis was part of the wider project of neoliberalism with the emphasis on "management" replacing the emphasis on "leadership" (Nettleford 1993, 21–22, 28n.6). The main feature emphasized by Compton for his selection of Lewis was his "pedigree"—a reference to Lewis's image as a leading Caribbean academic and the fact of his blood relation to W. A. Lewis. Vaughan Lewis campaigned on the slogan: "The Doctor is in the House."

18. Odlum, in his capacity as St. Lucian ambassador to the United Nations, had played a critical role in exposing the machinations of his predecessor, Stephen Flemming, in the events surrounding the U.N. funds inquiry. This had further served to strengthen his credibility among the populace.

CHAPTER 6. GLOBAL NEOLIBERALISM AND THE LEFT AGENDA

1. Anthony was a distinguished Caribbean academic holding a Ph.D. in law from the University of Birmingham. At the time of his assumption of the role of party leader of the SLP he had been serving as chief legal counsel to the CARICOM secretariat, to which he had been seconded from his post of senior lecturer at the law faculty of the University of the West Indies.

2. Only three returning incumbents contested the election under the SLP banner in 1997 (Midgett 1998, 8).

3. Odlum would later complain that the creation of two posts of deputy political leader within the party hierarchy (none of which he occupied) was intended to signal to him that he was "two removes from the red meat of power" (see *St. Lucia Hansard*, 2000 Budget Debate).

4. This led to a formal complaint by Vaughan Lewis of British interference in the St. Lucian electoral process (see *Electronic Telegraph*, 23 May 1997).

5. This development led to an acrimonious exchange of words between Taiwan's OECS ambassador and the prime minister of St. Lucia. Accusing the Chinese government of "buying" the friendship of St. Lucia, Taiwan's representative controversially intimated that the changing of relations was due to pressures placed upon Anthony by the foreign minister, George Odlum. This led to the response from Anthony that the ambassador's remarks were "not only grossly out of place, but also represented a crude and rude interference in the internal affairs of St. Lucia" (*St. Lucia Mirror*, 12 September 1997, 9).

6. Odlum appeared surprised to have been told by the premier of China that "it is economics and trade that count" in a manner that implied that "you must forget all politics" (Odlum, interview).

7. By the time of the electoral defeat of the SLP in 2006, the cultural complex and the two hospitals had not been built. These unfinished projects became major sources of controversy, as will be seen later, when Taiwan, with whom the UWP had established ties, appeared unwilling to complete the projects.

8. A promised visit by Castro to attend St. Lucia's 1999 independence celebrations was canceled due to security concerns.

9. Under the process of "corporatization," the former WASA was registered as a private company, WASCO, with the government as the main shareholder. The company was granted a

twenty-five-year lease to operate (see *St. Lucia Mirror Online*, 4 February 2000). The government guaranteed a loan of EC$40,741,000 to facilitate the transformation of WASCO into a business entity (*St. Lucia Mirror*, 24 December 1999, 19).

10. In 1998 WASA's outstanding debts stood at EC$110 million (Anthony, Budget Address 1998, 100).

11. Calderon had resigned from the SLP prior to the 1997 election after failing to be selected as a candidate. Calderon was one of the leading neoliberal ideologues in the party prior to his resignation (Poyotte, interview).

12. These assurances were seen as necessary given the fact that the ILO's legal consultant on the Labour Code was the wife of the prime minister. Her relationship with the prime minister was used by the employer group to seek to discredit the objectivity with which she undertook her task.

13. This constant demand for loyalty and patience was the subject of a popular 1999 calypso by The Invader, in which the government's exhortation to St. Lucians to "hold tight" was mocked. Another calypso by Lord Bingo, entitled "Kenny and Tony," sought to highlight the schizophrenic nature of the SLP government in its pursuit of neoliberalism. These calypsos (an important barometer of Caribbean political opinion) indicate a growing impatience with the SLP's neoliberalism.

14. As will be seen later, the earliest years of the UWP following its victory in 2006 opened up another round of public disaffection given the failure of the UWP to deliver the "moon," particularly in light both of the death of the popular leader John Compton and the emergence of the global financial crisis.

15. The April 2000 budget noted that the banana industry declined by 8 percent from the previous year (see Anthony, Budget Address 2000, 6).

CHAPTER 7. "SOVEREIGNTY FOR SALE"

1. Compton turned eighty-two on 1 May 2006, seven months before the 2006 election.

2. When the question of his age and physical capacity was brought up by a reporter in a televised interview, Compton dismissively responded by threatening to remove his shirt to provide empirical proof of his physical strength.

3. The election was closer than is suggested by the margin of seats. A mere 2,000 votes separated the two parties.

4. Among the defeated incumbents, only Perry Christie's PLP had served one term in office.

5. http://thevoiceslu.com/features/2008/january/22_01_08/DPP_on_Criminal_Investigations.htm.

6. http://www.htsstlucia.com/2008_News/January/HTS_News_January_17th_2008.html.

7. The Taiwanese embassy was opened on the very day of the establishment of diplomatic relations (see *The Voice*, 3 May 2007, 1).

8. Grenada's break with Taiwan proved particularly acrimonious. On 21 December 2006 the Import/Export Bank of Taiwan filed a motion for summary judgment against the government of Grenada in a New York court. The bank was seeking to recover a sum U.S.$21.6 million for loans contracted from Taiwan (*Grenada Today*, 3 February 2007).

9. http://commons.globalintegrity.org/2009/04/in-latin-america-presidential.html.

10. These developments illustrate the degree of instability that has characterized St. Lucia's politics under the leadership of Stephenson King, Compton's chosen successor. Lacking the technical and academic background to prepare him for the role of prime minister, his accession to the office has been marked by internal revolts, the most prominent of which was led by Bousquet in

his effort to be returned to the cabinet. In April and May 2009 King presided over the longest and most enduring strike witnessed in St. Lucia since the mid-1990s. With the deepening of the economic difficulties after 2008, further disruptions are likely.

11. http://www.rslonline.com/news/slp-slams-taiwanese-ambassador.xhtml.

12. http://www.thevoiceslu.com/let_and_op/2009/march/26_03_09/archive_date_list.htm.

13. The Taiwanese embassy explained the incident as a traditional expression of gratitude and goodwill. At the time of the incident, the government of St. Lucia was seeking to quell instability arising out of the appointment of the commissioner of police (a British national). The actions of the Taiwanese president and the belated acknowledgment of the receipt of the cash-filled envelope by the commissioner added fuel to the already troubled domestic political situation.

14. http://www.htsstlucia.com/2008_News/November/HTS_News_November_12th_2008 .html.

15. http://www.guardian.co.uk/world/2008/nov/12/chen-arrest-taiwan Time.com—http:// www.time.com/time/world/article/0,8599,1858363,00.html.

16. http://www.stlucia.gov.lc/primeminister/statements/2007.

17. http://www.cananews.net/news/127/ARTICLE/32445/2008-12-12.html.

Bibliography

BOOKS, ARTICLES, AND PAMPHLETS

Abbot, G. 1969. "Size, viability, nationalism and politico-economic development." *International Journal* 35(1): 56–68.

Acosta, Y., and Casimir, J. 1985. "Social origins of the counter-plantation system in St. Lucia." In Gomes 1985, 34–59.

Adrien, P. 1996. *Metayage, Capitalism, and Peasant Development in St. Lucia, 1840–1957.* Kingston: Consortium Graduate School of the Social Sciences, University of the West Indies.

Agnew, J. 2009. *Globalization and Sovereignty.* Boulder, Colo.: Rowman and Littlefield.

Allahar, A., ed. 2001. *Caribbean Charisma: Reflections on Leadership, Legitimacy and Populist Politics.* Boulder, Colo.: Lynne Rienner.

Alleyne, K. n.d. *Memoir of the Constitutional Development of St. Lucia: Commemorating the 25th Anniversary of Elected Representatives to St. Lucia.* N.p: n.p.

Amoore, L., et al. 1997. "Overturning 'globalisation': Resisting the teleological, reclaiming the 'political.'" *New Political Economy* 2(1): 179–195.

Anderson, B. 1983. *Imagined Communities: Reflections on the Origin and Spread of Nationalism.* London: Verso.

Andrew, M. 1999. "The new international economic environment: The WTO and implications for the OECS." *Journal of Eastern Caribbean Studies* 24(2): 69–92.

Anthony, K. D. 1998. "Caribbean integration: The future relationship between Barbados and the OECS." *Journal of Eastern Caribbean Studies* 23(1): 35–50.

———. 2004. *At the Rainbow's Edge: Selected Speeches of Kenny D. Anthony.* Edited by Didacus Jules and Tennyson S. D. Joseph. Kingston: Ian Randle.

Archibugi, D., and D. Held eds. 1995. *Cosmopolitan Democracy: An Agenda for a New World Order.* Cambridge: Policy Press.

Arthur, O. S. 1998. "Prospects for Caribbean political unity." *Journal of Eastern Caribbean Studies* 23(1): 27–34.

Barbados Export Promotion Division. 1985. "An overview of the Caribbean Basin Initiative." *Bulletin of Eastern Caribbean Affairs* 11(3): 7–17.

Barrow, C. 1992. *Family Land and Development in St. Lucia.* Bridgetown: University of the West Indies, Institute of Social and Economic Research.

Barrow-Giles, C. 1992a. "St. Lucia's foreign policy and the fall of Communism in Eastern Europe and the Soviet Union." *Caribbean Affairs* 5(2): 10–17.

Barrow-Giles, C., and T. S. D. Joseph. 2006. *General Elections and Voting in the English-Speaking Caribbean 1992–2005.* Kingston: Ian Randle.

Barrow-Giles, C., and J. Soomer. 1996. "The politics of John Compton: Its impact on the political future of St. Lucia." *Bulletin of Eastern Caribbean Affairs* 21(3): 20–35.

Barry, T., B. Wood, and D. Preusch. 1984. *The Other Side of Paradise: Foreign Control in the Caribbean.* New York: Grove Press.

Beckford, G. 1972. *Persistence Poverty: Underdevelopment in Plantation Economies of the Third World.* London: Oxford University Press.

Beckles, H. 1990. *A History of Barbados: From Amerindian Settlement to Nation-State.* Cambridge: Cambridge University Press.

———. 1992. "Independence and the social crisis of nationalism in Barbados." *Bulletin of Eastern Caribbean Affairs* 17(3): 1–18.

Bell, W., ed. 1967. *The Democratic Revolution in the West Indies: Studies in Nationalism, Leadership and the Belief in Progress.* Cambridge, Mass.: Schenkman.

———. 1973. "New states in the Caribbean: A grounded theoretical account." In Eisenstadt and Rokkan 1973, 177–208.

———. 1980. "Equality and social justice: Foundations of nationalism in the Caribbean." *Caribbean Studies* 20(2): 5–36.

Belle, G. 1994. "The collapse of the Soviet system: Implications for the Caribbean Left." In Cobley 1994, 94–110.

Best, L., and K. Levitt. 1968. "Outlines of a model of pure plantation economy." *Social and Economic Studies* 17(3): 283–326.

Bgoya, W., and G. Hyden. 1987. "The state and the crisis in Africa: In search of a second liberation." *Development Dialogue* 2:5–29.

Bienefeld, M. 1994. "The new world order: Echoes of a new imperialism." *Third World Quarterly* 15(1): 31–48.

Bishop, L. B., and A. Payne. 2010. "Caribbean regional governance and the sovereignty/statehood problem." Centre for International Governance Innovation, Caribbean Paper No. 8, February, 1–22.

Blackman, C. 1984. "New horizons for private enterprise in the decade ahead." In Caribbean Association of Industry and Commerce 1984, 29–50.

Blaut, J. 1986. "A theory of nationalism." *Antipode* 18(1): 5–10.

———. 1987. *The National Question: Decolonising the Theory of Nationalism.* London: Zed Books.

Bogues, A. 1994. *The Limits of Political Sovereignty: A Review of the Jamaican Experience 1989–1991.* Kingston: Friedrich Ebert Stiftung.

Bolland, N. O. 1995. *On the March: Labour Rebellions in the British Caribbean, 1934–1939.* London: James Curry and Ian Randle.

Bonefeld, W., and J. Holloway. 1996a. "Conclusion: Money and class struggle." In Bonefeld and Holloway 1996b, 210–227.

———., eds. 1996b. *Global Capital, National State and the Politics of Money.* London: MacMillan.

Breen, H. 1844. *St. Lucia: Historical, Statistical and Descriptive.* London: Longman, Brown, Green and Longmans.

Brenner, R. 1998. *The Economics of Global Turbulence: A Special Report on the World Economy, 1950–1998.* New Left Review No. 229. London: New Left Review.

Broderick, M. 1968. "Associated Statehood: A new form of decolonisation." *International and Comparative Law Quarterly* 17(2): 368–403.

Brown, D. 1992. "The aims of privatization." In Ryan and Brown 1992, 270–273.

———. 1997. "Barbados to join the OECS?" *Journal of Eastern Caribbean Studies* 23(1): 80–82.

Brzezinski, Z. 1970. *Between Two Ages: America's Role in the Technocratic Era.* New York: Viking Press.

Camilleri, J. A. 1990. "Rethinking sovereignty in a shrinking, fragmented world." In Walker and Mendlovitz 1990, 13–44.

Camilleri, J. A., and J. Falk. 1992. *The End of Sovereignty? The Politics of a Shrinking and Fragmenting World.* London: Edward Elgar.

Carasco, F. J. 1979. "The development of trade unionism in St. Lucia, 1938–1978." In *The Crusader,* 17 February, 11, 14; 24 February, 9–10.

Caribbean Association of Industry and Commerce. 1984. *Symposium on the Role of the Private Sector in the Caribbean—The 1980s and Beyond.* Curacoa: Curacoa Chamber of Commerce and Industry.

Caribbean Bananas Exporters' Association (CBEA). 1994. *The Banana Regime and the Lomé Convention.* N.p: CBEA.

———. 1997. *The Renegotiation of the Lomé Convention. Submission to the International Development Committee, UK Parliament.* N.p.: CBEA.

CARICOM. 1984. *The Nassau Understanding: Structural Adjustment and Closer Integration for Accelerated Development in the Caribbean Community.* Nassau: CARICOM.

Carnegie, A. R. 1978. "The approach of independence for the Associated States: A constitutional law perspective." *Bulletin of Eastern Caribbean Affairs* 4(2): 7–12.

Cerny, P. G. 1996. "What next for the state?" In Kofman and Youngs 1996, 123–137.

———. 1997. "Paradoxes of the competition state: The dynamics of political globalization." *Government and Opposition* 32(2): 251–274.

Charles, G. F. L. 1994. *The History of the Labour Movement in St. Lucia 1945–1974: A Personal Memoir.* Castries: Folk Research Centre.

Chen-Young, P. 1973. *Report on Private Investment in the Caribbean.* Kingston: Atlas.

Chomsky, N. 1991. "The struggle for democracy in a changed world." *Review of African Political Economy* 50:12–20.

Clapham, C. 1996. *Africa and the International System: The Politics of State Survival.* Cambridge: Cambridge University Press.

———. 1998. "Degrees of statehood." *Review of International Studies* 24:143–157.

Cobley, A., ed. 1994. *Crossroads of Empire: The Europe-Caribbean Connection 1492–1992.* Bridgetown: Department of History, University of the West Cave Hill Campus.

Collective for Caribbean Project for Justice and Peace. 1982. *The Logic Behind the Caribbean Basin Plan: Capitalist Development or Militarization.* N.p: American Friends Service Committee.

Dabreo, D. S. 1981. *Of Men and Politics: The Agony of Saint Lucia.* Castries: Commonwealth Publishers International.

———. 1982. *Facing the Truth Eyeball to Eyeball: A Letter of Love to the People of St. Lucia.* Castries: Commonwealth Publishers.

Davidson, B. 1987. *African Nationalism and the Problems of Nation Building.* Lecture Series No. 42. Lagos: Nigerian Institute of International Affairs.

———. 1992. *The Black Man's Burden: Africa and the Curse of the Nation-State.* London: James Curry.

Davis, H. B. 1978. *Towards a Marxist Theory of Nationalism.* New York: Monthly Review Press.

Deere, C., et al. 1990. *In the Shadow of the Sun: Caribbean Development Alternatives and U.S. Policy.* Boulder, Colo.: Westview Press.

Devaux, R.J. 1997. *They Called Us Brigands: The Saga of St. Lucia's Freedom Fighters.* Castries: Optimum Printers.

Domínguez, J. I. 1993. "The Caribbean question: Why has liberal democracy (surprisingly) flourished?" In Domínguez, Pastor, and Worrell 1993, 1–25.

Domínguez, J. I., R. A. Pastor, and D. Worrell, eds. 1993. *Democracy in the Caribbean: Political, Economic and Social Perspectives*. Baltimore: Johns Hopkins University Press.

Du Boff, R. B., and E. S. Herman. 1997. "A critique of Tabb on globalisation." *Monthly Review* 49(6): 27–35.

Duncan, N. 1995a. "Globalisation or re-colonisation: Forcing the integration imperative?" In Duncan 1995b, 29–35.

———, ed. 1995b. *Caribbean Integration: The OECS Experience*. Kingston: Friedrich Ebert Stiftung.

Dunn, J. 1969. *The Political Thought of John Locke: An Historical Account of the Argument of "Two Treatise of Government."* Cambridge: Cambridge University Press.

———, ed. 1995. *Contemporary Crisis of the Nation State?* Oxford: Blackwell.

Easter, B. H. 1965. *St. Lucia and the French Revolution*. The 1965 Tom Ferguson Memorial Lecture. Castries: Voice Publishing.

Edie, C. J. 1991. *Democracy by Default: Dependency and Clientelism in Jamaica*. Kingston: Lynne Rienner.

———. 1994. *Democracy in the Caribbean: Myths and Realities*. London: Praeger.

Emerson, R. 1960. *From Empire to Nation: The Rise to Self-assertion of African and Asian Peoples*. Cambridge, Mass.: Harvard University Press.

Emmanuel, P. 1976. "Independence and viability: Elements of analysis." In Lewis 1976b, 1–15.

———. 1992. *Elections and Party Systems in the Commonwealth Caribbean, 1944–1991*. Bridgetown: Caribbean Development Research Services (CADRES).

Fanon, F. 1983. *The Wretched of the Earth*. Reprint, London: Penguin Books.

Farrell, T. M. 1983. "Decolonization in the English-speaking Caribbean: Myth or reality?" In Henry and Stone 1983, 3–13.

Feinberg, R. E., and R. Newfarmer, eds. 1984. *From Gunboats to Diplomacy: New U.S. Policies for Latin America*. Baltimore: Johns Hopkins University Press.

Ferguson, T. 1988. *The Third World and Decision Making in the IMF: The Quest for Full and Effective Participation*. London: Pinter.

Finlayson, J. A., and M. W. Zacher. 1981. "International trade institutions and the North-South dialogue." *International Journal* 36(4): 732–765.

Forman-Peck, J. 1983. *A History of the World Economy: International Economic Relations since 1850*. Brighton: Wheatsheaf.

Francois, M. 1994. *George Odlum: Hero or Villain*. Castries: Voice Press.

———. 1996. *The Rise and Fall of John Compton: St. Lucia's Julius Caesar*. Castries: National Freedom Party.

Frank, A. G. 1984. *Critique and Anti-critique: Essays on Dependence and Reformism*. London: Macmillan Press.

———. 1991. "No escape from the laws of world economics." *Review of African Political Economy* 50:21–32.

Fraser, C. 1994. *Ambivalent Anti-colonialism: The United States and the Genesis of West Indian Nationalism*. Westport, Conn.: Greenwood Press.

Furedi, F. 1994. *The New Ideology of Imperialism: Renewing the Moral Imperative*. London: Pluto Press.

Gaspar, B. D. 1997. "La guerre des bois: Revolution, war, and slavery in St. Lucia, 1793–1838." In Gaspar and Geggus 1997, 102–130.

Gaspar, B. D., and D. P. Geggus, eds. 1997. *A Turbulent Time: The French Revolution and the Greater Caribbean*. Indianapolis: Indiana University Press.

Gellner, E. 1964. *Thought and Change*. London: Weidenfeld and Nicolson.

Ghai, D., ed. 1991. *The IMF and the South. The Social Impact of Crisis and Adjustment*. London: Zed Books/UNRISD and ISER/UWI.

Gill, S. 1993a. "Gramsci and global politics: Towards a post-hegemonic research agenda." In Gill 1993b, 1–18.

———. 1993b. *Gramsci, Historical Materialism and International Relations*. Cambridge: Cambridge University Press.

———. 1995. "Globalisation, market civilization and disciplinary neo-liberalism." *Millennium* 24(3): 447–470.

Girvan, N., and O. Jefferson, eds. [1971]. *Readings in the Political Economy of the Caribbean*. Kingston: New World Group.

Gittens, T. 1982. "The post-colonial state, class formation and social transformation: A return to theory." *Transition* 5:21–41.

———. 1983. "Political parties, electoral politics and democracy in post-colonial societies: The demobolisation of mass mobilisation." *Transition* 7:14–30.

———. 1987. "The political economy of neo-colonialism: A short interpretative essay on the post-colonial social formation." *Transition* 15:47–67.

Gomes, P. I., ed. 1985. *Rural Development in the Caribbean*. London: C. Hurst/St. Martin's Press.

Gordon, D. M. 1988. "The global economy: New edifice or crumbling foundations?" *New Left Review* 168:25–64.

Gordon, G. 1966. *Two Political Essays*. Castries: Voice Press.

Goss, B., and D. Conway. 1992. "Sustainable development and foreign direct investment in the Eastern Caribbean: A strategy for the 1990s and beyond?" *Bulletin of Latin American Research* 11(3): 307–326.

Griffith, W. H. 1990. "CARICOM countries and the Caribbean Basin Initiative." *Latin American Perspectives* 17(1): 33–54.

———. 1994. "Appropriate economic theory for the Caribbean." In Watson 1994, 31–48.

Grossman, L. 1994. "British aid and Windwards bananas: The case of St. Vincent and the Grenadines." *Social and Economic Studies* 43(1): 151–179.

———. 1998. *The Political Ecology of Bananas: Contract Farming, Peasants and Agrarian Change in the Eastern Caribbean*. Chapel Hill: University of North Carolina Press.

Gruhn, I. V. 1983. "The recolonisation of Africa: International organisations on the march." *Africa Today* 30(4): 37–48.

Halliday, F. 1986. *The Making of the Second Cold War*. London: Verso.

Harker, T. 1993. "A brief overview of economic performance in the eighties." In Lalta and Freckleton 1993, 17–34.

Harris, C. 1960. "The constitutional history of the Windwards." *Caribbean Quarterly* 6(3&4): 160–176.

Harris, N. 1990. *The End of the Third World: Newly Industrialising Countries and the Decline of an Ideology*. London: Penguin Books.

Hart, R. 1989. *Rise and Organise: The Birth of the Workers' and National Movement in Jamaica (1936–1939)*. London: Karia Press.

———. 1998. *From Occupation to Independence: A Short History of the Peoples of the English-Speaking Caribbean Region*. London: Pluto Press.

———. 1999. *Towards Decolonisation: Political, Labour and Economic Development in Jamaica 1938–1945*. Kingston: Canoe Press, University of the West Indies.

Harvey, D. 2005. *A Brief History of NeoLiberalism*. Oxford: Oxford University Press.

Hawthorn, G. P. 1994. "The crisis of southern states." In Dunn 1995, 130–145.

Hawthorn, G. P., and P. Seabright. 1996. "Governance, democracy and development: A contractualist view." In Leftwich 1996, 74–93.

Held, D. 1991a. "Democracy, the nation-state and the global system." In Held 1991b, 197–235.

———, ed. 1991b. *Political Theory Today*. Cambridge: Polity Press.

———. 1995. "Democracy and the new international order." In Archibugi and Held 1995, 96–120.

Helleiner, Eric. 1994. *States and the Re-emergence of Global Finance: From Bretton Woods to the 1990s*. Ithaca, N.Y.: Cornell University Press.

Hintjens, H. M. 1995. *Alternatives to Independence: Explorations in Post-Colonial Relations*. London: Dartmouth.

Hirst, P., and G. Thompson. 1995. "Globalisation and the future of the nation state." *Economy and Society* 24(3): 408–442.

———. 1996. *Globalisation in Question*. Cambridge: Polity Press.

Hobsbawm, E. 1977. "Some reflections on 'The Break-up of Britain.'" *New Left Review* 105:3–23.

———. 1990. *Nations and Nationalism since 1780: Programme, Myth, Reality*. Cambridge: Cambridge University Press.

Hoogvelt, A. M. 1994. *The Third World in Global Development*. London: MacMillan.

———. 1997. *Globalisation and the Post-colonial World: The New Political Economy of Development*. London: MacMillan.

Horsman, M., and A. Marshall. 1994. *After the Nation-State: Citizens, Tribalism and the New World Disorder*. London: Harper Collins.

Huntley, E. 1978. "The foreign affairs of independent St. Lucia, St. Vincent, St. Kitts-Nevis and Dominica." *Bulletin of Eastern Caribbean Affairs* 4(2): 13–16.

Hurrel, A., and N. Woods. 1995. "Globalisation and inequality." *Millennium* 24(3): 447–470.

Ince, B. 1976. "The administration of foreign affairs in a very small developing country: The case of Trinidad and Tobago." In Lewis 1976b, 307–339.

Jackson, R. H. 1990. *Quasi-states: Sovereignty, International Relations and the Third World*. Cambridge: Cambridge University Press.

———. 1992. "Jurdical statehood in sub-Saharan Africa." *Journal of International Affairs* 46(1): 1–16.

———. 1998. *Surrogate Sovereignty? Great Power Responsibility and Failed States*. University of British Colombia, Institute of International Relations, Working Paper No. 25.

Jackson, R. H., and A. James, eds. 1993. *States in a Changing World*. Oxford: Clarendon Press.

Jagan, C. 1954. *Forbidden Freedom: The Story of British Guiana*. New York: International Publishers.

James, A. 1984. "Sovereignty: Ground rule or gibberish?" *Review of International Studies* 10(2): 1–18.

James, C. L. R. 1984. *Party Politics in the West Indies*. San Juan: Inprint Caribbean.

———. 1989. *The Black Jacobins: Toussaint L'Ouverture and the San Domingo Revolution*. New York: Random House.

James, W. n.d. *St. Lucia's Turmoil*. Castries: Voice Press.

Jesse, C. 1964. *Outlines of St. Lucia's History*. Castries: St. Lucia Archeological and Historical Society.

Johnson, C. 1980. "The emergence of political unionism in economies of British colonial origin: The case of Jamaica and Trinidad." *American Journal of Economics and Sociology* 39(2&3): 151–164.

Johnston, R. J., B. Knight, and E. Kofman, eds. 1988a. *Nationalism, Self-Determination, and Political Geography*. London: Croon Helm.

———. 1988b. "Nationalist self-determination and the world political map." In Johnston, Knight, and Kofman 1988a, 1–17.

Joseph, T. S. D. 1997. "'Old expectations, new philosophies': Adjusting state-society relations in the post-colonial Anglophone Caribbean." *Journal of Eastern Caribbean Studies* 22(4): 31–67.

Kelly, D. M. 1986. "St. Lucia's female electronics factory workers: Key components in an export-oriented industrialisation strategy." *World Development* 14(7): 823–838.

———. 1987. *Hard Work, Hard Choices: A Survey of Women in St. Lucia's Export-Oriented Electronics Factories.* Cave Hill, Barbados: University of the West Indies, Institute of Social and Economic Research.

Kemp, E. 1985. "CBI: The promise and the reality." *Bulletin of Eastern Caribbean Affairs* 11(3): 1–16.

Klak, T., ed. 1998a. *Globalisation and Neoliberalism: The Caribbean Context.* Lanham, Md.: Rowman and Littlefield.

———. 1998b. "Is the neo-liberal industrial export model working? An assessment from the Eastern Caribbean." *European Review of Latin America and Caribbean Studies* 65:67–90.

———. 1998c. "Thirteen theses on globalisation and neo-liberalism." In Klak 1998a, 3–23.

Klak, T., and G. Myers. 1997. "The discursive tactics of neo-liberal development in small third world countries." *Geoforum* 28(2): 133–149.

———. 1998. "How states sell their countries and their people." In Klak 1998a, 87–109.

Klak, T., and J. Rulli. 1993. "Regime of accumulation, the Caribbean Basin Initiative, and export-processing zones: Scales of influence on Caribbean development." In Goetz and Clarke 1993, 117–150.

Koester, S. 1981. "Hess twin tactics: Play island against island, bypass U.S. shipping costs." *Multinational Monitor* (April): 10.

———. 1990. "Social transformation and development capitalism: A case study in St. Lucia." *El Caribe Contemporeaneo* 2 (January–June): 51–72.

Kofman, E., and G. Youngs, eds. 1996. *Globalisation: Theory and Practice.* London: Pinter.

Krasner, S. D. 1985. *Structural Conflict: The Third World Against Global Liberalism.* Berkeley: University of California Press.

———. 1993. "Economic interdependence and independent statehood." In Jackson and James 1993, 301–321.

Kreisky, B., and H. Guaher, eds. 1987. *Decolonisation and After: The Future of the Third World.* London: South Publications.

Lalta, S., and M. Freckleton, eds. 1993. *Caribbean Economic Development: The First Generation.* Kingston: Ian Randle.

Leftwich, A. 1996. *Democracy and Development: Theory and Practice.* Cambridge: Polity Press.

Lewis, G. K. 1968. *The Growth of the Modern West Indies.* New York: Monthly Review Press.

Lewis, P. 1999. "The failed OECS political union initiative: Lessons of regional integration in the Anglophone Caribbean." *Journal of Eastern Caribbean Studies* 24(4): 30–54.

Lewis, V. A. 1976a. "The Commonwealth Caribbean and self-determination in the international system." In Lewis 1976b, 227–247.

———, ed. 1976b. *Size, Self-determination and International Relations: The Caribbean.* Kingston: University of the West Indies, Institute of Social and Economic Research.

———. 1988a. "Small states and foreign policy: The CARICOM states from the 1970s to the 1980s." In Heine and Maingot 1988, 133–143.

———. 1993. "The Eastern Caribbean states: Fledgling sovereignties in the global environment." In Domínguez, Pastor, and Worrell 1993, 99–121.

———. 1999. "Future Caribbean commitment to regionalism." *Journal of Eastern Caribbean Studies* 24(1): 51–63.

Lewis, W. A. 1977. *Labour in the West Indies: The Birth of a Workers' Movement*. Reprint, London: New Beacon Books.

Lindsay, A. D. 1975. *The Myth of Independence: Middle-Class Politics and Non-mobilisation in Jamaica*. Kingston: University of the West Indies, Institute of Social and Economic Research.

Long, F. 1980. *The Political-Economy of EEC Relations with African, Caribbean and Pacific States: Contributions to the Understanding of the Lomé Convention on North-South Relations*. Oxford: Perganon Press.

Lowenthal, D., and L. Comitas, eds. 1973. *The Aftermath of Sovereignty: West Indian Perspectives*. New York: Anchor Books.

Lyon, P. 1993. "The rise and fall and possible revival of international trusteeship." *Journal of Commonwealth and Comparative Politics* 31(1): 96–110.

Lyons, G. M., and M. Mastanduno, eds. 1995. *Beyond Westphalia? State Sovereignty and International Relations*. Baltimore: Johns Hopkins University Press.

Marazzi, C. 1996. "Money in the world crisis: The new basis of capitalist power." In Bonefeld and Holloway 1996b, 69–91.

Marshall, D. 1996. "National development and the globalisation discourse: Confronting 'imperative' and 'convergence' notions." *Third World Quarterly* 17(5): 875–901.

Marshall, W. K., ed. 1988. *Emancipation III: Aspects of the Post-slavery Experience in Barbados*. Bridgetown: University of the West Indies, Department of History, and the Barbados National Cultural Foundation.

Mayall, J. 1990. *Nationalism and International Society*. Cambridge: Cambridge University Press.

Mazrui, A. 1991. *The World with One Superpower: Is It a More Dangerous Place?* The 16th Sir Winston Scott Memorial Lecture. Bridgetown: Central Bank of Barbados.

McAffee, K. 1990. "Hurricane: IMF, World Bank, USAID in the Caribbean." *NACLA Report on the Americas* 23(5): 13–41.

———. 1991. *Storm Signals: Structural Adjustment and Development Alternatives in the Caribbean*. London: Zed Books.

Meeks, B. 1996. *Radical Caribbean: From Black Power to Abu Bakr*. Kingston: The Press, University of the West Indies.

Midgett, D. 1983. *Eastern Caribbean Elections, 1950–1982. Antigua, Dominica, Grenada, St. Kitts-Nevis, St. Lucia and St. Vincent*. Institute of Urban and Regional Research Development Series No. 13. Iowa City: University of Iowa, Center for Development Studies.

———. 1985. "The Caribbean Basin Initiative: Salvation or cynicism?" *Bulletin of Eastern Caribbean Affairs* 11(3): 36–43.

———. 1998. "The St. Lucia Labour Party victory of 1997 and the decline of the conservative movements." *Journal of Eastern Caribbean Studies* 23(4): 1–24.

Mohan, G. 1996. "Globalisation and governance: The paradoxes of adjustment in sub-Saharan Africa." In Kofman and Youngs 1996, 289–303.

Moran, J. 1998. "The dynamics of class politics and national economies in globalization: The marginalisation of the unacceptable." *Capital and Class* 66:53–83.

Mordecai, J. 1968. *The West Indies: The Federal Negotiations*. London: George Allen and Unwin.

Morris, C. W. 1998. *An Essay on the Modern State*. Cambridge: Cambridge University Press.

Moskos, C., and W. Bell. 1964. "West Indian nationalism." *New Society* 69:16–18.

———. 1967a. "Attitudes towards democracy." In Bell 1967, 68–85.

———. 1967b. "Attitudes towards equality." In Bell 1967, 100–113.

Munroe, T. 1972. *The Politics of Constitutional Decolonisation: Jamaica 1944–1962*. Kingston: University of the West Indies, Institute of Social and Economic Research.

Nairn, T. 1975. "Marxism and the modern janus." *New Left Review* 94:1–21.

———. 1977. *The Breakup of Britain*. London: New Left Books.

National Development Corporation (NDC). 1973. *St. Lucia: Advantages for Industrial Development*. Castries: NDC.

Navarro, L. 2000. "Globalizing liberation." *NACLA Report on the Americas* 33(6): 4–43.

Nettleford, R. 1993. *Inward Stretch, Outward Reach: A Voice from the Caribbean*. London: MacMillan.

Nkrumah, K. 1961. *I Speak of Freedom: A Statement of African Ideology*. London: Heinemann.

———. 1965. *Neo-colonialism: The Last Stage of Imperialism*. London: Thomas Nelson and Sons.

Nurse, K., and W. Sandiford. 1995. *Winaward Island Bananas: Challenges and Options under the Single European Market*. Kingston: Friedrich Ebert Stiftung.

Odlum, G. n.d.a. *Crusader Vignettes*. Castries: Offset Printers.

———. n.d.b. *The Banana Agenda: Five Editorials by George Odlum*. N.p: n.p.

OECS. 1981. *Treaty Establishing the Organisation of the Eastern Caribbean States*. Castries: OECS.

———. 1988. *Forms of Political Union: A Discussion Paper on a Union to Suit our Needs*. Castries: OECS.

———. n.d. *Fourth and Final Report of the Regional Constituent Assembly of the Windward Islands*. Castries: OECS.

Ohmae, K. 1990. *The Borderless World*. London: Collins.

———. 1993. "The rise of the region state." *Foreign Affairs* 72(2): 78–87.

O'Loughlin, C. 1963. *A Survey of Economic Potential and Capital Needs of the Leeward Islands, Windward Islands, and Barbados*. Overseas Research Publication No. 5. London: HMSO, Department of Technical Co-operation.

———. 1968. *Economic and Political Change in the Leeward and Windward Islands*. New Haven, Conn.: Yale University Press.

O'Neal, H. W. 1964. "The economy of St. Lucia." *Social and Economic Studies* 13(4): 440–470.

Overbeek, H., ed. 1993. *Restructuring Hegemony in the Global Political Economy: The Rise of Transnational Neo-Liberalism in the 1980s*. London: Routledge.

Oxaal, I. 1968. *Black Intellectuals Come to Power: The Rise of Creole Nationalism in Trinidad and Tobago*. Cambridge, Mass.: Schenkman.

Pantin, D. 1994. "Techno-industrial policy in the restructuring of the Caribbean: The missing link in Caribbean economic thought." In Watson 1994b, 49–64.

Partington, I. 1989. *Applied Economics in Banking and Finance*. Oxford: Oxford University Press.

Pastor, R. A. 1992. *Whirlpool: U.S. Foreign Policy towards Latin America and the Caribbean*. Princeton, N.J.: Princeton University Press.

Payne, A. 1994. "U.S. hegemony and the reconfiguration of the Caribbean." *Review of International Studies* 20:149–168.

Peck, J., and A. Tickell. 1994. "Jungle law breaks out: Neoliberalism and global-local disorder." *Area* 26(4): 317–326.

Peoples Progressive Party (PPP). 1950. Outline of Ten-year Program (1951–1960).

———. 1957. Election Manifesto, 18 September.

Persuad, W. 1993. "Europe 1992 and the Caribbean: Crisis, challenge and opportunity." In Lalta and Freckleton 1993, 189–199.

Peters, D. C. 1992. *The Democratic System in the Eastern Caribbean*. New York: Greenwood Press.

Petersman, E. 1997. *International Trade Law and the GATT/WTO Dispute Settlement System*. London: Kluwer Law International.

Phillips, F. A. 1960. "1959—A summary of constitutional advances—The Leeward and Windward Islands." *Caribbean Quarterly* 6(3&4): 230–232.

———. 1977. *Freedom in the Caribbean: A Study in Constitutional Change.* New York: Oceana Publications.

Polanyi-Levitt, K. 1985. "The origins and implications of the Caribbean Basin Initiative: Mortgaging sovereignty?" *International Journal* 11(2): 229–281.

Post, K. 1969. "The politics of protest in Jamaica, 1938: Some problems of analysis and conceptualisation." *Social and Economic Studies* 18(4): 374–390.

———. 1978. *Arise Ye Starvelings: The Jamaican Labour Rebellion of 1938 and Its Aftermath.* The Hague: Martinus Nijhoff.

———. 1981. *Strike the Iron: A Colony at War—Jamaica 1939–45.* Vol. 1. Atlantic Highlands, N.J.: Humanities Press.

Premdas, R. 2002. "Self-determination and sovereignty in the Caribbean: Migration, transnational identities, and deterritorialisation of the state." In Ramsaran 2002, 47–63.

Quick, S. A. 1993. "The international economy and the Caribbean: The 1990s and beyond." In Domínguez, Worrel, and Pastor 1993, 212–228.

Raghavan, C. 1990. *Recolonisation: GATT, the Uruguay Round and the Third World.* London: Zed Books.

Ramsaran, R. 1982. "The U.S. Caribbean Basin Initiative." *The World Today* 38(11): 430–436.

———. 1989. *The Commonwealth Caribbean in the World Economy.* London: Macmillan Caribbean.

———. 1992. *The Challenge of Structural Adjustment in the Commonwealth Caribbean.* New York: Praeger.

———. 1993. "Domestic policy, the external environment, and the economic crisis in the Caribbean." In Payne and Sutton 1993, 238–258.

———. 1998. *An Introduction to International Money and Finance.* London: Macmillan.

———, ed. 2002. *Caribbean Survival and the Global Challenge.* Kingston: Ian Randle.

Resource Center. 1984. *Focus on the Eastern Caribbean Bananas, Bucks and Boots.* Albuquerque, N.M.: Resource Center.

Riviere, B. 1990. *State Systems in the Eastern Caribbean: Historical and Contemporary Features.* Kingston: University of the West Indies, Institute of Social and Economic Research.

Roberts, K. J. 1998. "Multilateral agreement on investment." *Monthly Review* 50(5): 23–32.

Robinson, W. R. 2004. *A Theory of Global Capitalism: Production, Class and State in a Transnational World.* Baltimore: Johns Hopkins University Press.

———. 2008. *Latin America and Global Capitalism: A Critical Globalization Perspective.* Baltimore: Johns Hopkins University Press.

Rodney, W. 1990. *The Groundings with My Brothers.* Reprint, London: Bogle-L' Ouverture.

Romalis, R. 1975. "Economic change and peasant political consciousness in the Commonwealth Caribbean." *Journal of Commonwealth and Comparative Politics* 12(3): 225–241.

Rosenau, J. 1995. "Sovereignty in a turbulent world." In Lyons and Mastanduno 1995, 191–227.

Ruigrok, W., and R. Van Tuldor. 1995. *The Logic of International Restructuring.* London: Routledge.

Ryan, S. 1972. *Race and Nationalism in Trinidad and Tobago: A Study of Decolonisation in a Multiracial Society.* Toronto: University of Toronto Press.

———. 1989. *The Disillusioned Electorate: The Politics of Succession in Trinidad and Tobago.* Port of Spain: Inprint Caribbean.

———. 1994. "Problems and prospects for the survival of liberal democracy in the Anglophone Caribbean." In Edie 1994, 233–250.

Sabine, G. H. 1937. *A History of Political Theory*. London: George G. Harrop.

Sandiford, E. 1992. *Governance in Recessionary Times: Speeches April 1991–June 1992*. Bridgetown: Barbados Government Information Service.

Sassen, S. 1996. *Losing Control? Sovereignty in an Age of Globalization*. New York: Columbia University Press.

———. 1998. *Globalization and Its Discontents*. New York: New Press.

Sathyamurthy, T. V. 1983. *Nationalism in the Contemporary World: Political and Sociological Perspectives*. London: Pinter.

Scholte, J. A. 1996. "Beyond the buzzword: Towards a critical theory of globalisation." In Kofman and Youngs 1996, 43–57.

Schumpeter, J. A. 1950. *Capitalism, Socialism and Democracy*. London: George Allen and Unwin.

Serbin, A. 1998. *Sunset Over the Islands: The Caribbean in an Age of Global and Regional Change*. New York: St. Martin's Press.

Sheppard, J. 1987. *Marryshow of Grenada: An Introduction*. Bridgetown: Letchworth Press.

Sim, R., and J. Anderson. 1980. "The Caribbean strategic vacuum." *Conflict Studies* 121:1–23.

Slater, D. 1996. "Other contexts of the global: A critical geo-politics of North-South relations." In Kofman and Youngs 1996, 273–288.

St. Lucia Labour Party (SLP). 1957. *Election Manifesto: Forward St. Lucia*. N.p: n.p.

———. 1978. *Independence? Do It Right. Let the People Decide*. Castries: The Voice Press.

———. 1979. *Election Manifesto*. Castries: SLP.

———. 1997. *Election Manifesto: New Vision, New Directions for a New Century*. Castries: SLP.

Stiglitz, J. 2002. *Globalization and Its Discontents*. London: Allen Lane.

Stone, C. 1980. *Democracy and Clientelism in Jamaica*. New Brunswick, N.J.: Transaction Books.

Strange, S. 1996. *The Retreat of the State: The Diffusion of Power in the World Economy*. Cambridge: Cambridge University Press.

Tabb, W. K. 1997a. "Contextualising globalization: Comments on Du Boff and Herman." *Monthly Review* 49(6): 35–39.

———. 1997b. "Globalization is *an* issue: The power of capital is *the* issue." *Monthly Review* 49(2): 20–30.

Thomas, C. Y. 1978. "The 'non-capitalist path' as theory and practice of decolonisation and socialist transformation." *Latin American Perspectives* 5(2): 10–28.

———. 1991. "The economic crisis and the Commonwealth Caribbean: Impact and response." In Ghai 1991, 43–68.

———. 1996. "A state of disarray: Public policy in the Caribbean." *Bulletin of Eastern Caribbean Affairs* 20(2): 46–56.

———. 2000. "The economic development of the OECS in the emerging international economic order." *Journal of Eastern Caribbean Studies* 25(1): 58–78.

Thomas, M. 1989a. *Agricultural Diversification: The Experience of the Windward Islands*. Institute of Development Studies, Discussion Paper Series, No. DP 257.

———. 1989b. *Cash Crops and Development: Bananas in the Windward Islands*. Institute of Development Studies, Discussion Paper Series, No. DP 258.

Thomson, R. 1987. *Green Gold: Bananas and Dependency in the Eastern Caribbean*. London: Latin American Bureau.

Thorndike, A. E. 1979a. "The politics of inadequacy: A study of the Associated Statehood negotiations and constitutional arrangements for the Eastern Caribbean, 1965–67." *Social and
Economic Studies* 28(3): 597–617.

Toffler, A. 1981. *The Third Wave*. London: Pan Books.

United Workers' Party (UWP). 1992. *Election Manifesto: A Secure Future for St. Lucia*. Castries:
UWP.

Van der Pijl, K. 1993a. "State socialism and passive revolution." In Gill 1993b, 237–258.

Walker, R. B. J., and S. H. Mendlovitz, eds. 1990a. *Contending Sovereignties: Redefining Political
Community*. Boulder, Colo.: Lynne Rienner.

Wallerstein, I. 1983. "Nationalism and the world transition to socialism: Is there a crisis?" *Third
World Quarterly* 5(1): 95–102.

Watson, A. 1997. *The Limits to Independence: Relations between States in the Modern World*.
London: Routledge.

Watson, H. 1990. "Recent attempts at industrial restructuring in Barbados." *Latin American
Perspectives* 17(1): 10–32.

———. 1994a. "Beyond nationalism: Caribbean options under global capitalism." In Watson
1994b, 225–231.

———, ed. 1994b. *The Caribbean in the Global Political Economy*, Boulder, Colo.: Lynne Rienner.

———. 1994c. "Global restructuring and the prospect for Caribbean competitiveness: With a case
study from Jamaica." In Watson 1994b, 67–90.

Watson, H. 1988. "The changing structure of world capital and the development options in the
Caribbean." In *Symposium on the Future of the Caribbean in the World System: Proceedings of a
Symposium*, 1–46. Kingston: Friedrich Ebert Stiftung.

Wayne, R. 1977. *It'll Be Alright in the Morning*. Castries: Star Publications.

———. 1986. *Foolish Virgins*. Los Angeles: Star Publications.

———. 2010. *Lapses and Infelicities: An Insider Perspective of Politics in the Caribbean*. Castries:
Star Publications.

Welch, B. 1994. "Banana dependency: Albatross or liferaft for the Windwards." *Social and
Economic Studies* 43(1): 123–149.

Williams, M. 1996. "Rethinking sovereignty." In Kofman and Youngs 1996, 109–122.

Williams, O., and R. Darius. 1998. "Bananas, the WTO and adjustment initiatives in the Eastern
Caribbean area." In Eastern Caribbean Central Bank 1998, 100-111.

Wiltshire-Brodber, R. 1983. "The instability and crisis in the Caribbean: The demystification of
the Caribbean Basin Initiative." *CARICOM Bulletin* 4:16–28.

Wood, E. M. 1997a. "A note on Du Boff and Herman." *Monthly Review* 49(6): 39–43.

———. 1997b. "A reply to Sivanandan." *Monthly Review* 48(9): 21–32.

World Bank. 1979. *Economic Position and Prospects for St. Lucia*. Report No. 2440-CRB, 19 April.
Washington, D.C.: World Bank.

———. 1985. *St. Lucia: Economic Prospects and Performance*. Washington, D.C.: World Bank.

———. 1992. *St. Lucia Country Economic Memoranda*. Report No. 10431. Washington, D.C.:
World Bank.

———. 1997. *The State in a Changing World: World Development Report 1997*. Oxford: Oxford
University Press.

World Trade Organization. 1999. Annual report.

Worrell, R. D. 1987. *Small Island Economies: Structure and Performance in the English-Speaking
Caribbean since 1970*. New York: Praeger.

———. 1993. "The economies of the English-speaking Caribbean since 1960." In Domínguez,
Pastor, and Worrell 1993, 189–211.

UNPUBLISHED THESES, MANUSCRIPTS, AND SEMINAR AND CONFERENCE PAPERS

Anthony, K. D. 1978. "St. Lucia, economic and social development of the countryside." In Rural Transformation Collective 1978, 2–12.

Antoine, R. 2007. "Why you need a labour code." Public lecture delivered to the George Charles Foundation, Castries, 13 November.

Barrow-Giles, C. 1992b. "Political development and foreign affairs of a mini-state: A case study of St. Lucia 1979–1987." Master's thesis, University of the West Indies.

———. 1999. "Dangerous waters—sovereignty and self-determinism under attack: Resistance, cultural and regional assertion as a means of capturing some semblance of that elusive dream." Paper presented at the twentieth anniversary of St. Lucia's independence, February.

———. n.d. "The 1997 vote in St. Lucia: The beginning of a new era?" Unpublished manuscript, University of the West Indies.

Barrow-Giles, C., and T. S. D. Joseph. 2008. "General elections in the Caribbean from St. Lucia to Barbados (2006–2008): Towards a tentative explanation of a trend." Paper presented at the 2008 Caribbean Studies Association Conference, San Andreas, Colombia, 26 May–1 June.

Belle, G. 1977. "The politics of development: A study in the political development of Barbados." Ph.D. diss., University of Manchester.

———. 1984. "U.S.A. imperialism and the English-speaking Caribbean." Paper presented at the second Caribbean Conference of Intellectual Workers, Trinidad, 13–14 January.

———. 1996. "Against colonialism: Political theory and re-colonisation in the Caribbean." Paper presented at the Conference on Caribbean Culture, University of the West Indies, Mona Campus, 3–5 March.

Bowen, S. 1992. "The O.E.C.S. experience with structural adjustment: Dominica, St. Lucia, and St. Vincent." Unpublished manuscript, Institute of Commonwealth Studies Library, University of London.

Demas, W. G. 1987. "Seize the time: Towards OECS Political Union." Bridgetown, mimeographed.

Duncan, N. 1980. "Aspects of statehood in the peripheral societies of the Anglophone Eastern Caribbean: A preliminary statement." Paper presented at the conference "LDCs of the Commonwealth Caribbean: Domestic, Regional and International Perspectives," Antigua, 4–7 June.

Eckstein, J. 1978. "CARICOM: An evaluation of its prospects for survival." Unpublished manuscript, Department of Management Studies, University of the West Indies, St. Augustine, Trinidad, April.

Emmanuel, P. 1974. "Independence, viability and conflict in very small states." Paper presented at the conference "Independence of Very Small States with Special Reference to the Caribbean," Cave Hill, Barbados, 25–28 March.

Francois, H. J. 1977. "Morning: A review of Rick Wayne's 'It'll Be Alright in the Morning.'" Castries, mimeographed.

Giacalone, R. 1993. "CARICOM-private sector relations and the West Indies Commission Report." Paper presented at the eighteenth annual conference of the Caribbean Studies Association, Kingston and Ocho Rios, 26–29 May.

Gonsalves, R. 2007. "The modern, competitive, post-colonial economy: The case of St. Vincent and the Grenadines." Unpublished manuscript, Office of the Prime Minister, Government of St. Vincent and the Grenadines.

Held, D. 1998. "The changing global contours of political community: Rethinking democracy in the context of globalization." Graduate Working Paper Seminar Series, Faculty of Social and Political Sciences, University of Cambridge.

Koester, S. 1986. "From plantation agriculture to oil storage: Economic development and social transformation." Ph.D. diss., University of Colorado.

Kunsman, C. 1963. "The origin and development of political parties in the British West Indies." Ph.D. diss., University of California at Berkeley.

Lewis, V. A. 1970. "The structure of small state behaviour in contemporary international politics." Ph.D. diss., University of Manchester.

———. 1988b. "The organisation of Eastern Caribbean States: Its current orientation." Paper presented at the Colloquium on the Geo-politics of the Eastern Caribbean at the Maison Francaise, Oxford University, 8–9 January.

———. 2009. "Presentation to the CARICOM heads of state and government on the report of the task force on the Trinidad and Tobago-Eastern Caribbean States Integration Initiative." Port-of-Spain, Trinidad and Tobago, 24 May.

Lewis-Meeks, P. 1991. "The integration of the Eastern Caribbean through the Organisation of the Eastern Caribbean States (OECS)." Ph.D. diss., University of Cambridge.

Louis, M. 1981. "'An equal right to the soil': The rise of a peasantry in St. Lucia—1838–1900." Ph.D. diss., Johns Hopkins University.

Michel, M. 2007. "St. Lucia's Labour Code: Old law or new law?" Public lecure delivered to the George Charles Foundation, Castries, 20 November.

Midgett, D. n.d. "The political economy of electoral corruption in the Eastern Caribbean." Unpublished manuscript, Department of Anthropology, University of Iowa.

Nurse, K. 1995 "Sustaining bananas: The socio-economic and cultural dimensions of change in the Windward Islands." Paper presented at the nineteenth annual conference of the Society for Caribbean Studies, Institute of Commonwealth Studies, London, 5–7 July.

Phillips, L. n.d. "Interview with Earl of Oxford, former administrator of St. Lucia." Unpublished manuscript, Rhodes House Library, Oxford.

Reeve, R. 1999. "The rock and the deep blue sea: Revolution, re-alignment, and realism in the foreign policy of the post-colonial micro-state." Master's thesis, London School of Economics, Faculty of Economics.

Romalis, C. 1969. "Barbados and St. Lucia: A comparative analysis of social and economic developments in two British West Indian islands." Ph.D. diss., Washington University.

Romalis, R. 1968. "The rural community and the total society during economic change in St. Lucia: A case study." Ph.D. diss., McGill University.

Rural Transformation Collective. 1978. "Bananas and poverty." Castries, mimeographed.

Salz, B. 1961. "Government and politics in St. Lucia." Unpublished manuscript, University of Puerto Rico.

Slocum, K. 1996. "Producing under a globalizing economy: The intersection of flexible production and local autonomy in the work lives and actions of St. Lucian banana growers." Ph.D. diss., University of Florida.

Thomas, A. 1987. "Associated statehood in the Leeward and Windward Islands: A phase in the transition to independence 1967–1983." Ph.D. diss., City University of New York.

Thorndike, A. E. 1979b. "The concept of Associated Statehood with special reference to the Eastern Caribbean." Ph.D. diss., University of London.

Workers' Revolutionary Movement (WRM). 1981. "Our country is in danger." WRM pamphlet, 27 April.

———. 1982a. "Workers must lead struggle." WRM pamphlet, 12 January.

————. 1982b. "No to foreign soldiers." WRM pamphlet, 15 January.

————. 1982c. "More layoffs capitalism responsible." WRM pamphlet, 24 July.

————. 1982d. "Why Labour lost and what is to be done?" WRM pamphlet, 7 May.

NEWSPAPER AND NEWSLETTER SOURCES

Advocate News (Barbados), 21 April 1971

CANA Online News, http://www.cananews.net/

Caribbean and West Indies Chronicle, October/November 1979–December/January 1984

Caribbean Insight, 1978–2000

Combat (organ of the National Workers Union) (St. Lucia), 1974–1984

The Crusader (St. Lucia), 1978–2010

The Economist, 7 October 1995, 27 November–3 December 1999, 3–11 December 1999

Electronic Telegraph (U.K.), 23 May 1997, http://www.telegraph.co.uk

Financial Times, 29 April 1974, 8 April, 1 September 1999

The Gleaner (Jamaica), 9 August 1995

The Gleaner (Jamaica) (online)

Global Integrity Commons (online), http://commons.globalintegrity.org/

Government Information Service–St. Lucia (online), http://www.st.lucia.gov.lc/gis/

Government Information Service-St. Lucia News, 21 March 1979

Grenada Today, Internet edition, 3 February 2007

The Guardian (U.K.), 27 January, 6, 8 April 1999

Guyana Chronicle Online, http://www.guyanachronicleonline.com/site/

Helen Television System (HTS) News Online (St. Lucia)

Keesing's Contemporary Archives, 1945–1980

Korea Newsreview, 19 November 1989

Multinational Monitor, April 1981

The Nation/Weekend Nation/Sunday Sun (Barbados), 29 August 1997, 26 July 2009

News Analysis, 1 February 1982

Newsweek, 28 April 1997

New York Times, 30 July 1987

The Observer (Jamaica), 8 February 1998

One Caribbean (St. Lucia), 4 October 1999

Outlet (Antigua), 25 February, 3, 10 March 2000

Radio St. Lucia Online News, http://www.rslonline.com/

St. Lucia Gazette, 1944–1979

St. Lucia Mirror, 1994–2010

St. Lucia Mirror Online, http://www.stluciamirror.com

St. Lucia Onestop News, http://sluonestop.com

St. Lucia Online News, 29 April, 13 May 2000, http://www.slucia.com/news_media.html

The Times (online), times.co.uk/ttt/news/

Trinidad and Tobago Review, March 1997, Divali [November] 1999

UN Chronicle, July–September 1979

UN General Assembly Official Records, 1965–1968

UN Monthly Chronicle, April 1967

The Vanguard (organ of the United Workers' Party, St. Lucia), 28 January 1978

The Voice of St. Lucia/Weekend Voice, 1930–2010

The Voice Online, http://www.thevoiceslu.com/
Week in Europe (weekly report by David Jessop on Europe and the Caribbean), 10 March–24 August 2000
West Indian World, 14 October 1976
West Indies Chronicle, February/March 1975–August/September 1978
Workers' Clarion (organ of the SLP and SLCWU), 1952–1958

OFFICIAL REPORTS AND PUBLICATIONS

Government of St. Lucia (GOSL) (Pre- and Postindependence)
1952. Report of the Commission of Enquiry into the Stoppage of Work at the Sugar Factories in St. Lucia in March 1952 and into the Adequacy of the Existing Wage Fixing Machinery in that Colony (Chairman, C. Malone).
1952–2006. Reports on Legislative Council and General Elections to the St. Lucia House of Assembly.
1957. Report of the Commission Appointed to Investigate the Causes of the Stoppage of Work in the Sugar Industry during March and April in St. Lucia (Chairman, D. Jackson).
1960. Report of the Commission of Enquiry into the Sugar Industry of St. Lucia (Chairman, A. MacKenzie).
1962. Report of the Commission of Enquiry into the Actions of Members of the St. Lucia Police Force and Special Reserve Police on 2nd, 3rd, and 4th days of November, 1961 and the Circumstances and Events Leading Thereto (Chairman, E. Hallinan).
1973. Report on the Prolonged Stoppage of Work on the Cul-de-sac and Roseau Group of Estates during the Months of April and May 1973, and Other Matters Connected Therewith (Chairman, K. Stoby).
1977. Report of the St. Lucia Public Services Review Committee (Chairman, H. Dolly).
1977. National Development Strategy.
[1978]. Independence for St. Lucia [government "Green Paper" on independence].
1979. Report into a Trade Dispute between the Government of St. Lucia and the Public Service Associations, 5 April (Chairman, C. Hewlett).
1993. Report of the Banana Review Committee.
1995. Report of a Commission of Inquiry Appointed by His Excellency the Governor General of St. Lucia (Chairman, F. Phillips).
1998. Report into the Socio-Economic Impact of Banana Restructuring in St. Lucia (Cargill Technical Services).
1999. Country Strategy Paper for the Banana Industry, Agricultural Diversification and Social Recovery of Rural Communities (St. Lucia Government, Ministry of Agriculture).

St. Lucia Legislature (Pre- and Postindependence)
1938. Debate on the Motion for the First Reading of the Labour Ordinance Bill, 14 June.
1938–1939. Minutes of the St. Lucia Legislative Council, 8 December.
1948. Debate on a Resolution for Constitutional Reform, 9 September.
1964. Address by the Acting Administrator, Gerald Jacks Bryan, at the opening of the Legislative Council, 25 February.
1964. Address by the Acting Administrator, Gerald Jacks Bryan, at the Opening of the Legislative Council, 14 July.
1964. Address by the Acting Administrator, Gerald Jacks Bryan, at the Opening of the Legislative Council, 17 December.

1965. Address by the Acting Administrator, Gerald Jacks Bryan, at the Opening of the Legislative Council, 30 December.

1968. Throne Speech, Frederick Clarke, 2nd Session of St. Lucia House of Assembly, 4 January.

1969. Throne Speech, Frederick Clarke, 2nd Session of St. Lucia House of Assembly, 30 December.

1969–2009. Budget Addresses in the St Lucia House of Assembly, 10 January.

1970–2009. Throne Speeches to the St. Lucia House of Assembly, 29 December.

1977–2008. *St. Lucia Hansard* (Parliamentary Debates)

Acts of Parliament

1976. Public Order Act.

1977. Oil Refinery Act.

U.K. Legislature

1922. House of Commons Debates, 4 July, Sessional Papers, Vol. 156, 3 July–21 July.

1966–1967. House of Commons Debates, Sessional Papers, Vol. 740, 30 January–10 February.

1978–1979. House of Commons Debates, Sessional Papers, Vol. 960, 11 December–11 January.

1978–1979. House of Lords Debates, Sessional Debates, Vol. 397, 5 December–25 January.

U.K. Government Parliamentary Papers

1922. Cmnd. 1679. Report of the Hon. E. F. L. Wood on His Visit to the West Indies and British Guiana, 1921–1922.

1930. Cmnd. 3517. Report of the West Indian Sugar Commission.

1945. Cmnd. 6607. West India Royal Commission Report (Chairman, Lord Moyne).

1947. Cmnd. 7120. Circular Despatch of Secretary of State for the Colonies to Governors of All West Indian Colonies on Closer Association for the British West Indian Colonies, 14 February.

1948. Cmnd. 7291. Report of Conference on the Closer Association of the British West Indian Colonies, September 1947, Montego Bay, Jamaica, Part I. Part II, Proceedings in Col. 218.

1953. Cmnd. 8895. The Plan for a British Caribbean Federation.

1953. Cmnd. 8837. Report by Conference on West Indian Federation, London, April.

1955. Cmnd. 9618. The Plan for a British Caribbean Federation: Report of the Fiscal Commissioner.

1956. Cmnd. 9733. Report by Conference on British Caribbean Federation, London, February.

1959. Cmnd. 804 Report of the Leeward and Windward Islands Constitutional Conference.

1961. Cmnd. 1417. Report of the West Indies Constitutional Conference.

1965. Cmnd. 2865. Constitutional Proposals for Antigua, St. Kitts-Nevis-Anguilla, Dominica, St. Lucia, St. Vincent, Grenada.

1966. Cmnd. 3021. Report of the Windward Islands Constitutional Conference.

1978. Cmnd. 7328. Report of the St. Lucia Constitutional Conference, London, 5 April.

U.K. Government Miscellaneous Papers

1930–1946. Annual Colonial Report (St. Lucia).

1948. Col. 218. Conference on the Closer Association of the British West Indian Colonies (Part Two: Proceedings).

1950. Col. 255. Report of the British Caribbean Standing Closer Association Committee 1948–1950.

1998. House of Commons International Development Committee, Fourth Report on the Renegotiation of the Lomé Convention, 21 May.

Government of Canada
2002. Ombudsman of Manitoba. Access and Privacy Annual Report.

PUBLIC RECORDS OFFICE DOCUMENTS

1952. PRO-CO 1031/267.
Extract from Windward Islands Political Report, January.
Summary of Sugar Strike.
1953. PRO-CO 1031/267.
St. Lucia Sugar Strike: Acting Governor of Windward Islands to Colonial Secretary, 2 February.
1954. PRO-CO 1031/1528.
Correspondence between Windward Islands Governor and Colonial Office on W. G. Brown.
1955. PRO-CO 1031/1408.
Verbatim Report of the Debate in the St. Lucia Legislative Council, on a Resolution for Adoption of Proposals for Introduction of the Ministerial System, 25 February.
1957. PRO-CO 1031/2808.
Address by Hon. G. F. L. Charles, Made on the Castries Market Steps at Labour Party Meeting, 4 April.
1957. PRO-CO 1031/2809.
Record of Meeting of St. Lucia Executive Council, 22 April.
List of Persons Charged and Taken to Court between 3 and 26 April, 27 April.
Windward Islands Governor to Colonial Secretary on the Political and Industrial Background, 1 May.
Acting Governor to Colonial Secretary, 15 May.
Intelligence Report: Public Meeting held at Dennery under the Chairmanship of Hon. G. F. L. Charles, 12 July.
Administrator to Colonial Office via Windward Islands Governor, 17 July.
1958. PRO-CO 1031/2178.
Windward Islands Governor to Colonial Office on Political Parties in St. Lucia, 4 June.
1960. PRO-CO 1031/3422.
Note of Meeting between Colonial Office and Van Geest, 23 November.
1962. PRO-CO 1031/3702.
Some Notes on the Political and Security Situation in St. Lucia, January.

POLITICAL SPEECHES AND PUBLIC BROADCASTS

Anthony, K. D. 1996. "Setting the agenda for change." Address to the Convention of the Unity Labour Party (St. Vincent and the Grenadines), 24 November. wysiwg://http:www.geocities .com/capitolHill/6116/slpchng.html.
———. 1997. "New vision, new direction, a new Government for the next century." Address to the Annual Conference of Delegates of the St. Lucia Labour Party, 2 November.
———. 1998b. Address to the nation on the banana industry, 25 August. http://www.st.luciagov.lc.
———. 1999b. Statement on the impending election of a new SLBC board, 20 October 1994. http://www.stluciagov.lc.
———. n.d. Address on the impact of the WTO ruling in respect of the EU banana import regime on the banana industry of the Windward Islands. http://www.stluciagov.lc.
Arthur, O. S. 2000. "The future of the Caribbean Community and Common Market." Address

to the third Media Conference in Georgetown, Guyana, 5 May. http://www.Caricom.org/press50_00.html.

Compton, J. 1979a. Address on the continued strike action by members of the public services, 11 March.

———. 1979b. Address to the thirteenth annual UWP Conference of Delegates, 1 May.

———. 1979c. Preelection public broadcast, 1 July.

———. 1980. Address to fourteenth annual UWP Conference of Delegates, 5 October.

———. 1994. Address on the occasion of the fifteenth anniversary of the independence of St. Lucia.

Skerrit, R. 2008. Address to the nation, 28 February.

PRESS RELEASES

1982. St. Lucia Chamber of Commerce, Industry and Agriculture, 12, 13 January.

1982. St. Lucia Manufacturers' Association, 12 January.

1982. St. Lucia Small Business Association, 12 January.

PUBLIC AND PERSONAL LETTERS

1957. Sugar Manufacturers Ltd. to Administrator: "Draft Minutes of General Shareholders Meeting of Sugar Manufacturers Ltd.," 6 May.

1957. Claudius S. Chase, President of St. Lucia Chamber of Commerce and Agriculture; F. J. Carasco, Chairman of St. Lucia Sugar Association Ltd.; Norman Moffat, Chairman of St. Lucia Banana Growers' Association; Lewis Floissac, Chairman of St. Lucia Agriculturist Association; and Milne Marshall, Chairman of St. Lucia Coconut Growers Association, to Eric Williams, Premier of Trinidad and Tobago, 17 May.

1982. St. Lucia Teachers Union, St. Lucia Seamen and Waterfront Workers' Union, Civil Service Association, National Workers Union, and St. Lucia Workers' Union to Prime Minister Winston Cenac, 14 January.

1994. Patrick Joseph, Secretary, Banana Salvation Committee, to Ira d'Auvernge, Minister of Agriculture, 2 February.

1994. Patrick Joseph, Secretary, Banana Salvation Committee, to Ira d'Auvernge, Minister of Agriculture, 3 May.

PERSONS INTERVIEWED

Anthony, Kenny	Leader of the SLP (1997–present)	11 January 1998
Charles, George	Retired Chief Minister of St. Lucia	19 September 1997
Compton, John	Retired Prime Minister of St. Lucia	4 November 1997
d'Auvergne, Ausburt	Former Permanent Secretary, Ministry of Planning (1987–1994)	5 November 1997
Fletcher, James	Permanent Secretary, Ministry of Agriculture (1998–)	11 January 2000
Francois, Hunter J.	Former President of the PPP (1961–1964); Founding Member of the UWP; Former Minister of Education (1964–1972)	15 October 1997
George, Calixte	Minister of Communications and Works	18 November 1997

Huntley, Earl	Permanent Secretary, Ministry of Foreign Affairs	3 November 1997
Lewis, Vaughan	Former Prime Minister of St. Lucia (1996–1997)	3 December 1997
Odlum, George	Minister of Foreign Affairs and International Trade	27 September 1997
Poyotte, Lawrence	General Secretary of the CSA (1999–)	26 September 1997 and 12 January 2000

INTERNET AND OTHER SOURCES

Daher Broadcasting Television. Video Recording of Panel Discussion on the May 1997 General Elections in St. Lucia. Panelists: Cynthia Barrow-Giles and Anthony Darius. 23 May 1997.
Government of St. Lucia: http://www.stluciagov.lc.
Political Database of the Americas: www.georgetown.edu/pdba/elecdata.

Index

Acosta, Yvonne, on small banana grower empowerment, 44–45

ACP states, impact of trade liberalization upon, 113–15

Agnew, Jonathan, description of global neoliberalism, 8

ALBA (Bolivarian Alternative for Latin America), relationship of SLP towards, 147

ALP. *See* Antigua Labour Party

Amerada-Hess: terms of establishment in St. Lucia, 55–56; SLP accommodation to, 68–70

Anthony, Kenny: accommodation to neoliberalism, 152–54, 162–63; on adjustment of banana industry, 121–22; criticism of Compton's independence foreign policy, 64; criticism of Taiwanese interference, 178; electoral defeat of, 166–69; emergence as leader of SLP, 131–32; involvement in the WRM, 61; on land ownership distribution, 54; response to protests against Labour Code, 158–60; role in internal transformation of SLP, 137–38, 140, 142–43; role in the SLP 1979 manifesto, 63; social democratic agenda of, 145–46, 148–49

Antigua Labour Party (ALP), electoral defeat of, 170

Antoine, Rosemarie, role in the Labour Code, 156–57

Arthur, Owen, electoral defeat of, 169

Associated Statehood: Compton's arguments against, 49, 51; main features of, 42–44

Augustin, Grace: in legislative council, 23; stance on ministerial system, 23, 31

Banana companies: Anthony administration's policy towards, 121–22; Joseph's management of, 162

Banana economy: early emergence of, 44–45; impact of New Banana Regime on, 113–14; neoliberal restructuring in, 62, 117–21; political significance of, 47, 164

Banana Salvation Committee (BSC): demonstrations against UWP government by, 125–28; ideological weaknesses of, 134; role of Joseph in, 119

Barbados Labor Party (BLP): electoral defeat of, 169, 171; electoral victory of, 135

Barbados National Bank (BNB), ownership of shares in NCB, 151–52

Barnard, Denis, planter class membership, 22

Barrow-Giles, Cynthia: on Caribbean electoral outcomes, 107, 134, 169, 171; on the politics of the banana industry, 40; on post–Cold War foreign policy, 97–98; on St. Lucia's economic dependence, 54, 56, 68–69, 92

Beaubrun, Clive, 23

Belle, George, on re-colonization, 18

Bishop, Matthew, on new understanding of sovereignty, 16–17

Bishop, Maurice, influence on St. Lucian Left, 62, 65

Blaut, James, on theories of nationalism, 19–20

BLP. *See* Barbados Labor Party

BNB. *See* Barbados National Bank

Bousquet, Earl: criticism of neocolonialism, 63; on the WRM stance on independence, 66

Bousquet, Rufus: incarceration in the USA, 171; involvement in UN Funds scandal, 131;

challenges to administration of, 64–65, 102–3; 2006 re-election of, 166

Constitutional development: chronology of, 28–29; Left notions of, 58; middle class notions of, 40–41

Crusader, The: on link between bananas and politics, 47; on G. Odlum's opposition to independence procedure, 66

Cuba: Anthony administration ties with 146–47; Louisy opposition to ties with, 80; 1979 SLP's ties with, 72, 74

d'Auvergne, Ausbert, opposition to Taiwanese interference, 178–80

d'Auvergne, Ira, Joseph communication with, 128

Democratic Labour Party (DLP): electoral defeat of, 135; electoral victory of, 171; impact on Anthony's accommodation to neoliberalism, 143

Deterville, Hilford: in the Forum, 61; indication of SLP's technocratic managerialism, 138; involvement in 1970s trade union agitation, 64; membership in CDP, 132

Devaux, Harold: membership of legislative council, 27; opposition to labor nationalism, 35; prominence in plantation sector, 23

DLP. *See* Democratic Labour Party

Dominica: China-Taiwan politics in, 178; commitment to the defeat of socialism in, 99–100; commitment to Windward Islands' unification in, 105–6; levels of nontraditional exports to U.S. by, 93; 1930s levels of representation in, 24; SLP's links to Left in, 72; St. Lucia's levels of 1980s growth compared with, 85; U.S. military spending in, 75

Douglas, Denzil, electoral victory of, 170

Douglas, Rosie, electoral victory of, 134

Downes, Modeste, opposition to banana privatization, 120

Duboulay, Andre, as pro-colonial planter in legislative council, 23

Duncan, Neville, on SLP's reversal of its anti-Hess radicalism, 69

EAI. *See* Enterprise for the Americas Initiative

EC. *See* European Union

Economic Partnership Agreement (EPA), early indications of, 116

Elias, Cass, on privatization of banana companies, 153

Emmanuel, Patrick A. M., electoral analysis by, 105, 107, 135–36

Enterprise for the Americas Initiative (EAI), deepening levels of liberalism in, 98

EPA. *See* Economic Partnership Agreement

Estaphane, Edmund, arrest of, 171

EU. *See* European Union

EU banana regime, U.S. challenges to, 115

European Community. *See* European Union

European Union (EU): Compton's views on economic crises in, 82; consolidation of neoliberal ideas in, 120, 147; implications for Associated Statehood, 51–52; U.S. challenge to banana regime of, 113–16

Flemming, Charles, involvement in UN Funds Scandal, 131

Fletcher, James, indication of SLP's managerialism, 138

Foreign investments: Compton's policy on, 57, 81, 93; extent of, 84–85, 93–94; SLP policies on, 145; WRM critique of, 54

Foreign policy, G. Odlum's expression of radical versions of, 71–73

Forum, The: associations with Caribbean Left, 62; entry into the SLP by members of, 64; main ideas of, 60–61; membership of, 61

Francois, Hunter J.: criticism of Compton, 105; on the PPP, 35

Francois, Martinus: criticism of amendment to Criminal Code, 126–27; on physical attack on Compton during BSC riots, 130

Frederick, Richard, arrest of, 171

Gairy, Eric, St. Lucian parallels with political approach of, 62

GATT. *See* General Agreement on Tariffs and Trade

Geest, Van, secret discussions with Compton by, 40

Geest Industries: Anthony criticism of land ownership by, 54; BSC strikes against, 125; domination of banana industry by, 46–47;

www.ingramcontent.com/pod-product-compliance
Lightning Source LLC
Chambersburg PA
CBHW030647270326
41929CB00007B/251